Latino/a Rights and Justice in the United States

Latino/a Rights and Justice in the United States

in the United States

Perspectives and Approaches

José Luis Morín
John Jay College of Criminal Justice
City University of New York

Carolina Academic Press
Durham, North Carolina

Library of Congress Cataloging-in-Publication Data

Morín, José Luis.
    Latino/a rights and justice in the United States : perspectives and approaches / by José Luis Morín.
        p.   cm
    Includes bibliographical references and index.
    ISBN 1-59460-086-4
1. Hispanic Americans--Civil rights. 2. United States--Race relations.
I. Title.

E184.S75M675 2004
323.1168'073--dc22

                                                                2004021706

Carolina Academic Press
700 Kent Street
Durham, NC 27701
Telephone (919) 489-7486
Fax (919) 493-5668
www.cap-press.com

Printed in the United States of America

Sin dignidad no hay vida.

Without dignity there is no life.

— Eugenio María de Hostos

CONTENTS

TABLE OF CASES

ACKNOWLEDGMENTS

Any endeavor of this kind typically draws on many sources of support. This book is no exception. I wish to thank my colleagues at the Puerto Rican/Latin American Studies Department at John Jay College of Criminal Justice-CUNY—Professors Luis Barrios, Francisco Chapman, Marcia Esparza, Jodie Roure, and Luis Álvarez—who individually and collectively provide the foundation for the important work that is advanced through the department. I am especially grateful to Marta Morales, Charles Frederick, Luis Barrios, and Edgar Rivera Colón for their assistance and constructive comments. I also wish to thank my research assistant, Rafael Torruella, and my department's office assistant, Christopher Aviles, for their help and commitment.

The research and other tasks involved in the production of this book would not have been possible without the support of two PSC/CUNY Research Grant Awards, along with the institutional support given by President Gerald W. Lynch, Provost Basil Wilson, Jacob Marini, and the Office of Sponsored Programs of John Jay College of Criminal Justice. Other colleagues at John Jay College who have lent direct or indirect support for this project include Professors Dorothy Moses Schulz, David Brotherton, and Michael Blitz. I am especially grateful for the efforts and support given by Timothy Stevens to this project. I am also deeply indebted to my students at John Jay College, who are an endless source of reflection and inspiration.

At John Jay College, I have also been fortunate to have been part of an important and dynamic initiative, the John Jay College-Family Life Center/*Palenque*, which is discussed in this book. I wish thank the many people who have served as part of the staff of the program for their contributions and dedication to its success, including Luis Barrios, Marta Morales, Rafael Torruella, Claudia De La Cruz, Reynaldo García-Pantaleón, Dió-genes Abréu, Héctor Rivera, Sandra Maria Esteves, Dagoberto López, Luisa Sánchez, Randol Contreras, and the John Jay College students who participated as mentors/facilitators. I also wish to acknowledge the support of the program's community-based partnership agencies, including *Alianza Dominicana* and the Dominican Women's Development Center, as well as the funding assistance provided by the Family and Community Violence Prevention Program (FCVP) headed by Dr. Laxley W. Rodney at Central States University in Ohio and the Office of Minority Health. Most importantly, I thank the youth of the *Palenque* program, who have consistently proven that Latina and Latino youth have much to offer to their communities and the greater society.

My appreciation is also extended to those who provided an array of information and assistance at different points during this project, including attorney Jorge González, Michael Zinzum of the Coalition against Police Abuse, Vina Camper of Police Watch, Elizabeth Schroeder of the ACLU Foundation of Southern California, Anthony Miranda, the Latino Officers Association, Iris Báez, the Anthony Báez Foundation, Alex Sánchez, Homies Unidos, Ralph Rivera, Klaudia M. Rivera, and Raul Añorve of the Instituto de Educación Popular del Sur de California.

I am grateful to the many Latina and Latino law enforcement personnel and Latina and Latino youth who have provided insights and encouragement for this work. This book was written in the hope of improving the lives of our Latina and Latino youth and communities.

A special final word of appreciation is reserved for my wife, Jeanette Guillén-Morín. I was truly blessed to have had her steadfast assistance and support throughout the duration of this project. I dedicate this book to her.

Latino/a Rights and Justice in the United States

CHAPTER 1

INTRODUCTION: TOWARD AN UNDERSTANDING OF LATINOS/AS IN THE UNITED STATES

More than two-thirds of all persons arrested for all criminal offenses are White, leading prominent criminologists to conclude that the typical criminal offender in the United States is White (Walker, Spohn, and DeLeone 2004, 40). Yet Latinos and Latinas, commonly perceived and treated as non-White, are disproportionately depicted in the media as criminals (Dorfman and Schiraldi 2001) and disproportionately incarcerated nationwide (Villarruel et al. 2002).

What was long predicted has come to pass: The U.S. Census Bureau has proclaimed officially that Latinos/as have become the "largest minority community" in the United States, surpassing African Americans in total numbers (Bureau of the Census 2003b; Cohn 2003, A1). It is a population projected to continue to grow at a rapid pace well into the foreseeable future (Schaefer 2001, 3). Indeed, for many years now, Latinos/as have hardly been a "minority" in such cities as San Antonio, Texas, where the population of persons of Mexican descent comprises a majority. In many other cities, such as New York or Los Angeles, Latinos/as make up ever-growing segments of the population. But in spite of their emerging demographic presence in the United States, Latinos and Latinas remain poorly understood. In the area of law and criminal justice policy, Latinos/as, commonly categorized with other "minority groups" or people of color, are almost singularly understood as a population that is overrepresented in incarceration rates, juvenile justice, and crime statistics.

As the italicized statements at the head of this chapter suggest, however, unresolved questions persist as to whether Latinos/as are fairly perceived and treated in the area of criminal justice. Additionally, there are the persistent

While it is common for Latinos/as to be absent from network news and prime time television, it is also true that when Latinos/as do appear their depiction is typically disparaging. The National Association of Hispanic Journalists reports that 66 percent of network news stories about Latinos/as focused exclusively on three topics: crime, terrorism, or illegal immigration. In 2002, suspected terrorist José Padilla, who was suspected of, but not charged with, involvement in a plot to detonate a "dirty bomb," was found to occupy "a central role in the coverage of Latinos…with 21 network stories or 18 percent of all stories aired on Latinos" (Méndez-Méndez and Alverio 2003, 3).

The results of the National Association of Hispanic Journalists study support the conclusions of other research conducted on local news coverage showing that Latinos/as and African Americans are often overrepresented as criminals while Whites are usually underrepresented. In a report examining studies on local television news, Dorfman and Schiraldi (2001, 13) found that nine out of twelve or 75 percent of the studies showed "minorities" as overrepresented as perpetrators of crime. With respect to Latinos/as, Dorfman and Schiraldi explain that

> Hispanics were 14% more likely to be depicted as committing violent crime than nonviolent crime, whereas Hispanics were 7% more likely to be arrested for a violent crime than a nonviolent crime. Some might argue that this is simply because violent crime is more newsworthy than nonviolent crime. But Whites were 31% more likely to be depicted committing a nonviolent crime than a violent crime, whereas Whites were in fact only 7% more likely to be arrested for a nonviolent crime. Thus, while Blacks and Hispanics were overrepresented as violent offenders, Whites were underrepresented as violent offenders on the evening news. (15)

These and other studies raise serious concerns, not only about the invisibility of Latinos/as in the United States, but also about negative and one-sided representations that contribute to public misperceptions and the preservation of prejudice, discrimination, and injustice. The dearth of reliable information, data, and analyses about Latino/a communities invariably results in uninformed or misinformed policymakers as well as a misguided general public. It is a problem that cries out for greater attention. As the New Jersey State Troopers racial profiling scandal of recent years reminds us—a scandal in which the state governor and attorney general conceded that for at least a decade state troopers engaged in systematic and illegal racial profiling of Latinos/as and African Americans—Latinos/as are among the groups most adversely affected by police prejudice and discrimination (see New Jersey Black and Latino Caucus 2002). The imbalance in what is known of Latinos/as, their past and present reality, and how they are viewed, categorized, and treated are among the many dimensions that need to be studied and understood in the quest for fair and appropriate public policies toward Latino/a communities.

The perpetuation of misinformation about Latinos/as has played an unfortunate role in the United States. In addition to advancing stereotypes about Latino/a communities, it has helped promote a false sense among Whites that the United States does all that it can for Latinos/as and the countries from which they originate. For Latinos/as, the conspicuous absence of Latinos/as in U.S. history reinforces the notion that they have no history or culture worthy of being recorded. Stripped of the means through which to learn about themselves, Latinos/as become disconnected from their own history, culture, and identity Latinos/as are also made to feel that to retain a link to their heritage, language, and culture is futile and counterproductive. For Latinos/as, the recurring message in the United States is usually that English, and only English, is worth learning; speaking and learning your native Spanish will only set you back. Ubiquitous negative depictions of Latinos/as in the news and in the entertainment media only serve to instill a sense of being "other" and "less than" the dominant White society.

Latino/a Populations in the United States

In an effort to fill the information gap, a look at present-day demographics can serve as a point of departure in moving toward an understanding of Latino/a communities in the United States. As Table 1 indicates, Latinos/as do not comprise a single homogenous group. They originate from many countries and regions of Latin America that differ in culture and experiences as well as share points of commonality.

Table 1.   Latinos/as in the United States by Origin in 2002

Place of National Origin	Percentage
Mexican	66.9%
Puerto Ricans	8.6%
Central and South Americans	14.3%
Cubans	3.7%
Other Hispanic	6.5%

Source: U.S. Census Bureau, Demographic Supplement to the March 2002 Current Population Survey (Bureau of the Census 2002b, 1). The above figures do not include the islands of Puerto Rico, the U.S. Virgin Islands, American Samoa, and the Northern Mariana Islands.

The U.S. Census Bureau uses the category "other Hispanic" to include persons who identify themselves with terms such as Dominican, Tejano, or Spaniard (Bureau of the Census 2003e). These categories must be examined carefully, as they can obscure what are increasingly significant and growing numbers of Latino/a communities. For instance, Dominicans who are grouped with "other Hispanics" represent an increasing segment of New York City's population that is having a considerable impact on the city's political, economic and social dynamics. In 2001, the U.S. Census Bureau estimated the Dominican population in the United States at 765,000 persons or 2.2 percent of all Latinos/as (Bureau of the Census 2001b, 3). It is also essential to bear in mind that the comprehensiveness and accuracy of the census data collection process in Latino/a communities is often questioned and, therefore, regarded as an undercount, especially with respect to the number of undocumented persons.

Of persons from Central America who represented 4.8 percent of the total Latino/a population in 2001, Salvadorans made up the largest Central American group at 655,000 persons or 1.9 percent of all Latinos/as in 2001. They were followed by Guatemalans with 372,000 or 1.1 percent and Hondurans at 218,000 or 0.6 percent. Among South Americans, a group that comprised 3.8 percent of all Latinos/as in 2001, Colombians accounted for 471,000 persons or 1.3 of the total Latino/a population; 261,000 or 0.7 percent were Ecuadorians; and 234,000 or 0.7 percent were Peruvians (Bureau of the Census 2001b, 2).

Current data reflect that the Latino/a population in the United States grows at a faster rate than the entire U.S. population. From April 1, 2000 to July 1, 2002, the number of U.S. Latinos/as increased from 35.3 million to 38.8 million, accounting for half of the U.S. population growth during that time period (Bureau of the Census 2003b). Given the marked expansion in the presence of Latinos/as in the United States found in the census data, it should be obvious that more should be known and understood about Latinos/as within the larger U.S. society. The absence of an informed general population in the United States provides fertile ground for the preservation of forms of prejudice and discrimination that inhibit the realization of full and equal rights for Latinos/as.

"LATINO" OR "HISPANIC"?

In any discussion of racial and ethnic groups, questions eventually arise about the proper nomenclature. In the same way that the term "African American" became accepted and adopted over time, the use of the term "Latino" over "Hispanic" has sparked debate while gaining considerable acceptance. The label most traditionally used—and arguably imposed—by the U.S. government is "Hispanic," as a general ethnic classification for a person of Latin American descent whose country of origin was a former colony of Spain. But the term "Hispanic" has undergone considerable reexamination.

Increasingly, "Hispanic" is viewed as deficient and inaccurate. The term "Hispanic" has been deemed inappropriate, as an ethnic designator that homogenizes and subsumes millions of persons in the United States from diverse racial and ethnic origins and broad national and cultural experiences under one label (Oboler 1995, xiii–xiv). It also overemphasizes the legacy of European and Spanish colonial rule in Latin America, rather than representing and validating the diversity of racial and cultural characteristics, including the indigenous and African heritages of vast numbers of persons from Latin America (Perea et al. 2000, 4; Flores, et al 2002, 83). Indeed, that Latinos/as often manifest strong African or indigenous roots racially and culturally becomes important in analyzing racial and ethnic prejudice and discriminatory treatment of Latinos/as in the United States under U.S. law and by U.S. law enforcement agencies, as will be explored later in this volume.

"Hispanic" is also an "ahistorical" term that draws attention to the European colonial past while diverting attention away from the longstanding historical assertion of U.S. domination and control over Latin America as well as Latin Americans in the United States (Oboler 1995, 4). It is a term that obscures the political struggle for identity by Latin Americans in the United States. In critically analyzing the term "Hispanic," some have even challenged its use as divisive within the social construction of race in the United States that places a premium on "White" over "Black." As such, it encourages Latinos/as to choose the term "Hispanic" in an attempt to avoid racially discriminatory treatment (Martínez 1993).

In contrast, the use of the term "Latino" represents a form of self-definition, re-thinking, and empowerment on the part of Latinos and Latinas, particularly in response to a government-imposed classification (Oquendo 1995). "Latino" has been employed as a more precise description of "a geographically derived national origin group, that has been constantly and consistently viewed and treated as a racial group, in both individual and institutional interaction while in the United States" (Hayes-Bautista and Chapa 1987, 66). Its use has become so prevalent that the U.S. Census Bureau has now begun to use the term "Latino" interchangeably with "Hispanic" in accordance with the new standards issued by the Office of Management and Budget in 1997 (Bureau of the Census 2001b, 1). Therefore, the term used primarily in this book is "Latino/a," rather than "Hispanic," in a form that also accounts for gender. "Hispanic" is used only in instances to reflect its use by another source. As Latinos/as do not comprise a homogeneous group, they are referred to herein in the plural as Latino/a communities, populations, or groups.

Cultural and other differences among Latino/a groups also appear to be relevant to the manner in which Latinos/as tend to identify themselves. As a survey by the Pew Hispanic Center/Kaiser Family Foundation revealed (2002), most Latinos/as prefer to identify themselves first according to their countries of origin and as either "Latino" or "Hispanic" second. The study describes that the "tie to home country is much more salient than any pan-ethnic or 'Latino/Hispanic' identity" (23). Nonetheless, a majority of Latinos/as also recognizes a "unified Latino culture" and prefers to identify their race as "Latino" or "Hispanic," feeling that they do not fit into any single racial category used by the U.S. government (23).

Another label often applied to Latinos/as is "minority." "Minority," when used most sensibly, attempts to describe a group that experiences a pattern of disadvantage or inequality that also shares a visible trait usually determined at birth (Healey 2003, 10). However, the term is found frequently to have offensive and belittling connotations (Walker et al. 2004, 1), and therefore is not used in this book. "People of color" is used instead.

Race, Racism, and Racialized "Others"

To help bridge the gap in understanding Latinos/as in relation to issues of justice, this book seeks to provide an examination of the history and evolution of law and justice issues as they affect Latino/a communities in the United States. As Perea, Delgado, Harris, and Wildman stress (2000, 246), U.S. history insufficiently covers U.S. relations with Latin America and the history of Latinos/as in the United States. As these scholars point out, seldom is the history of the conquest of Latin America—not just by Spain, but by the United States—studied in U.S. schools. Even less attention is given to the underlying racial premises that have shaped U.S. government policies and practices (247–48). Absent is the history of the use of race as an instrument to suppress the rights of Latinos/as in ways similar to other people of color—Native Americans who endured genocide, the conquest of their lands, and forced assimilation; African Americans who suffered slavery, segregation, and the legacy of these horrific institutions; Chinese immigrants who experienced discrimination and exploitation as cheap labor; Japanese who lost their homes and property and were interned during World War II (Perea et al. 2000).

The history of conquests covered in Chapter Two of this volume provides the background for understanding the long trajectory of U.S.-Latin American relations that have given rise to the presence of Latinos/as in the United States. From its earliest beginnings as a country, the United States established a relationship with Latin America grounded in ideas that justified U.S. expansionism through military conquests. The legal framework constructed to delimit the rights of Mexicans and Puerto Ricans who found themselves under U.S. territorial designation in the 1800s is, in great measure, a product of the hegemonic aspirations and racial assumptions of U.S. policymakers that formed part of the ideology known as "manifest destiny."

Mexicans and Puerto Ricans are the two largest and earliest Latin American peoples to have encounters with U.S. desires to realize its "destiny." Understanding the history of Mexicans and Puerto Ricans in relation to the United States is vital since the impact of the events on them have set the course for other Latino/a groups that followed. As Suzanne Oboler observes (1995, 16), "the experiences of more recent Latin American immigrants cannot be understood without serious consideration of the context of historical discrimination shaped in relation to Chicanos and Puerto Ricans." In consideration of this fact, the experience of other Latinos/as will be discussed in this text in view of the events preceding the arrival of other Latino/a groups and the legacy of discrimination derived from the earlier actions taken to restrict the fundamental rights of Mexicans and Puerto Ricans.

This book examines the pursuit of U.S. hemispheric dominance and the persistent undercurrent of racism that was influential in the formation of U.S. law and foreign policy toward Latin America and Latin Americans historically and the manner in which hegemony and racism have shaped the rights of Latinos/as in the United States. Also explored is the historical linkage between U.S.-Latin America relations and the Latino/a presence within the territorial boundaries of the United States as well as the present-day flow of Latinos/as between Latin America and the United States.

The crucial role that race has played historically cannot be underestimated. The issue of race helped set the pattern for the limitation of rights for Latinos/as in the United States, a pattern that resonates into the present. Upon close examination, the record is clear: Latino/a communities remain challenged by prejudice and discrimination in U.S. society and by problems that stem from institutionalized forms of inequality and injustice, including racial profiling and police brutality within the criminal justice system. Therefore, the question of race as it affects Latino/a communities must be addressed.

The federal government's current ethnic and racial classification system depicts Latinos/as as an ethnic group, based on the premise that Latinos/as may be of any race. Nevertheless, Latinos/as are also regularly compared and grouped with racial "minority" groups in the United States, as demonstrated in Table 2 below. Table 2 presents estimates for the year 2002 by the Census Bureau of the U.S. population according to the number of people who identified with one race in the census, whether or not they reported any other races.

Table 2.   U.S. Population by Race and Persons of Latino/a Origin: 2002

Race	Population
Latino/a	38.8 million
White	236.2 million
African American	38.3 million
Asian	13.1 million
American Indian and Alaska Natives	4.3 million
Native Hawaiian and Other Pacific Islanders	943,000

Source: U.S. Bureau of the Census. 2003b. *Hispanic population reaches all-time high of 38.8 million, new census estimates show.* United States Commerce News, Economics and Statistics Administration, Bureau of the Census. Washington, D.C. Available from www.census.gov/Press-Release/www/2003/cb03-1000.html.

However, if race has no basis in science and is merely a social construction, as has been well established (Ferrante and Browne 2001), why does racial and ethnic prejudice and discrimination persist? Latinos/as have and continue to occupy a "racialized" status within the United States. As described by historian Edward J. Escobar (1999, 7), the racialization of Latinos/as in the United States involves a process through which social assumptions have prevailed that preserve Latinos/as as racially "other" in relation to the dominant White society. The group considered to be "other" is consigned to a place of subordination in relation to those who dominate. As racialized "others," Latinos/as have and continue to be perceived as somehow "foreign" and "less than" the White dominant population. Subordination, in turn, serves as the necessary prerequisite that justifies and explains the exercise of control and/or exploitation of the racialized group.

Incorporated into the discussion of race and the racialization of Latinos/as is a look at historical and contemporary forms of discrimination against Latino/a communities (Chapter Three). Indeed, discrimination—as manifested within the criminal justice system through the enduring problems of police brutality, corruption, racial profiling, and inequality in the courts, sentencing, and incarceration—is a pressing concern among Latinos/as as much as it is in the areas of housing, employment, health care, and voting rights.

The lack of adequate representation in U.S. law enforcement and judicial institutions poses other obstacles for Latino/a communities. Yet, as described in Chapter Four, increases in numerical representation alone do not necessarily guarantee equal access to justice. Other inadequacies, such as the lack of Latino/a involvement in policy making and the absence of culturally competent services, cannot be overlooked. For Latinos/as, the ability to make decisions that promote meaningful change in the institutions that affect their lives and the ability to retain and assert their identity within institutions more inclined to promote conformity than diversity are essential elements in making society more responsive to Latino/a community needs.

The Latino Officers Association represents an example of the many ways that Latinos/as have organized to advocate for change, reassert Latino/a identity, and open new opportunities. Indeed, the experience of Latino/a police officers in New York City also allows us to reflect upon whether the level of Latino/a representation as legal professionals—lawyers, judges, and others working within the judicial system—is adequate and on the consequences of an insufficient pool of Latino/a legal professionals on Latino/a communities.

Given the diversity of Latinas and Latinos in the United States—their many countries of origin, and even their cultural and linguistic differences—it is difficult for one book to be all-encompassing of the experiences of all Latinos/as in the United States. For this reason, New York City and Los Angeles—cities with significant and varied Latino/a populations—have been chosen for a specific discussion of justice issues in relation to the various Latino/a groups that reside in these two major urban centers. The discussion of the circumstances of Latinos/as in these cities is found in Chapter Five. Highlighted in this chapter are the police policies, practices, and scandals in New York City and Los Angeles that have long been at the center of police-Latino/a community tensions. The perspectives of two public figures, Alex Sánchez and Iris Báez, are provided to illustrate how their lives have been transformed in the midst of the harsh realities of life and justice in Los Angeles and New York City.

Beyond Defining the Problem: Finding Solutions

The story of Latinos/as in the United States is a story of hope, struggle, and commitment to the realization of Latino/a identity and justice. In the search for solutions, Chapter Six focuses on a program that seeks to address the needs of Latino/a youths and their families. The John Jay College-Family Life Center (*Palenque*), organized by members of the Puerto Rican/Latin American Studies Department of John Jay College of Criminal Justice in New York City, provides an alternative to traditional modes of viewing and assisting youths who are routinely labeled as "at risk."

A program that works with youth from the Washington Heights/Inwood community of New York City consisting largely of Latinos/as from the Dominican Republic, *Palenque* approaches its work with Latino/a youth and families from a culture-based perspective to counteract the detrimental effects of marginalization and lack of self-esteem common among these youths. The program attempts to fill the void left by a neighborhood rampant with "at risk" institutions—schools, medical facilities, and other public institutions and services unable to serve adequately the community. In this neighborhood, problems related to poverty combine with poor police-community relations and a myriad of structural circumstances that breed despair and undermine individual and collective advancement. By providing a range of academic, cultural, career, and personal and family development activities that emphasize the cultural background of the participants, *Palenque* helps these young people confront problems of personal and collective alienation.

In the search for alternative models and effective solutions to the problems faced by Latinos/as in the United States, Chapter Seven looks at the application of international human rights laws, norms, principles, and standards that protect minority group rights, linguistic human rights, and other forms of economic, social, and cultural rights. Indeed, *Palenque* is itself an initiative consistent with principles found in international human rights law that provide for the respect and protection of the economic, social, linguistic, and cultural needs of persons not part of the majority group in the country.

Recognizing that the issues addressed in this book are not one-dimensional in nature, this book takes a multidisciplinary approach to give a more comprehensive picture of Latino/a groups in connection to the larger society, the law, and the legal system. Historical, sociological, political, ethnographic, and legal elements are brought together in this book to provide the reader with a depth of understanding. In this volume, knowledge of the past is considered to be essential to improving the present. For this reason, a premium is placed on providing the historical context of the subject matter. Equally important is the need to broaden the scope of inquiry to include advancements made in the field of international human rights and, in particular, the development of economic, social, and cultural rights that are applicable to Latino/a groups in the United States.

As it is impossible for one book to represent all of the perspectives of the many diverse communities and people who make up Latino/a communities in the United States, this volume attempts to draw together information that is vital to understanding the general historical trajectory of Latinos/as. It explores contemporary patterns relating to justice issues affecting substantial numbers of Latinos/as, and it includes data of an ethnographic nature drawn from interviews of various Latinos and Latinas to delve into the lives, experiences, and perspectives of U.S. Latinos/as. Latino/a perspectives are presented at various points in this book to allow sectors of Latino/a communities to have their voices heard, their stories told in the context of a society where Latinos and Latinas are often invisible. Latino/a views are also presented to help us re-think and challenge the conventional wisdom about Latinos/as. Both quantitative and qualitative data have a place in this study of Latinos/as, with qualitative data providing insights that help explain why, rather than just how much or how often.

Latino/a Rights and Justice in the United States seeks to advance a discussion about broadening our concept of rights, respect, and dignity. It endeavors to provide the means to re-envision the ways that all persons can have access to educational, social, and economic progress and to deepen our appreciation about the ways in which we all have a stake in insuring progress for all. It is from this standpoint that the concluding chapter proposes to place in perspective the various experiences of Latinos/as along with a discussion of strategies to right wrongs and improve conditions for Latinos/as in their quest for equality and justice. While this book focuses on the elusiveness of equality and justice for Latinos/as in the United States, it also attempts to posit ideas, recommendations, and approaches to correct and reduce discrimination and inequality. In this sense, this book is meant to be a reflection about the absence of justice as well as the continuing quest for justice—recurring themes in the lives of Latinos and Latinas in the United States.

CHAPTER 2

THE ORIGINS OF LATINOS/AS IN THE UNITED STATES: AN ENCOUNTER WITH THE HISTORY OF U.S.-LATIN AMERICAN RELATIONS

Familiarity with the history of relations between the United States and Latin America is indispensable to unraveling the often forgotten events and circumstances that account for the Latino/a presence in the United States. In many instances, U.S. policies toward Latin America have been directly responsible for the influx of Latinos/as in the United States. But many today misconstrue that presence as one based solely on immigration when, in fact, Latinos/as inhabited what now comprises the Southwest and Western states of United States—approximately one-third of the continental United States—long before most other European settlement of North America (see Perea et al. 2000, 248).

Absent from the collective consciousness of most U.S. citizens are the wars of territorial conquests of the late 1800s. With the end of the U.S.-Mexican War in 1848, Mexicans were subsumed along with the land that was previously sovereign Mexican territory into the United States. Following the United States' war with Spain in 1898, Puerto Ricans became subjects of the United States and their land a possession of the United States even though they had already achieved political autonomy from Spain in 1897. Thus, immigration alone does not account for the number of Latinos/as currently in the United States. In point of fact, recent census data reveals that three in five Latinos/as are U.S. born (Bureau of the Census 2002b, 3).

The conspicuous lack of awareness of this history provides fertile ground for the preservation of forms of prejudice and discrimination that inhibit the realization of full and equal rights and justice for Latinos/as. This chapter seeks to ground the discussion about rights and justice in its historical context to better inform our understanding of the present-day condition of Latinos/as.

IMPERIAL DESIGNS ON LATIN AMERICA

Before reviewing the early history of U.S. foreign policy toward Latin America, it is necessary to clarify that the United States, notwithstanding its anti-colonial beginnings, occupies a place in history as one of the world's greatest empires and its ascent to this status was not accidental. By the end of the nineteenth century, the United States had successfully positioned itself as an imperial power with territorial possessions around the globe. It had also claimed a special dominant role over all of the Americas—a role that it maintains to the present. It is now well established that U.S. imperialism was not a passive endeavor, but a concerted effort to expand U.S. territorial reach for new markets and other economic, social, and political gains (LaFeber [1963] 1998, xiv–xix; Smith 2000, 12; Schoultz 1998, 78–90; Morín 2000, 9).

However much it has been couched in benevolent terms or justified in the name of spreading democracy, acquiring territories through wars of conquest places the United States squarely in the league of other imperial powers in world history that have engaged in the systematic violation of the right of self-determination of peoples (LaFeber [1963] 1998, xiv–xix; Smith 2000, 11–12). Indeed, as with all other imperial powers, the United States has used war and the threat of war as indispensable instruments to attain hegemony. Stated clearly, it is through conquest that the United States was able to wrest approximately half of the lands of Mexico and gain control over a series of island nations—including Puerto Rico, Cuba, the Philippines, Guam, and Hawaii—by the end of the 1800s.

The conquests of the 1800s were rooted in the longstanding and deeply held desires among many of the founders of the United States to construct an empire. As early as 1767, Benjamin Franklin articulated aspirations for the expansion of U.S. territory, including intentions to make Mexico and Cuba part of the United States (Perea et al. 2000, 258). Thomas Jefferson contended that the United States "has a hemisphere to itself. It must have a separate system of interest which must not be subordinated to those of Europe" (quoted in Smith 2000, 17). By the 1780s, Jefferson avowed that the Spanish empire should be taken over by the United States "peice by peice [sic]" (18). These expansionist designs were not simply the whimsy of Franklin and Jefferson; they became an integral part of the ambitions of U.S. policymakers who followed. The goal of seizing other lands to advance U.S. global economic and political interests could not be more plain than when in 1891 Secretary of State James Blaine in a letter to President Benjamin Harrison wrote, "I think there are only three places that are of value enough to be taken that are not continental.... One is Hawaii and the others are Cuba and Porto Rico [*sic*]" (quoted in LaFeber [1963] 1998, 110).

THE RACIAL JUSTIFICATIONS FOR U.S. IMPERIALISM

U.S. domination over Latin American lands and peoples was made palatable and justifiable to the U.S public in large measure through the perpetuation of racist ideologies. Manifest destiny, a dominant and influential belief system boldly advanced in the 1800s, touted the divine right of Anglo-Saxon U.S. citizens to territorial expansion based on purported racial and cultural superiority (Cabán 1999, 83; Stephanson 1995). The influence of the racist assumptions inherent in the notion of the "White man's burden" together with manifest destiny provided the requisite pretext for justifying Anglo-American dominance and territorial conquests (Stephanson 1995).

Policymakers and the major news media coalesced around the idea that the United States was governed by persons of a superior race, religion, and culture distinguishable from all others, and, therefore, the United States was uniquely and rightfully entitled to claim dominance over other lands and other peoples. So deeply held were these beliefs that all non-Anglo Saxons, even those from Europe, were considered threats to the nation. By 1751, Benjamin Franklin (1959, 234) voiced his beliefs about the racial and cultural threat that non-Anglo Americans posed, including German immigrants, who in his words "will shortly be so numerous as to Germanize us instead of our Anglifying them, and will never adopt our Language and Customs, any more than they can acquire our complexion" (see also Portes and Schauffler 1996, 433).

In spite of the diversity of people and races in the United States in its early years—Native Americans, Europeans of different countries of origin, and Africans—prominent leaders and founders of the United States regarded the country as one only of and for Anglo Americans. John Jay in *The Federalist Papers* ([1788] 2003, 32) remarked that

> Providence has been pleased to give this one connected country to one united people—a people descended from the same ancestors, speaking the same language, professing the same religion, attached to the same principles of government, very similar in their manners and customs.

Very early in U.S. history, Latin Americans were singled out as racially inferior to Anglo-Saxon Americans. James Buchanan denounced "the imbecile and indolent Mexican race," and in the press, the *New York Evening Post* in the late 1840s categorized Mexicans as "*Indians*—Aboriginal Indians. Such Indians as Cortez conquered three thousand [*sic*] years ago, only rendered a little more mischievous by a bastard civilization…. They do not possess the elements of an *independent* national existence…and they must share the destiny of their race" (quoted in Smith 2000, 47).

As historian Howard Zinn documents (2003, 154–55), major U.S. newspapers and political leaders repeatedly championed the idea of Anglo superiority as justification for the conquests of Mexico. The *New York Herald* in 1847 stated unequivocally: "The universal Yankee nation can regenerate and disenthrall the people of Mexico in a few years; and we believe it is part of our destiny to civilize that beautiful country" (155). Invoking God as further justification, Senator H. V. Johnson stated:

> I believe we should be recreant to our noble mission, if we refuse acquiescence in the high purposes of a wise Providence. War has its evils…but however inscrutable to us, it has also made, by the Allwise Dispenser of events, the instrumentality of accomplishing the great end of human elevation and happiness…. It is in this view, that I subscribe to the doctrine of 'manifest destiny.' (155)

Throughout the 1800s, words, cartoons, and photographs reinforced demeaning, negative stereotypes of the conquered peoples of Cuba, Puerto Rico as well as the Philippines and Hawaii. In an examination of the degrading representations of the peoples of these island nations in 1898, Frederic W. Gleach of Cornell University notes that "[r]acialization, infantilization, primitivization, and feminization were all used to construct our newly-interior Others as inferior to real Americans…. This was not a passing way of viewing them, but a persistent one—and a problematic one, even to the present" (2002, 68).

The notion that Latin American peoples' own racial and cultural deficiencies rendered them unable to govern properly their own nations laid the foundation for a foreign policy grounded on achieving and maintaining U.S. hegemony over the Americas. The foreign policy initiative that enshrined U.S. hegemony is the Monroe Doctrine of 1823. It is a doctrine that many historians agree still remains influential in U.S.-Latin American relations (see, e.g., Schoultz 1999; Smith 2000; LaFeber 1993). Racially negative characterizations of Latin Americans not only helped to rationalize the wars of conquest with Mexico and Spain in the 1800s, they were followed by U.S. government policies, practices, laws, and judicial decisions that relegated other Latin Americans subordinate to Anglo Americans.

The acceptance in the United States of Latin Americans as representing a separate and inferior race rendered uncontroversial numerous military interventions throughout Latin America. In the case of Cuba, Orville H. Platt, author of the notorious Platt Amendment, vehemently opposed Cuba's incorporation into the United States because "The people of Cuba, by reason of their race and characteristic, cannot be easily assimilated by us.... Their presence in the American union, as a state, would be most disturbing" (quoted in Smith 2000, 49). Since under U.S. policy Cubans were unworthy of incorporation into the union by virtue of their race, they could not be trusted with full political independence. As a result, the Platt Amendment of 1904 relegated Cuba to a neocolonial status and insured complete U.S. authority to intervene in Cuba's internal affairs, including control over Cuba's economy and politics. While the Platt Amendment was in effect (1904–1932), the U.S. military forces invaded and/or occupied Cuba in 1906–1909, 1912, and 1917–1922 (51).

Throughout the nineteenth century and into the twentieth century, Latin Americans were openly and continually depicted in Washington and throughout the United States as inferior and racialized "others," prone to uncivilized behavior, and undeserving of self-government. Simultaneously, the U.S. public was fed a steady diet of news stories and media portrayals that vividly reinforced in the hearts and minds of U.S. citizens that the U.S. government was acting benevolently and justifiably in pursuing its colonial agenda (Gleach 2002; *Journal of el Centro de Estudios Puertorriqueño* 1998, 155–63). Casting Latin Americans as racialized "others" helped to rationalize in the minds of the U.S. public their government's actions. It offered a vision of a government carrying out a benign mission among inherently inept peoples. Thus, U.S. policies were not to be interpreted as those of a colonial power acting in contravention of its own founding democratic principles, but in furtherance of those ideals. Professor Peter H. Smith (2000, 38–39) explains that projecting the United States as a nation imbued with the higher goal of spreading democracy among these racially, culturally, and religiously backwards peoples was vital not only to justify and mobilize domestic support and resources for its imperial ventures, but to validate its actions to rival powers as well. In addition, he points out that the projection of lofty goals served to indoctrinate and thereby control the peoples of the subjugated societies themselves.

Racism and a racialized vision of the peoples of the developing world also proved useful in the establishment of a legal framework for the unequal application of the law toward Latinos/as in the United States. For example, in the case of Puerto Ricans, U.S. Supreme Court judgments governing the rights of Puerto Ricans have been compared to the condition of separate and unequal experienced by African Americans in the United States for more than half a century (Torruella 1988). Indeed, virtually the same group of Supreme Court justices responsible for *Plessy v. Ferguson,* 163 U.S. 537 (1896)—the case establishing the notorious legal doctrine of separate but equal—decided the *Insular Cases,* which, as explained further in this chapter, continue to delimit the rights of Puerto Ricans. As with the *Plessy* case, the restrictions imposed on the rights of Puerto Ricans were grounded in the racist and racialized perceptions of Puerto Ricans and Latin Americans that prevailed throughout all branches of the U.S. government. Unlike *Plessy,* however, the *Insular Cases* have never been overturned, and as a result, significant restrictions on the most fundamental rights of the peoples of Puerto Rico are still applied.

During the Congressional debate about whether constitutional protections should be extended to Puerto Ricans in 1900, Puerto Ricans were characterized as follows:

> They are of the Latin race, and are of quick and excitable tempers, but they are at the same time patient, docile, frugal, and most of them industrious. (U.S. Senate 1900, 4875)

Given such characterizations, it is not surprising that Puerto Ricans were not accorded full constitutional rights, a condition that still exists today. As persons who collectively comprise a racially inferior group, the conclusion drawn was that Latin Americans present a danger to the dominant, White U.S. population and its institutions (Torruella 1988). As a consequence, it was imperative to restrict Latino/a rights through legislation and other legal obstacles to protect Anglo-American power and authority over the status and condition of Latinos/as in the United States (see Delgado and Stefancic 1998; Perea et al. 2000; Torruella 1988).

U.S. CONQUESTS IN MEXICO AND PUERTO RICO

The two largest Latino/a populations in the United States today, Mexicans and Puerto Ricans, share a history linked inexorably to the U.S. imperial expansion of the 1800s. As mentioned in Chapter One, familiarity with the historical experiences of these two groups is essential to understanding the treatment of Latin Americans who later came to the United States and the contemporary situation of Latinos/as.

Contrary to the depiction of Latinas and Latinos as primarily "illegal immigrants" to the United States, many Mexicans lived on the lands that presently comprise roughly one-third of the continental United States, including the present-day states of California, Texas, New Mexico, Arizona, Nevada, and parts of Colorado, Utah, and Kansas (Perea et al. 2000, 248). At the end of the U.S.-Mexican War in 1848, approximately 75,000 Mexicans living on the lands acquired by the United States through the war were forced to decide whether to become U.S. citizens (Perea et al. 2000, 248; Acuña 2000, 50).

The conquest of these lands and the people who inhabited them was possible through the efforts of President James K. Polk. By stationing troops at the border with Mexico, Polk intentionally instigated hostilities with Mexico (Smith 2000, 20–22; Zinn 2003, 149–69). In view of the vast territories and resources taken as part of the Treaty of Guadalupe Hidalgo that ended the U.S.-Mexican War, it was not unexpected that the purpose of a $15 million payment to Mexico at the conclusion of this war has been construed to have been nothing more than an attempt to legitimize a patent seizure of land in violation of the sovereignty of another nation (Zinn 2003, 169).

Drafted by a victorious U.S. government after Mexico's military defeat, the Treaty of Guadalupe Hidalgo of 1848 between the United States and Mexico failed to protect the rights of Mexicans who became U.S. citizens. Mexicans within the territories acquired by the United States were reduced to second-class citizenship, subjected to the loss of their lands in spite of preexisting land grants, and denied the right to vote and political representation (Perea et al. 2000, 260–91; Acuña 2000, 53–55).

Although the treaty in large measure did intend originally to extend full rights to Mexicans consistent with international law, in its final version the Treaty of Guadalupe Hidalgo was modified in significant ways to appease the concerns raised in Congress over the racial threat that Mexicans represented to Anglo-American rule (Perea et al. 2000, 263). As a result, article IX of the treaty was amended to grant Congress the ultimate power to decide at what time Mexicans could be granted full rights as U.S. citizens. Article IX of the Treaty of Guadalupe Hidalgo (1848), thus, reads:

> The Mexicans who, in the territories aforesaid, shall not preserve the character of citizens of the Mexican Republic, conformably with what is stipulated in the preceding article, shall be incorporated into the Union of the United States and be admitted, *at the proper time (to be judged of by the Congress of the United States)* to the enjoyment of all the rights of citizens of the United States, according to the principles of the Constitution; and in the mean time, shall be maintained and protected in the free enjoyment of their liberty and property, and secured in the free exercise of their religion without restriction [emphasis added].

Any reference to protecting liberty and property in the treaty turned out to be disingenuous. Not only were full constitutional rights withheld in the amendment to article IX, article X of the Treaty of Guadalupe Hidalgo, anticipated to protect "[a]ll grants of land made by the Mexican government or by the competent authorities, in the territories previously appertaining to Mexico," was completely stricken from the final version of the treaty (Perea et al. 2000, 261). As further discussed in Chapter Three of this volume, this action insured that Mexicans with valid land grants would eventually lose lands to White settlers who systematically challenged and won title over those lands in court (Perea et al. 2000, 270–92; Acuña 2000, 54–55; Ebright 1994, 45–50).

In 1898, the U.S. war with Spain—sold to the U.S. public by government officials and the news media as a crusade to end the brutality of Spanish colonial rule in Cuba—resulted in one colonial power replacing another. As with the Treaty of Guadalupe Hidalgo, the Treaty of Paris of 1898, which ended the war, fell short of granting equal rights to the peoples of the lands transferred to the United States as the spoils of war. Article IX of the treaty states that the U.S. Congress shall determine the "civil rights and political status of the native inhabitants of the territories...ceded to the United States" (U.S. Department of State 1898). The ceded territories included the Philippines, Guam, and other islands of the Pacific, as well as Puerto Rico. Fears about the "alien nations" that inhabited these territories and the possibility that they might contaminate U.S. society by incorporating these "mongrel" races into the United States ran rampant at the time. Hence, the U.S. government inserted language in the Treaty of Paris that insured that the inhabitants of these conquered lands could not exercise full citizenship and constitutional rights (Torruella 1988).

In one of a series of cases known as the *Insular Cases*, the U.S. Supreme Court determined it impossible to confer full constitutional rights to Puerto Rico because its "alien races" are not ready for having "the blessings of a free government under the Constitution extended to them" (*Downes v. Bidwell*, 182 U.S. 244, 286 (1901)).[1] The Court based its decision, *inter alia*, on the Doc-

---

1. In its narrowest sense, the term *Insular Cases* refers to the decisions of the U.S. Supreme Court dealing with the status of the territories the United States acquired pursuant to the Treaty of Paris of 1898, 30 Stat. 1754, T.S. 343, following the U.S. war with Spain (see Torruella 1988, 3). These cases include *De Lima v. Bidwell*, 182 U.S. 1 (1901); *Goetze v. United States* (*Crossman v. United States*), 182 U.S. 221 (1901); *Dooley v. United States*, 182 U.S. 222 (1901); *Armstrong v. United States*, 182 U.S. 243 (1901); *Downes v. Bidwell*, 182 U.S. 244 (1901) and *Huus v. New York & P. R. Steamship Co.*, 182 U.S. 392 (1901). More broadly defined, the term includes decisions that follow this original line of cases that also relate to the status of other U.S. colonies—such as Hawaii. Hence, the *Insular Cases*

trine of Conquest set forth in *Johnson v. McIntosh*, 21 U.S. 543, 590 (1823)—
a racially-charged doctrine that justified the granting of title to land in North
America to the far superior persons from the "civilized" nations of Europe over
Native Americans, who were nothing more than "fierce savages." Creating a
legal rationale for U.S. colonial expansion was of such importance that Justice Henry Billings Brown in the *Downes* case conceded that any other decision could "be fatal to the development of…the American Empire" (*Downes
v. Bidwell*, 182 U.S. 244, 286 (1901)).

As a result, the *Downes* case and subsequent U.S. Supreme Court cases have
allowed the U.S. Congress to retain plenary (that is, absolute) power to determine the civil rights of Puerto Ricans and the political status of Puerto Rico.
As an unincorporated territory—one of several territories that "belong to but
are not a part of the United States" (*Downes v. Bidwell*, 182 U.S. 244, 287)—
full and equal constitutional protections need not apply to Puerto Ricans.

In 1917, Puerto Ricans were made U.S. citizens with the passage of the
Jones Act by the U.S. Congress. Yet U.S. citizenship—imposed without the
consent of the Puerto Rican people and in disregard for the unanimous vote
of the Puerto Rican legislature to preserve Puerto Rican citizenship (Fernandez 1994, 67)—still did not guarantee full and equal protection under the U.S.
constitution for persons residing in Puerto Rico. The U.S. Supreme Court in
Balzac v. People of Porto Rico [*sic*], 258 U.S. 298 (1922), in fact, held that the
right to a jury trial and other such rights under the U.S. Constitution are not
applicable to the inhabitants of Puerto Rico unless granted by the U.S. Congress. The court's reasoning, which still stands today, is that Puerto Rico remains an unincorporated territory of the United States, even after the enactment of the Jones Act, and as such, the U.S. Congress retains plenary powers
to determine the rights of Puerto Ricans under the Territorial Clause of the
U.S. Constitution, article IV, section 3, paragraph 2.

Notwithstanding Justice John Marshall Harlan's dissent in *Downes*, which
maintained that colonies and colonial subjects run contrary to the very spirit
and letter of the U.S. Constitution (*Downes v. Bidwell*, 182 U.S. 244, 380
(1901)), the *Insular Cases*, and even the Supreme Court's decision in *Johnson*

---

may also include *Fourteen Diamond Rings v. United States*, 183 U.S. 176 (1901); *Hawaii v.
Mankichi*, 190 U.S. 197 (1903); *Gonzales v. Williams*, 192 U.S. 1 (1903); *Kepner v. United
States*, 195 U.S. 100 (1904); *Dorr v. United States*, 195 U.S. 138 (1904); *Rassmussen v. United
States*, 197 U.S. 516 (1905); *Dowdell v. United States*, 221 U.S. 325 (1911); *Ocampo v. United
States*, 234 U.S. 91 (1914); *Balzac v. People of Porto Rico* [*sic*], 258 U.S. 298 (1922). For a
further discussion of the *Insular Cases* as a part of U.S. imperial expansionism and their
role in undermining self-determination, see Rivera Ramos (2001, 73–142).

v. McIntosh, have never been overturned. They remain binding precedents in U.S. law, an affirmation of Puerto Rico's colonial status and a confirmation of second-class legal status for Puerto Ricans in contravention of the universal prohibition against colonialism established under international law (see, e.g., United Nations 1960). Moreover, U.S. Supreme Court decisions of more recent years reaffirm the denial of equal protection under the U.S. Constitution to Puerto Ricans in cases that cite the *Insular Cases* as the legal precedent (see, e.g., *Califano v. Torres*, 435 U.S. 1 (1978); *Harris v. Rosario*, 446 U.S. 651 (1980)).

Not surprisingly, all political parties in Puerto Rico presently denounce Puerto Rico's ongoing colonial situation (Trías Monge 1997, 138). They have also made their dissatisfaction with the enduring U.S. colonial scheme known to the United Nations. As a result, since the 1970s, the United Nations committee responsible for the implementation of the decolonization process has recognized repeatedly the Puerto Rican peoples' right to the exercise of self-determination under U.N. standards for decolonization, standards that the United States has failed to meet (Trías Monge 1997, 138; Fernandez 1994; Gautier Mayoral and Del Pilar Arguelles 1978).[2] Indeed, it is abundantly clear from the Congressional Record that labeling Puerto Rico a "commonwealth" in the 1950s was never meant to change the political, economic, and social relationship between the United States and Puerto Rico (Fernandez 1994, 85).

---

2. The term "peoples" is used here in a manner consistent with its meaning under international law and in the manner in which the U.N. Special Committee on decolonization uses the term with respect the case of Puerto Rico. That is, that "all peoples have the right to self-determination; by virtue of that right they freely determine their political status and freely pursue their economic, social and cultural development" (United Nations 1960, para. 1; 1966a, art. 1; 1966b, art. 1). The U.N. Decolonization Committee, formally known as the Special Committee on the Situation with regard to the Implementation of the Declaration of the Granting of Independence to Countries and Peoples, is mandated to implement U.N. General Assembly Resolution 1514 (XV) of 1960, the Declaration of the Granting of Independence to Countries and Peoples (United Nations 1960; see Appendix B). Specifically with respect to the case of Puerto Rico, the Special Committee in 2003 adopted a resolution which echoed past resolutions, stating that it "*Reaffirms* the inalienable right of the people of Puerto Rico to self-determination and independence in conformity with General Assembly Resolution 1514 (XV) and the applicability of the fundamental principles of that resolution concerning Puerto Rico." The resolution further called upon "the Government of the United States to assume its responsibility of expediting a process that will allow the Puerto Rican people fully to exercise their inalienable right to self-determination and independence, in conformity with General Assembly 1514 (XV) and the resolutions and decisions of the Special Committee concerning Puerto Rico" (United Nations 2003b).

Congress's authority over the island nation and its peoples remains absolute, and thus, it maintains Puerto Rico as a U.S. colony (Trías Monge 1997, 161–63; Rivera Ramos 2001, 225).[3] The United States retains complete power to unilaterally nullify all or parts of the Puerto Rican Constitution. In fact, the U.S. Congress actually eliminated Article 2, Section 20 on economic and social rights of the 1952 Commonwealth Constitution, overriding the work of the Puerto Rican Constitutional Convention (García Martínez 1989, 229). Puerto Ricans do not share equal rights with U.S. citizens in the United States: they serve and die in U.S. wars, but cannot vote for the President who can send them into battle; U.S. laws apply to Puerto Rico without the consent of Puerto Ricans; Puerto Ricans have no say in treaties and foreign affairs that affect them; Puerto Ricans have no voting representation in the U.S. Congress; trade, shipping, immigration, and monetary policies are all controlled by the United States; U.S. federal courts operate in English, rather than in the native language of Puerto Rico; and the "commonwealth" status continues out of compliance with United Nations decolonization requirements (Trías Monge 1997, 161–63; Rivera Ramos 2001, 130; Fernandez 1994, 61–94; Maldonado-Denis 1972, 189–208). This situation has led former Chief Justice of Puerto Rico José Trías Monge to conclude that "[t]here is no known noncolonial relationship in the present world where one people exercises such vast, almost unbounded power over the government of another" (1997, 163).

Why the United States maintains colonies in the face of the worldwide repudiation of colonialism in the post-World War II era becomes apparent when one considers the enormous benefits that accrue to the U.S. government and U.S. corporate interests (Maldonado-Denis 1972, 151–88; Lewis 1963, 167–236).[4] Net profits from Puerto Rico to U.S. corporations surpass the profits of all other industrial countries, including the United Kingdom, Germany

---

3. Puerto Ricans are not the only ones over whom the U.S. Congress exerts plenary powers. Based on a U.S. Supreme Court decision that has never been reversed, the U.S. government has maintained that the U.S. government's relationship with Native Americans is one between a guardian and ward. The U.S. Supreme Court in *Cherokee Nation v. Georgia*, 30 U.S. (5 Pet.) 1, 17 (1831), declared that "Indian tribes" pursuant to the U.S. Constitution were "domestic dependent nations," whose relationship with the United States "resembles that of a ward to his guardian. They look to the U.S. government for protection; rely upon its kindness and its power; appeal to it for relief to their wants; and address the President as their great father." Accordingly, the U.S. government retains plenary or absolute control over Native Americans, their lands, and their federally-recognized tribal status.

4. Today, the Decolonization Committee of the United Nations not only oversees the case of Puerto Rico's status, but of other U.S. colonies—i.e., non-self-governing territo-

and Japan (Gonzalez 2000, 249–50). Puerto Rico serves as a captive market for U.S. goods; its population is a source of low-wage labor; 14 percent of the land is used for U.S. military bases; and Puerto Ricans can be readily drafted or they volunteer to serve and fight in the U.S. military (Gonzalez 2000, 251–53; Maldonado-Denis 1972).

Contrary to popular beliefs, Puerto Rico is not an example of U.S. magnanimity or a model for Third World development. Puerto Rico is an impoverished nation with 60 percent of its people living below the poverty line (Gonzalez 2000, 250). According to Trías Monge (1997, 3–4),

> Per capita income in Puerto Rico is still only about one-third of that of the United States and half of Mississippi. In the Caribbean, eleven other areas enjoy a higher per capita income: the Cayman Islands, Aruba, Montserrat, the Bahamas, Martinique, the American Virgin Islands, the British Virgin Islands, the Netherlands Antilles, Guadeloupe, French Guiana, and Barbados. The per capita income of the poorest of these areas is 20 percent higher than that of Puerto Rico.

Consolidating Hemispheric Hegemony

Beyond the assertions of U.S. power over Mexico and Puerto Rico, the history of U.S.-Latin American relations abounds with examples of instances in which the U.S. government has sought to extend its political, economic and cultural domination. The forms of racism and paternalism evident in manifest destiny, the *Insular Cases*, and the other examples cited previously, have also been discernible in U.S. actions toward other Latin American countries. The seemingly countless number of U.S. interventions of Latin America's so-called "banana republics" reeks of condescension and paternalism (see LaFeber 1993).

The cornerstone of U.S. policy toward Latin America has been the Monroe Doctrine of 1823. As most of Latin America broke away from Spanish and Portuguese colonial rule by the 1820s, President James Monroe's administration moved quickly to stave off any additional interventions or colonization by other European powers, declaring such attempts "dangerous to our peace and safety" (Holden and Zolov 2000, 13). The Monroe Doctrine's silence on U.S. colonial aspirations opened the door for the use of force against any al-

---

ries—including Guam, American Samoa, and the U.S. Virgin Islands (see, e.g., United Nations 2003a).

leged outside threat to U.S. interests in the hemisphere, and consequently, any obstacle in the way of achieving complete hegemony over the Americas.

To advance U.S. interests in the Americas, the 1904 Roosevelt Corollary to the Monroe Doctrine laid out the ground rules that justified U.S. military interventionism. In the words of Theodore Roosevelt:

> Chronic wrong-doing, or an impotence which results in a general loosening of the ties of civilized society, may in America, as elsewhere, ultimately require intervention by some civilized nation, and in the Western Hemisphere the adherence of the United States to the Monroe Doctrine may force the United States, however reluctantly, in flagrant cases of such wrongdoing or impotence, to the exercise of an international police power. (Department of State 1905, xli–xlii)

Of course, the "civilized nation" to oversee this extension of the Monroe Doctrine was the United States, and U.S. desires to intervene in Latin America were far from reluctant. Commonly referred to as the "Big Stick" doctrine, the Roosevelt Corollary to the Monroe Doctrine legitimized the use of U.S. armed force, but it did little to "civilize" or democratize the region. Between 1898 and 1934, the United States militarily invaded and/or occupied Latin American countries on more than thirty occasions and "despite high-minded rhetoric and ostensible nobility of purpose, not a single U.S. intervention led to installation of democracy" (Smith 2000, 60).

In the Dominican Republic, U.S. military interventions begun under Theodore Roosevelt's administration spanned many decades and included the U.S. invasions and military occupations in 1903, 1904, 1914, 1916–1924, and 1965 (51, 169–172). These interventions provided direct control over the Dominican Republic's economy for the benefit of U.S. banking and commercial interests, most clearly evident in U.S. seizure of the customhouses (54–56). Instead of spreading democracy, U.S. policies supported brutal dictators, as in the Dominican Republic's Rafael Trujillo, who could safeguard U.S. business interests and profits (Schmitz 1999; Roorda 1998). Into the later half of the twentieth century, the 1965 U.S. military occupation of the Dominican Republic guaranteed that the democratically elected government of Juan Bosch would never return, paving the way for Trujillo's right-hand man Joaquín Balaguer (Moya Pons 1995, 381–404; Smith 2000, 169–72).

For the United States, adherence to the norms of international law was at best an afterthought. As U.S. power and control over the region grew, justifying violations of international law became increasingly insignificant to U.S. government leaders. In a moment of complete candor in reference to the intervention of Panama, Theodore Roosevelt offered no explanation other than

"I took the Isthmus" (quoted in Schoultz 1998, 173). From as early as the 1850s, the U.S. government preferred to recognize William Walker as the legitimate president of Nicaragua—a North American filibuster who orchestrated an illegal coup to install himself as president, declare English the official language, and legalize slavery—than to respect the rights of Nicaraguans to self-determination (Holden and Zolov 2000, 39).[5] Into the twentieth century, the United States abused its self-ordained "police power" to impose a brutally racist and autocratic U.S. military regime upon the people of Haiti during the U.S. occupation of Haiti from 1915–1934 (Schmidt 1995).

Having already significantly consolidated its hegemony by the 1930s (Smith 2000, 64), the United States moved toward a policy of acting as a "good neighbor," adopting a noninterventionist stance, in words if not deeds. This shift was based, in part, on the implementation of international agreements, most notably the Convention on the Rights and Duties of States adopted at Montevideo in 1933, that reinforced the concept of the equality of states and specifically declared in article 8 that "[n]o state has the right to intervene in the internal or external affairs of another" (Convention on the Rights and Duties of States 1933). Although the "good neighbor" policy ostensibly sought to demonstrate U.S. intentions to act in accordance with international law in an effort to salvage its international reputation, the policy change was undercut, not by a return to overt military interventionism, but by U.S. resort to the installation of puppet governments and support for military dictatorships responsible for egregious human rights violations throughout Latin America (Schoultz 1998).

In the name of fighting communism, U.S. policy took an especially brutal turn at the expense of human rights in Latin America. Similar to the neo-colonial relationship maintained with the Dominican Republic, the United States propped up and sustained ruthless dictators and oligarchs throughout Latin America. The Somoza family dynasty (1934–1979) in Nicaragua, a family "[t]hat seized most of the wealth, including a land area equal the size of Massachusetts" and the infamous "Fourteen Families" of El Salvador who still control almost 60 percent of the land were among the most notorious examples (LaFeber 1993, 10–11). In Cuba, the United States backed the government of Fulgencio Batista, a dictator who tolerated gross economic disparities, poverty, unemployment, illiteracy, and racial exclusion for the protection of U.S. busi-

---

5. Filibuster is a term derived "from the Spanish *filibustero*, for freebooter or buccaneer" (Holden and Zolov 2000, 39). LaFeber describes the filibusters of the mid-1800s as "private adventurers who moved out of New Orleans, New York, and Baltimore to conquer the small countries [of Central America] for personal gain, the extension of slave territory, or usually both" (1993, 30).

ness interests (Pérez, Jr. 1995, 295–307). In these and other instances through-out Latin America, repression became the means by which social unrest in the face of economic injustice was quelled. Latin American armies trained and fi-nanced by the United States became the surrogates for U.S. marines, who in earlier times were readily called upon to intervene.

BEHIND THE RHETORIC OF DEMOCRACY

It would appear inconceivable that the United States—a country founded in a war against colonialism—would seek to subjugate other peoples or un-dermine the very principles of democracy that it purports to spread. The con-tradiction between its stated principles and its hegemonic ambitions has been and continues to be a central theme in U.S. foreign policy. However, a now familiar pattern was established early on in Latin America: U.S. global eco-nomic interests usually supercede even its best intentions. A U.S. marine in the 1930s, Smedley Darlington Butler, memorialized his recollection of decades of U.S. interventionism as such:

> I spent thirty-three years, most of my time being a high class muscle man for big business, for Wall Street and the bankers. In short, I was a racketeer for capitalism…. I helped make Mexico, especially Tampico, safe for American oil interests in 1916. I helped make Haiti and Cuba a decent place for the National City Bank boys to collect revenue in. I helped in the raping of half a dozen Central American republics for the benefits of Wall Street. The record of racketeering is long. I helped purify Nicaragua for the international banking house of Brown Broth-ers in 1909–1912. I brought light to the Dominican Republic for American sugar interests in 1916. (Butler [1935] 2003, 10)

But as Cornell University historian Walter LaFeber explains (1993), U.S. busi-ness interests were not alone in this venture; the U.S government worked ceaselessly to support U.S.-based commercial enterprises. By establishing and maintaining a system grounded in the Monroe Doctrine, the U.S. government could always provide direct assistance—including the use of military force—to protect U.S. corporate interests in the region (81–85).

Hegemony over the Western Hemisphere translated into securing a per-petual source of cheap and exploitable land, raw materials, human labor, and other resources. This held true as much for the Cold War era (1947–1989) as it did in earlier periods in U.S.-Latin American relations. In 1950, George Ken-nan, the chief State Department official responsible for the Cold War containment policy, outlined the goals of U.S. policy toward Latin America during the Cold War in order of importance, as follows:

1. The protection of our [sic] raw materials;
2. The prevention of military exploitation of Latin America by the enemy; and
3. The prevention of the psychological mobilization of Latin America against us. (quoted in LaFeber 1993, 109)

To these ends, in 1954, the U.S. government through the C.I.A. and the United Fruit Company combined to topple the democratically-elected government of Jacobo Arbenz, who sought land reform for impoverished peasants in Guatemala. Although not a communist, the U.S. government considered Arbenz "soft" on communism, creating the necessary pretext for the coup. For decades, U.S.-backed, right-wing military juntas in Guatemala crushed the opposition and committed countless atrocities and killings among civilians, peasants, and indigenous peoples (LaFeber 1993).

In El Salvador, the Salvadoran military engaged in bloody counterinsurgency operations backed by the U.S. government. Its mission to eliminate the opposition to the government resulted in innumerable deaths, including the assassinations of three U.S. nuns, a Catholic layperson, and Archbishop Oscar Romero in 1980; the massacre at El Mozote, where hundreds of men, women and children were slaughtered in 1981; and the murder of six Jesuit scholars, their housekeeper and her daughter in El Salvador in 1989 (LaFeber 1993; Danner, 1993; LeoGrande 1998, 570–71). The U.S. government continued to provide military aid to the government of El Salvador even as the U.S.-trained Salvadoran soldiers, such as the Atlactl Battalion, were being implicated in these murders. In lieu of sending its own troops (that is, the use of the "Big Stick"), the U.S. government preferred a policy that allowed the local armed forces to assume the role of assassins, saboteurs, and terrorists to protect U.S. interests in the region.

The 1975 Select Committee to Study Governmental Operations with Respect to Intelligence Activities, known as the Church Committee report after Senator Frank Church, revealed the extent of U.S. covert operations in Cuba, Chile, the Dominican Republic, and the Congo, including plots to kill Fidel Castro and Patrice Lumumba (Senate 1975a; Senate 1975b). The Church hearings and other disclosures established that the C.I.A.'s *Freedom Fighting Manual* and the School of the Americas' *Study Manual* were published and distributed to Latin American military personnel for the precise purpose of training in sabotage and torture (Holden and Zolov 2000, 297–99, 313–15).

In yet another successful attempt at "regime change" in Latin America, the United States in 1973 helped depose the democratically-elected government of Salvador Allende in Chile. Recently declassified C.I.A. documents directly implicate President Nixon and then Secretary of State Henry Kissinger in the covert operations to destabilize the Allende government (Kornbluh 2003a, 2003b). In an exposé of Henry Kissinger's involvement in the events that took place in Chile, Christopher Hitchens (2001, 55) observed that "the very name of Allende was anathema to the extreme Right in Chile, to certain powerful corporations (notably ITT, Pepsi Cola and the Chase Manhattan Bank) which did business in Chile and the United States, and to the CIA." General Augusto Pinochet—whose right-wing dictatorship unseated Allende's government and was recognized by the United States—has been accused of torture and other gross violations of human rights resulting in the deaths and disappearances of thousands persons following the 1973 coup (see, e.g., *Regina v. Bartle*, House of Lords, 24 March 1999 [1999] 2 All ER 97, [1999] 2 WLR 827). U.S. support for authoritarian regimes in Argentina, Paraguay, and Brazil had similar aims: violence—including torture, "disappearances," "dirty wars," and other violations of the most basic human rights—was to be deployed against anyone who opposed the established order of repressive, right-wing regimes that protected U.S. interests in the hemisphere.

In the case of Nicaragua, U.S. disregard for the human rights of Latin Americans under international law could not be more glaring. In 1986, the International Court of Justice (ICJ or the World Court) voted overwhelmingly to condemn U.S. support of the "contra war" and the mining of the Nicaraguan harbor in Nicaragua as blatant violations of international law that, *inter alia*, endangered the lives and wellbeing of civilians and infringed upon Nicaragua's territorial sovereignty (Military and Paramilitary Activities (Nicar. v. U.S.), 1986 I.C.J. 14 (June 27)). By any measure, such actions could be categorized as state-sponsored terrorism. The seriousness of U.S. violations against Nicaragua left the ICJ no option but to rule that the United States was obligated to make reparations to the Republic of Nicaragua for all the injuries caused to the country and its people, damage claims which had risen to $17 billion (Holden and Zolov 2000, 300). In defiance of the World Court's decision, the U.S. government refused to recognize the court's jurisdiction, shunning all accountability under international law (LaFeber 1993, 301; LeoGrande 1998, 333–34; Smith 2000).[6]

The resulting turmoil, death, and economic and social destruction left after decades of internal conflict in Central America cannot be underestimated:

---

6. At the behest of the United States, the U.S.-backed government of Violeta Chamorro withdrew Nicaragua's case before the World Court on September 12, 2001, denying the country the opportunity to obtain court-awarded monetary compensation (Holden and Zolov 2000, 300).

[T]he years from 1979–1991 turned out to be the bloodiest, most violent, and most destructive era in Central America's post-1820 history. The number of dead and 'disappeared' varies according to different sources. The minimum number is 200,000 (40,000 in Nicaragua, 75,000 in El Salvador, 75,000 in Guatemala, 10,000 in Honduras and the frontier fighting in Costa Rica), but this is only an estimate. Millions have been displaced or made refugees. If a similar catastrophe struck the United States in proportion, 2½ million North Americans would die and 10 to 20 million would be driven from their homes. (LaFeber 1993, 362)

Following this period of armed conflict in Central America, it was found that "[h]undreds of thousands of Central Americans (one out of four in the case of Salvadorans) have been uprooted by force, military pressure, or war destruction, becoming refugees either in their own countries or abroad" (Zea, Diehl and Porterfield 1997, 39). By the early 1990s, "more than a million Salvadorans and about 200,000 Guatemalan refugees resided in the United States alone…most of them children or young adults" (39–40).

The connection between U.S. policy and many documented human right atrocities of that era has been well established by respected sources, including the international commission of inquiry established under the Accord of Oslo of 1994 (United Nations 1994a). The commission of inquiry, officially named the Commission for Historical Clarification, concluded:

Whilst anti-communism, promoted by the United States within the framework of its foreign policy, received firm support from right-wing political parties and from various other powerful actors in Guatemala, the United States demonstrated that it was willing to provide support for strong military regimes in its strategic backyard. (1999, 19)

Throughout the Cold War period, as Smith asserts, "[f]ear of the 'communist threat' may have been greatly exaggerated, as now appears in retrospect" (2000, 2). In support for this assessment, the Commission for Historical Clarification found that

at no time during the internal armed confrontation did the guerilla groups have the military potential necessary to pose an imminent threat to the State. The number of insurgent combatants was too small to be able to compete in the military arena with the Guatemalan Army, which had more troops and superior weaponry, as well as better training and co-ordination…the State deliberately magnified the military threat of the insurgency, a practise justified by the concept of the internal enemy. The inclusion of all opponents under one banner, democratic or otherwise, pacifist or guerrilla, legal or illegal, communist or noncommunist, served to justify numerous and serious crimes. (1999, 22)

Thus, in hindsight it is plausible to conclude that U.S. policies in Latin America had less to do with fighting communism than with maintaining the old order in which U.S. economic interests could reign free to exploit Latin America's land, labor, and other resources. Certainly, U.S. support for brutal right-wing dictatorships belies any rhetoric about spreading freedom and democracy.

GLOBALIZATION'S IMPACT: MAINTAINING THE SYSTEM

Today, it is generally incontrovertible that the primary aim of U.S. policy toward Latin America historically was its maintenance of political and economic hegemony over the Americas. Tragically, this goal too often came at the expense of the human rights and dignity of peoples in Latin America. But it is also argued that the United States has not only reaped the benefits of its past domination over Latin America, but it also actively seeks to keep them in place through its present policies. After decades of consolidating its hegemony over the hemisphere, the United States in the post-Cold War era is able to deploy new justifications for the use of military force, and it utilizes global economic strategies to maintain its power over the region.

In its first military intervention in a Latin American country after the fall of the Soviet Union, the 1989 U.S. military invasion of Panama purported to fight the "war on drugs" by capturing the alleged drug-kingpin and head of state Manuel Antonio Noriega, a former C.I.A. operative who had been paid upwards of $200,000 annually from U.S. tax dollars (Scott and Marshall 1991, 67). However, as an anti-drug initiative, this military invasion today is widely considered a failure. "Operation Just Cause had virtually no effect on drug trafficking," and in reality, Noriega turned out to be "a minor player in the narcotics business" (Smith 2000, 297; see also Scott and Marshall 1991, 72). Analysts have documented how the invasion had nothing to do with fighting a war against drugs and virtually everything to do with how Noriega became increasingly expendable to U.S. policy and interests by the late 1980s (Scott and Marshall 1991, 65–73). In fact, Panama's new President, Guillermo Endara, had ties to the banks implicated in drug-money laundering (72–73).

Further belying President George H.W. Bush's justifications of the "war on drugs" for the invasion, the U.S. government's General Accounting Office reported increases in drug activity in Panama two years after the invasion, noting that the country "continues to be a haven for money laundering" (General Accounting Office 1991, 1).

The U.S. invasion of Panama endures today, along with past interventions, as another affront to human rights and international law. Critics charged that the U.S. military's use of excessive force caused the deaths of thousands of Panamanian civilians in violation of international law (see, e.g., Clark 1991). Numerous human rights groups reported that disproportionate numbers of Panamanian civilians were killed as a result of the invasion, and at the United Nations, the U.N. General Assembly vehemently condemned the invasion as a "flagrant violation" of international law (Smith 2000, 297). In the post–Cold War era, the U.S. invasion of Panama became symbolic of U.S. intentions to consolidate its authority over the Americas. Past pretexts—such as spreading democracy or the fight against communism—have been replaced with new justifications for U.S. interventionism, such as the war on drugs.

But it is crucial to note that direct military intervention—however much an option for U.S. policymakers—is superfluous in view of the United States' current global economic supremacy. The North American Free Trade Agreement (NAFTA) and other U.S. efforts to promote the neo-liberal agenda of free trade, open markets, privatization, and economic global integration have provided an international framework that facilitates and continues the flow of economic benefits to the countries of the "North"—the United States, Western Europe, and Japan—often with diminishing returns and growing economic inequality for a vast number of developing nations of the "South"— Latin America, Africa, and Asia.

There is mounting evidence that the free trade policies promoted by the United States have actually led to uneven development, favoring developed countries to the detriment of developing nations. "The income gap between the fifth of the world's people living in the richest countries and the fifth in the poorest was 74-to-1 in 1997, up from 60-to-1 in 1990 and 30-to-1 in 1960. By 1997, the richest 20% captured 86% of world income, with the poorest 20% capturing a mere 1%" (Wallach and Sforza 1999, 16). Throughout Latin America from the period of the 1980s to the 1990s, "the absolute number of people living under conditions of poverty swelled from 125 million to 186 million, an increase of 61 million, or nearly 50 percent" (Smith 2000, 272).

With the expansion of U.S. corporate interests, the exploitation of human labor and resources in Latin America by U.S. multinational corporations at the expense of human rights, labor rights, and environmental rights of Latin

Americans has become an increasing concern. Over the last decade, U.S. companies have been accused of engaging in illegal child labor and sweatshop practices and in creating gross environmental hazards in factories or *maquiladoras* that produce garments and other items for major U.S. corporations throughout Mexico, Central America, and the Caribbean (Gonzalez 2000, 228–45; Rosen and McFayden 1995). Free trade zones that offer tax breaks to global corporations in developing countries have frequently been cited for using repressive means "to keep free trade zones free of labor unions, as well as health and safety regulations" (Sklar 1995, 46). In El Salvador, U.S. clothing manufacturers have been able to pay as little as 33 cents an hour to factory workers (47).

As illustrated in a series of editorials in the *New York Times*, free trade, as it currently operates, provides an unfair advantage to U.S. business interests. Profits are harvested by developed countries on the backs of poverty-stricken nations. Huge sums in U.S. subsidies to the U.S. cotton and other industries virtually insure that developing nations will remain poor and unable to compete fairly with developed nations (*New York Times* 2003a, A18; 2003b, A14; 2003c, 10; 2003d, A20).

The model for development in Latin America touted by U.S. presidents has been NAFTA. Yet despite NAFTA's promise of economic development, poverty stands roughly the same in Mexico today—just over 50 percent—as it did in the early 1980s. But if one factors in population growth in Mexico, from 70 million to 100 million over the same period, Mexico can be considered worse off today with "19 million more Mexicans living in poverty than 20 years ago, according to Mexican government and international organizations.... What has become painfully clear in Mexico is that free trade—most famously NAFTA—has failed to lift the country out of poverty" (Jordan and Sullivan 2003, A10).

Indeed, nearly ten years after NAFTA began, a study sponsored by the Carnegie Endowment for International Peace concludes that "NAFTA has not helped the Mexican economy keep pace with the growing demand for jobs." The purported benefits of NAFTA for Mexico's poorest have not been realized. "Real wages for most Mexicans today are lower than they were when NAFTA took effect." Moreover, "NAFTA has not stemmed the flow of poor Mexicans into the United States in search of jobs; in fact there has been a dramatic rise in the number of migrants to the United States, despite an unprecedented increase in border control measures" (Audley et al. 2003, 6).

Nobel prize winner in economics Joseph E. Stiglitz has also voiced criticisms about the course that globalization has taken, noting that even in instances where growth has occurred in Mexico, "the benefits have accrued largely to the upper 30 percent, and have been even more concentrated in the top 10 percent. Those at the bottom have gained little; many are even worse off" (2002, 86). Stiglitz attributes the present-day attitude of developed countries to the persistence of the colonial mentality that presumes they know what is best for developing nations, and that the United States is still affected by the historical legacy of "manifest destiny" and expansionism, and to an even greater extent, "by the cold war, in which principles of democracy were compromised or ignored, in the all encompassing struggle against communism" (24–25).

Despite these criticisms, the United States is poised to begin another round of free trade initiatives throughout the Americas in the form of the Free Trade Area of the Americas and bilateral treaties with Central American countries. Considering the balance of power, it is questionable whether most Latin American countries truly have a choice in the matter.

Conclusions

As LaFaber explains (1993), the primary U.S. government objective in Latin America, past and present, has been to create and maintain a system that assures U.S. economic and political hegemony. The historical events outlined in this chapter have had a profound impact on Latinos and Latinas, including the following:

The Establishment and Fortification of a Dominant-Subordinate Paradigm

U.S. imperial conquests and interventionist policies have established a dominant-subordinate paradigm that persists to the present. The current global economic configuration maintains a system advantageous to U.S. government and corporate interests that had its origins in the hegemonic aspirations of the United States' earliest leaders. The consequences of U.S. hegemony over the Americas have been lasting and dramatic. Today, Latin American countries remain impoverished and, therefore, vulnerable to continued exploitation and subordination, nearly as easily as they were in the 1820s. The single-minded pursuit of U.S. foreign policy goals and economic interests has often blinded the U.S. government to the human suffering and the violations of sovereignty and other rights resulting from its own actions. The covert and overt use of force and direct and indirect forms of intervention throughout the region have become so regular as to have become normalized as a matter of U.S. policy.

From "manifest destiny" to "free trade," U.S. policies toward Latin Americans have been repeatedly couched in benign terms, but its undercurrents of paternalism and its human, economic, social, and environmental costs to Latin America are undeniable. While Latin America's social and economic troubles are also attributable to widespread and unrelenting corruption in many Latin American countries (Rosenberg 2003), it is equally true that the United States has traditionally played a key role in undermining democracy in support of corrupt and brutal regimes that sustained inequalities and hardships in their respective countries.

For much of its 71-year rule, the Institutional Revolutionary Party (PRI) in Mexico, for instance, engaged in fraudulent elections and other kinds of illegal, corrupt, and undemocratic behavior. Yet the United States government readily lent support for many of Mexico's leaders, including former President Carlos Salinas de Gotari, whose brother was implicated in illegal drug trafficking and who himself has been under a cloud of suspicion of corruption since the end of his term in office in 1994 (McKinley, Jr. 2004, A4).

Accountability also rests with the United States for the many ruthless Latin American dictators it has sponsored over the years, including Somoza in Nicaragua, Trujillo in the Dominican Republic, Strossener in Paraguay, the Duvaliers in Haiti, Pinochet in Chile, and military regimes in Argentina and Brazil. Given this record, it is no wonder that Latin America remains weak and impoverished.

The powerful forces of globalization, as they function presently, more often than not promote poverty and unfair treatment of Latin American workers, peasants, and indigenous peoples, placing ever-increasing pressure on the poor of Latin America to immigrate to the United States in hope of a better life. U.S. free trade policies actually appear to be worsening conditions in Latin America and are the cause of an increase of Latin American immigrants into the United States who are desperate for work (Audley et al. 2003).

Consistent with the theory of "push and pull" factors—"factors that cause a population to move out of an area (push) and into a new area (pull)" (Healey 2003, 610)—dire economic conditions that exist in Latin America provide a potent "push" incentive for Latin Americans to leave for the United States, as the economically dominant and powerful country where jobs and opportunities are purportedly abundant. Latin Americans will continue to try to migrate to the United States, where in turn, they are also susceptible to exploitation as low-wage factory or agricultural workers. Studies of the apparel industry in the United States show that U.S. companies continue to draw on or "pull" Latin American immigrants to the United States into industries where they serve as a source of cheap and exploitable labor (Gereffi, Spener, and Bair 2002; Sassen 1998).

The dominate-subordinate paradigm that characterizes U.S.-Latin American relations fulfills two major functions: (1) it keeps Latin America and its peoples poor and vulnerable to exploitation, and (2) it provides for a steady steam of immigrants from Latin America to meet the needs of U.S. businesses vying for cheap labor. The failure of U.S. policy to have a positive impact on economic development in Latin America will result invariably in increases in Latino/a immigration.

The Racialization of Latin Americans

In the pursuit of its foreign policy objectives, the United States has often been indifferent to the human rights and well-being of Latin Americans. The United States has not been immune to the hubris common to previous imperial powers that have believed that they knew what was best for the world. Powerful ideas about race, including the grand allure of manifest destiny, shaped not only U.S. foreign policy, but how the United States was to view Latin Americans. The absence of concern for the human rights of Latin Americans by the U.S. government, as much as it is rooted in its hegemonic ambitions, is also rooted in racist and racialized perceptions of Latin Americans. The racialization of Latin Americans as racially inferior not only served to justify U.S. conquests and policies, it helped rationalize the subsequent subordination of Mexicans and Puerto Ricans in the United States, establishing the pattern of treatment for Latinos/as who followed. As explored in the next chapter, this racialized image of Latin Americans formed the basis for prejudice and discrimination for all other Latinas and Latinos.

U.S.-Latin American Linkages and Their Consequences

Globalization and migratory patterns are likely to continue to strengthen linkages between Latinos/as in the United States and their native homelands. This phenomenon will make Latinos/as an ever-growing part of the future of the United States. U.S.-Latin American relations, thus, become an essential part of understanding the Latino/a experience in the United States today.

Latin Americans have endured an arduous historical trajectory. Centuries of colonialism, plunder, and exploitation have left a legacy that is present today. Vast economic and social inequalities and injustices still mar the Latin American landscape, with the effect of globalized corporate power on Latin America being but one example of how foreign interests and profits supercede the needs and concerns of contemporary Latin Americans and U.S. Latinos/as.

In his classic work *Open Veins of Latin America*, Eduardo Galeano poignantly reminds us of the impact of U.S. colonialism and neocolonial policies over time:

> Along the way we [Latin Americans] even lost the right to call ourselves Americans, although the Haitians and the Cubans appeared in history as new people a century before the *Mayflower* pilgrims settled on the Plymouth coast. For the world today, America is just the United States; the region we inhabit is a sub-America, a second-class America of nebulous identity. ([1973] 1997, 2)

Indeed, the possibility of Latin Americans achieving the full realization of the right to chart their own historical course, to determine their own social and cultural identity, and to control their own economic development appears as elusive as ever in contrast to the power of the North American behemoth. This reality presents equally difficult challenges for Latinos/as in the United States.

CHAPTER 3

DISCRIMINATION AND LATINOS/AS IN THE UNITED STATES

"Racial Profiling is a tool we use, and don't let anyone say otherwise. Like up in the valley, I knew who the crack sellers were—they look like Hispanics who should be cutting your lawn"—Deputy Bobby Harris, Los Angeles County Sheriff's Department. (Goldberg 1999, 57)

"Over eight in ten (82%) Latinos report that discrimination against Latinos is a problem in preventing Latinos from succeeding in the United States." (Pew Hispanic Center/Kaiser Family Foundation 2002, 70)

The history of U.S.-Latin American relations can be summed up as unequal: one country wealthy and dominant; the others poor and vulnerable. This relationship has been, and in many ways, continues to be fashioned by the inexorable drive of the United States to maintain a dominant-subordinate arrangement. To this end, racist ideologies, economic advantage, political power, and military might have all been deployed.

In the context of U.S.-Latin American relations, the concept of race as it has evolved in the United States has been an especially convenient device used to explain and legitimize the subordination of Latin American peoples. Racist and racialized categorizations in the United States have played a central role in justifying and unifying the country in the conquest of Latin American lands, the exploitation of Latin American workers, unrestricted and unfair access to Latin America's natural resources, and the exacting of unfair commercial and other economic advantages at the expense of Latin Americans' right to self-determination, well-being, and development.

Over time, concerns over European recolonization of the Western Hemisphere, the fear of the spread of Soviet communism in the post-World War II era, and the war on drugs have rationalized U.S. interventionism throughout Latin America. But an equally significant undercurrent of U.S. policy toward

43

Latin America has been its racialized, condescending, and paternalistic aspects that question the capacity of Latin Americans to govern themselves. Then as now, the United States has exhibited an inability to fully accept the exercise of the fundamental right of self-determination by Latin American peoples. Its actions demonstrate reluctance to treat Latin Americans as equals since that would, in almost all circumstances, impede U.S. commercial, military, and political interests. In the name of protecting those interests, the United States has not hesitated to stifle, rather than promote, human rights and democracy.

Latinos/as in the United States—the descendants of those who were conquered by the United States, as in the case of Mexicans after 1848 or Puerto Ricans after 1898, and those who followed, escaping economic and/or political hardships in their homelands—have been no less susceptible to racialized characterizations and unequal policies and practices that preserve economic, political, and social control in the hands of Anglo Americans. A definition of racial and ethnic discrimination is the unequal treatment based on membership in a particular racial or ethnic group (Healey 2003, 26). If applied to the situation of Latin Americans, such a definition makes plain that the United States has not treated Latin Americans as equals.

Similar to the use of race in U.S.-Latin American relations, race has been a powerful tool shaping attitudes, policies, practices, and laws affecting Latinos/as in the United States. This chapter explores the Latino/a experience with discrimination in the United States and Latino/a resistance to the injustice rendered by prejudice and discrimination.[1]

Latinos/as and Discrimination: 1848–Present

Understanding that U.S. policies toward Latin America have often been premised on ideas about the racial inferiority of Latin Americans, it follows that in the United States Latinos/as would not likely be treated as equals any more than Latin Americans abroad. With respect to the earliest Latinos/as in the United States, Martha Menchaca explains that

---

1. In contrast to discrimination or the "the unequal treatment of a person or persons based on group membership" (Healey 2003, 26), prejudice can be defined as "the tendency to think about other groups in negative ways, to attach negative emotions to those groups, and to prejudge individuals on the basis of their group memberships" (25).

Most [U.S.] government officials argued that Mexicans of predominantly Indian descent should be extended the same legal status as the detribalized American Indians. Mexicans, on the other hand, argued that under the Treaty of Guadalupe Hidalgo and international laws, the U.S. Government agreed to extend [to] all Mexican citizens—regardless of their race—the political rights enjoyed by white citizens. These rights were accorded to them on the basis of the international principle guaranteeing inhabitants of ceded territories the nationality of the successor state unless other provisions are made in the treaty of peace. (1993, 584)

Soon after the end of the U.S.-Mexican War in 1848, vast tracts of land inhabited by Mexicans pursuant to Spanish or Mexican land grants were swiftly wrested by Anglo Americans. Whites forcibly removed Mexicans from their lands; married wealthy, landowning Mexican women; or used the courts and claims procedures established by Congress—including the California Land Claims Commission and the Court of Private Claims—to gain title to lands (Perea et al. 2000, 270–71). Laws were created and the courts were used effectively to limit Latino/a rights to the advantage of Anglo Americans. Many land grants, for instance, were based on concepts of communal properties, conflicting with U.S. notions of private property. As a result, courts increasingly ruled in favor of Anglo claims over lands inhabited by Mexicans under the land grant system (Acuña 2000, 369; Ebright 1994). By 1897, the U.S. Supreme Court in *United States v. Sandoval*, 167 U.S. 278 (1897), ruled that property protected by article 8 of the Treaty of Guadalupe Hidalgo did not protect claims to communally held lands, as such lands had been under Spanish or Mexican authority government and, therefore, individual claimants lacked actual title.

The massive loss of land sparked resistance by Mexicans in the territories ceded to the United States. The insurgency movement led by Juan Cortina in 1859, known as the Cortina War, was among the earliest organized opposition efforts (Rosenbaum 1998). The fight over the seizure of land grants continued for many decades and included the organized resistance efforts of Reies López Tijerina's *La Alianza Federal de Mercedes* (the Federal Alliance of Land Grants) into the 1960s. The *Alianza's* protests "invoked the treaty of Guadalupe Hidalgo…. For them, it was problematic to force a defeated nation to 'sell' territory under duress" (Acuña 2000, 369). Unfortunately, a legacy of the Treaty of Guadalupe Hidalgo is its failure to adequately protect the most fundamental of rights for Mexicans to remain on their own lands. The treaty did not effectively prevent lands from ending up in the hands of Anglo settlers; it sim-

ply provided the appearance of a fair treaty in fulfillment with the requirements of international law.

Full and equal rights as U.S. citizens were denied to persons of Mexican ancestry after 1848 in other areas of life. For generations, school segregation was
as much a part of life for Chicanos as it was for African Americans in the
United States. It was not until 1946 in the case of *Mendez v. Westminster School
District of Orange County*, 64 F. Supp. 544, 549 (S.D. Cal. 1946), *aff'd*, 161
F.2d 774 (9th Cir. 1947)—a precursor to the landmark 1954 Supreme Court
decision in *Brown v. Board of Education*, 347 U.S. 483 (1954)—that it was held
that children of Mexican descent were deprived of equal educational opportunities in the public school system through segregation. The court in *Mendez*
quite pointedly found that "the methods of segregation prevalent in the defendant school districts foster antagonisms in the children and suggest inferiority among them where none exists" (*Mendez v. Westminster School District
of Orange County*, 64 F. Supp. 544, 549).

For decades, state-sanctioned segregation and exclusion was a fact of life
for Latinos/as in the United States as much as it was for African Americans.
As the Supreme Court acknowledged in *Hernandez v. Texas*, 347 U.S. 475,
479–80 (1954), two weeks before delivering its decision in the *Brown* case, the
subordination of persons of Mexican descent by Whites had been systematic
for many years and the evidence before the court confirmed this reality:

> The participation of persons of Mexican descent in business and
> community groups was shown to be slight. Until very recent times,
> children of Mexican descent were required to attend a segregated
> school for the first four grades. At least one restaurant in town promi-
> nently displayed a sign announcing 'No Mexicans Served.' On the
> courthouse grounds at the time of the hearing, there were two men's
> toilets, one unmarked, and the other marked 'Colored Men' and
> 'Hombres Aquí' ('Men Here').

Hernandez v. Texas—a case which struck down the practice of excluding persons of Mexican descent from service as jury commissioners, grand jurors,
and petit jurors—marked the first instance in which a Latino/a group was recognized as a "cognizable minority group for equal protection purposes" under
the Constitution's Fourteenth Amendment, transcending the commonly held
Black/White understanding of race and discrimination in the United States
(Perea 1997b, 1248–49).

Indeed, discrimination and second-class citizenship for Latinos/as took
many forms. Politically, California's first constitution granted voting rights
only to "white" Mexicans, as Mexicans were generally considered an inferior

race of indigenous ancestry (Perea et al. 2000, 265–70). The "Greaser Act," an anti-vagrancy law enacted in California in 1856 directed at "all persons who are commonly known as 'Greasers' or the issue [children] of Spanish or Native Blood," was a deliberate use of the law for purposes of discriminating against persons of Latin American descent and suppressing their rights based on a "racial" criteria (Acuña 2000, 144). In later years, the *Bracero* Program (1942–1964), the federal government's initiative to make up for labor shortages during World War II, represented another legal mechanism used to exploit Mexican workers for cheap labor. Legal challenges to the unjust treatment received under this program have endured into recent years, with Mexican workers still seeking just compensation for wages never paid (Louima 2002, 5).

With a rise in anti-immigrant and anti-Mexican sentiment in the 1950s came another federal government program, "Operation Wetback." Under this program, growing nativist demands to stop Mexican migration were satisfied through a military operation that purported to deport undocumented Mexicans in the United States. As its derogatory name implies, safeguarding human and civil rights was not a concern. In fact, it served as a smokescreen for illegal searches and seizures and resulted in the mass deportation of many Mexicans with U.S. citizenship (Mirandé 1987, 125–29; Acuña 2000, 304–5; Healey 2003, 361).

As with Mexicans after 1848, the rights of Puerto Ricans following the U.S. war with Spain in 1898 were also severely circumscribed. With the U.S. occupation of Puerto Rico in 1898, the United States imposed martial rule. In 1900, a civilian government with a U.S. appointed governor was installed in disregard for Puerto Rico's own constitutional government and political autonomy established in 1897. Puerto Rican culture, linguistic heritage, and identity also suffered a severe blow. In an attempt to force assimilation, the U.S. government banned Spanish as the language of instruction in public schools and imposed English as the official language of instruction from 1898 to 1948 (Zentella 1999).

Essentially the same Supreme Court that decided the notorious case of *Plessy v. Ferguson*, 163 U.S. 537 (1896), also decided the cases that define Puerto Rico's present status and rights vis-à-vis the United States under U.S. law. Similar to *Plessy*, the Insular Cases were designed, in part, to protect the United States from "alien races" (see *Downes v. Bidwell*, 182 U.S. 244 (1901); Toruella 1988). In keeping with the *Insular Cases*, the U.S. Congress today exerts absolute power over the civil rights of Puerto Ricans and the status of their homeland. Puerto Ricans benefit only from those rights that the U.S. Congress grants. Even though Puerto Ricans are U.S. citizens at birth, Puerto Ricans on their is-

Rights Act of 1964, 42 USC § 2000d (*Campaign for Fiscal Equity et al., v. State of New York et al.*, 187 Misc. 2d 1; 719 N.Y.S.2d 475 (2001)).

Agreeing with the trial court, the Court of Appeals found a "causal link" between the state's funding system and the provision of fewer resources to New York City schools—precisely those schools in the state with the greatest need and the schools attended overwhelmingly by students of color (*Campaign for Fiscal Equity v. New York*, 100 N.Y.S.2d 893 at 919). With approximately 1200 schools and 1.1 million students, the court found that about 84 percent of the New York City public school system's children were "racial minorities," which include Latinos/as and African Americans; "80 percent were born outside the United States; and 16 percent were classified as Limited English Proficient ('LEP'—persons who speak little or no English)—most of the State's students in each of these categories" (903–04). In addition, the schools' population was found in great numbers to be poor or in economic need: "Upwards of 73 percent were eligible for the Federal free or reduced lunch program; 442,000 City schoolchildren came from families receiving Aid to Families with Dependent Children" (904). In spite of the obvious need for resources, "[p]er-pupil expenditures in the New York City public schools, at $8171, were lower than in three-quarters of the State's districts, including all the other 'large city' districts, as classified by the SED [State Education Department]. The State's dollar contribution to this figure was also lower, at $3562, than its average contribution to other districts; and the City's, at about $4000, was likewise lower than the average local contribution in other districts" (905).

New York State's Governor, George Pataki, insisted on pursuing this case to the highest court in the state at taxpayer expense, arguing that the state's obligation only extends to providing an eighth grade education, as sufficient for a "sound basic education" (906). As a candidate for governor, Pataki made great attempts to woo Latino/a voters to his candidacy and to the Republican Party, but to the disappointment of many Latinos/as, it has appeared that the State under his leadership was willing to forego the education of the large number of the state's Latino/a children who rely on a public education.

In 2000–2001, close to 40 percent (37.8%) of New York City public school children were Latino/a (Citizens' Committee for Children 2002, 107). Yet the state's attorneys sought to sidestep the glaring problems of overcrowded classrooms, classes taught by unqualified teachers, and the lack of books and other necessary teaching instruments and facilities. In court, the state attorneys' argument, in large measure, amounted to blaming the victims: that educational failure was due to the students' poor socioeconomic situation, rather than any fault of the state's (*Campaign for Fiscal Equity v. New York*, 100 N.Y.2d 893 at 920). Fortunately for the children of New York City, the governor's position did not prevail. The court held instead that regardless of the socioeconomic condition of the children, the state is still obligated to meet the basic educational needs of all children, because the court deemed it an unacceptable "premise that children come to the New York City schools ineducable, unfit to learn" (921). Accordingly, the court ordered that the State of New York implement a new funding scheme that would insure a fair share of resources to educate children in New York City Schools (947–48).

Like other education cases, the *Campaign for Fiscal Equity* case brings to light the many years of unequal educational opportunities that Latino/a families and children have had to endure. It also demonstrates the great lengths that people of color have had to go to mount legal challenges against state officials indifferent to the discriminatory affects of their policies on Latinos/as and other communities of color. Taken in context, the *Campaign for Fiscal Equity* case, filed in the mid-1990s, was rapidly approaching a decade in litigation before the highest court of the state handed down its decision. As of the beginning of 2004, a corrective plan was not yet in place. Hence, for years before, during, and after this case, vast numbers of Latino/a children in the New York City school system have been without schools that adequately meet their educational needs. The New York Court of Appeals itself cited examples of "systemic breakdown" that still plague the system, including deplorable classroom conditions and a third of the city's third grade school children being "functionally illiterate" (*Campaign for Fiscal Equity v. New York*, 100 N.Y.2d 893 at 916). Despite reports of improvements in tests scores in New York City, school officials concede that in 2003 one out of two fourth-graders or "50 percent…aren't making the grade" (Herszenhorn 2003, A1).

As with other people of color, Latinos/as continue to be harmed by policies that discriminate and neglect their most basic of human needs. It is also symptomatic of the larger national trend to reduce spending on basic social services. As reported by the National Criminal Justice Commission, "[i]n 1991, for the first time in American history, several major cities spent more on law enforcement than on secondary education. In 1994 and 1995, several governors—including George Pataki in New York—proposed building new prisons while cutting back on social services. These funding choices affect the quality of life and the degree of opportunity available to all Americans" (Donziger 1996, 204). Given this gross injustice, the Commission's findings beg the question about whether Latinos/as and other communities of color are truly accepted as "Americans" in contemporary U.S. society and strongly suggest that the perceptions of Latinos/as as a racialized "other" relegate Latinos/as to obscurity and inequity.

RACIAL PROFILING AND BIAS IN THE CRIMINAL JUSTICE SYSTEM

A discussion about discrimination against Latinos/as would not be complete without delving into the Latino/a experience with law enforcement and the criminal justice system. The racialization of Latinos/as as inferior, dangerous, and criminal has manifested itself in the criminal justice system in many ways, and prejudice, stereotypes, and discrimination have taken many forms. The use of abusive language and racial and ethnic slurs against people of color has been a regular occurrence, according to studies of law enforcement behavior around the country (Walker et al. 2004, 119–20, Amnesty International 1998, 17–54). In many instances, the word "spic" has surfaced in police misconduct and brutality cases involving Latino/a victims (Morín and del Valle 1990). As a derogatory racial epithet and racial/ethnic identifier, the term "spic" differentiates Latinos/as from the dominant English-speaking society, reinforcing the idea of Latinos/as as "the other." Ostensibly, nothing more effectively drives home the message that Latinos/as are "the other" than abusive police behavior and brutality.[2]

The problem of police abuse and violence in Latino/a communities usually correlates with poor relations between police and Latino/a communities and prevailing attitudes on race and ethnicity. But contrary to the popular perception of people of color as society's criminal element, Walker, Spohn, and DeLone point out that the typical criminal offender is actually White:

> Examination of arrest statistics for all offenses, for instance, reveals that the typical offender is white; over two-thirds (69.7 percent) of those arrested in 2000 were white, less than one-third (27.9 percent) were African American, and less than 3 percent were Native American or Asian. Similarly, over half of those arrested for violent crimes and nearly two-thirds of those arrested for property crimes were white. (2004, 40)[3]

---

2. The term police brutality is used herein in reference to the use of excessive force, which as defined by Walker, Spohn, and DeLone (2004, 106), is "any physical force that is more than reasonably necessary to accomplish a lawful police purpose."

3. The data cited by Walker, Spohn, and DeLone for the year 2000 is derived from the U.S. Department of Justice Uniform Crime Reports (U.S. Department of Justice 2001). Statistics for 2001 are remarkably consistent. Figures on arrests by race for 2001 show that, for all criminal offenses, 69.5 percent were White, 28.1 percent were Black, 1.3 percent were

The government's Uniform Crime Reports (UCR), upon which the foregoing statistics are based, do not include a category for Latinos/as since Latinos/as are classified as an ethnic rather than a racial group. The result is that the UCR data does not accurately account for Latinos/as, who are usually categorized as either White or Black.[4] Nevertheless, it has been observed that in other instances Latinos/as are likely to be identified as "other," particularly in data collected based on the perception of the offender's race (45). In statistics where an "other" category is used, Whites, again, come up as the most common criminal offender. For instance, the Bureau of Justice Statistics (2000, 48) reports that for all crimes of violence in 1995 the perceived race of offenders for a single-offender crime was 63.1 percent White, 27.3 percent African American, and 8.0 percent "other." For all crimes of violence in 2002, the perceived race of offenders for a single-offender crime was 63.3 percent White, 22.8 percent African American, and 13.0 percent "other" (Bureau of Justice Statistics 2003a, table 40).

In spite of the data showing that criminal activity among Whites is common, law enforcement officers and the criminal justice system generally continue to be shaped by prejudices present in the larger society that promote the idea that people of color are primarily responsible for crime. Hence, it is common for cases of police brutality and misconduct throughout the United States to be linked to problems of racial and ethnic prejudice and discrimination, including bias directed at Latinos/as (Amnesty International 1998; Human Rights Watch 1998; Mirandé 1987). A clear example of systemic and institutionalized discrimination that has come to light in recent years is the case of racial profiling by New Jersey State Troopers. After years of denial, New Jersey government officials were forced to admit that their state troopers had engaged in the racial profiling of African Americans and Latinos/as. During the decade of the 1990s, at least eight out of every ten automobiles singled out for searches on the New Jersey Turnpike were cars driven by African Americans and Latinos/as (Kocieniewski and Hanley 2000, A1).

The issues of police misconduct and brutality are frequently countered with debates over the need for tougher policing methods. Although some newer

---

American Indian or Native Alaskan, and 1.1 percent were Asian or Pacific Islander (U.S. Department of Justice 2002, 252).

4. A recent study of Latina and Latino youth and the U.S. justice system criticizes the failure of the justice system to maintain separate data on ethnicity in addition to race (Villarruel et al. 2002, 46–49). The result of data that does not keep track of Latinos/as, *inter alia*, is that it masks the disparate treatment of Latino/a youths within the justice system (49).

Table 3. Street Searches ("Stops-and-Frisks") by Police in New York City

1998	Frisks	Arrests
	27,061 people frisked	4,647 people arrested of those frisked
	(22,414 persons searched were mistakenly thought to be armed.)	
1997	Frisks	Arrests
	18,023 people frisked	4,899 people arrested of those frisked
	(13,124 persons searched were mistakenly thought to be armed.)	

Table 4. Rates of "Stops" by Police in New York City for People of Color and Whites (January 1, 1998 through March 31, 1999)

- Blacks comprise 25.6% of the City's population, yet 50.6% of all persons "stopped" were black.
- Hispanics comprise 23.7% of the City's population, yet 33.0% of all persons "stopped" were Hispanics.
- Blacks comprise 62.7% of all persons "stopped" by the NYPD's Street Crime Unit.

The effect of differing crime rates in communities of color and white communities does not fully explain the increased rate of stops of people of color. After accounting for differences in crime rates:

- Blacks were stopped 23% more often than Whites across all crime categories.
- Hispanics were stopped 39% more often than Whites across all crime categories.

Source: Spitzer, Elliot. 1999. *The New York City Police Department's "Stop and Frisk" Practices: a Report to the People of the State of New York from the Attorney General.* New York: Civil Rights Bureau, vii–x.

Colombians, Puerto Ricans, African Americans and Nigerians" (49). Indeed, profiles used by federal agents at airports have included very long lists of seemingly odd and broadly-defined categories of persons suspected of carrying drugs, such as someone who "made a local call after deplaning...made a long-distance call after deplaning...carried a small bag...carried a medium-size bag...carried two bulky garment bags...dressed casually...left the airport by taxi" (Cole 1999, 47–49). Federal drug-courier profiles have specifically identified "Hispanics" as suspects (49).

Law enforcement agents assume that racial profiles used in anti-drug operations accurately determine which racial or ethnic groups are responsible for drug-related crimes. As Georgetown University Law Professor David Cole notes (2001, 248), "racial profiling studies...make clear that the war on drugs has largely been a war on minorities. It is, after all, drug enforcement that motivates most racial profiling." Racial profiles actually do not correctly reflect the racial description of illicit drug consumers or traffickers. In fact, U.S. government data about drug use indicate that Whites use drugs at much the same rate as persons from other racial or ethnic groups. The Substance Abuse and Mental Health Services Administration (2002, 1) finds that the "patterns of current use among major racial/ethnic groups in 2001 were similar to previous years. The rate among blacks was 7.4 percent, whites 7.2 percent, and Hispanics 6.4 percent."

In some instances, drug use among Whites is actually greater than among other racial and ethnic groups. Among youth ages 12–17, Whites were more likely to use some form of hallucinogen in their lifetime at a rate of 6.8 percent, African Americans 1.7 percent, Asians 5.2 percent, and Latinos/as 4.1 percent (Substance Abuse and Mental Health Services Administration 2003, 2). Moreover, it has been discovered that Latino/a and African American youths have been "more likely than whites and Asians to perceive great risk in trying LSD" (2).

The notion that Latinos/as and African Americans are more likely to be involved in distributing illegal drugs may also be inaccurate. As Professor Cole explains (2001, 247), a "Justice Department study [Riley 1997, 1] found that most [illicit drug] users report getting their drugs from dealers of the same race, so the demographics of distribution likely reflect the demographics of drug use."

The staying power of prejudice and stereotypes of Latinos and Latinas as drug suspects have produced negative repercussions for Latinos/as within the justice system. Prejudiced opinions have been found to permeate police departments throughout the country. In a 1999 cover story in the *New York Times Magazine*, police officers from different cities openly voiced an unwillingness to give up racial profiling in their day-to-day work, a reluctance principally grounded in bigoted attitudes about race and ethnicity (Goldberg 1999). With specific reference to Latinos/as, Deputy Bobby Harris of the Los Angeles County Sheriff's Department unabashedly stated that "[r]acial profiling is a tool we use, and don't let anyone say otherwise. Like up in the valley, I knew who the crack sellers were—they look like Hispanics who should be cutting your lawn" (57). This statement is in keeping with existing research that shows a pervasiveness of prejudiced attitudes among police officers (Walker et al. 2004, 120–21). In one study, for instance, 80 percent of Denver police officers were found to dislike persons with Spanish surnames (Bayley and Mendelsohn 1969). While holding prejudiced opinions does not necessarily mean that police officers will take discriminatory action, the evidence that there is openness to bigotry and an inclination to use racial profiling has mounted over the years, suggesting that prejudice forms the fertile ground upon which discriminatory action develops. The high incidence of racial profiling and racial and ethnic bias in law enforcement throughout the country, as documented in many studies (see, e.g., Amnesty International 1998; Human Rights Watch 1998; Cole 1999; Harris 2002; Meeks 2000) tends to support the position that prejudice frequently fosters discriminatory acts.

There has also been a growing body of evidence in cities such as New York and Los Angeles that police abuse and brutality is often directed against lesbians and gays (see Amnesty International 1998, 40–42). A report by the Audre Lorde Project (2000) finds that police misconduct and brutality has been particularly troubling in lesbian, gay, bisexual, two spirit, and transgender communities of color in New York City. As no one in society should be subject to unfair police practices and brutality, how lesbian, gay, bisexual, two spirit, and transgender persons in Latino/a communities are vulnerable to police abuse deserves further study and action.

For Latinos/as, racial and ethnic prejudice and discrimination in the courts appears to play a consistent role in the meting out of unequal justice. As one study in Los Angeles found, Latino males were regularly prosecuted to the fullest extent, with African American males, White males, and women of all ethnicities following in descending order (Spohn, Gruhl, and Welch 1987, 175–91). As further evidence of the impact of a criminal justice system prone to intentional and unintentional racial and ethnic discrimination, a major study conducted by Michigan State University/Building Blocks for Youth points to bias in the criminal justice system as a key factor in the high rates of incarceration among Latino/a youth (Villarruel et al. 2002). As a result, national data reveals that Latino/a youth are charged with violent offenses five times the rate of White youth and serve longer sentences than White youth—as much as 143 days longer for violent crimes (2–3). In Los Angeles, Latino/a youth are incarcerated at rates much higher than White youth—7.3 times as often from 1996–1998—and Latino/a youth are prosecuted as adults more often than White youth—2.4 times as often from 1996–1998 (2).

THE ECONOMIC AND SOCIAL COSTS OF DISCRIMINATION ON LATINOS/AS

Discrimination leads to economic, social, and cultural exclusion for those discriminated against, and discrimination provides the means through which the unequal distribution of opportunities and resources can be maintained. In many ways, the socioeconomic inequalities and injustices discernable in Latino/a communities today are products of past and present *de jure* and *de facto* discrimination (see Delgado and Stefancic 1998). For most Latinas and Latinos around the country, the effects of discrimination on their lives and on their ability to advance are very palpable. In their *2002 National Survey of Latinos*, the Pew Hispanic Center/Kaiser Family Foundation found that "[o]ver eight in ten (82%) Latinos report that discrimination against Latinos is a problem in preventing Latinos from succeeding in the United States" (2002, 70).

Today, poverty and other forms of social and economic disadvantages in Latino/a communities are comparable to that of African Americans, a community of color that has been subject to systemic exploitation, oppression, and discrimination throughout U.S. history. As Table 5 shows, the rate of poverty for Latinos/as, for instance, has been and continues to be nearest to that of African Americans. In 2001, Latinos/as and African Americans had poverty rates of 21.4 and 22.7 percent, respectively, while the poverty rate for Whites was 7.8 percent (Bureau of the Census 2002a, 4).

Table 5.   U.S. Poverty Rate According to Race and Ethnicity

Race/ethnic group	Percentage
Latinos/as	21.4
African Americans	22.7
Asians & Pacific Islanders	10.2
Whites	7.8

Source: U.S. Bureau of the Census. 2002a. *Poverty in the United States: 2001*. Current Population Reports, Consumer Income, P60–219. Prepared by Bernadette D. Procter, and Joseph Dalaker, Bureau of the Census. Washington, D.C.

Table 6 identifies where Latinos/as stand in relation to income in comparison to African Americans and Whites (Bureau of the Census 2001a, 4). Again, these statistics illustrate the similarity in income inequality experienced by both Latinos/as and African Americans.

Table 6.   U.S. Median Family Income for 2000

Race/ethnic group	Median Income
Latino/a	$33,447
African Americans	$30,439
Asians & Pacific Islanders	$55,521
Whites	$45,904

Source: U.S. Bureau of the Census. 2001a. *Money Income in the United States: 2000*. Current Population Reports, Consumer Income, P60–213. Prepared by Carmen DeNavas-Walt, Robert W. Cleveland, and Marc I. Roemer, Bureau of the Census. Washington, D.C.

In spite of increases in income detected in 2000 (Bureau of the Census 2001a), poverty rates overall have continued to rise. In 2001, the poverty rate for all families increased to 9.2 percent (6.8 million poor families in 2001 compared to 6.4 million in 2000) (Bureau of the Census 2002a, 6–7). From 2000 to 2001, the number of Latino/a families in poverty rose from 1.5 million to 1.6 million (7).

The economic disparities along racial and ethnic lines become more salient when one compares net worth or wealth as depicted in Table 7 (Bureau of the Census. 2003c, 12):

Table 7.   U.S. Median Net Worth or Wealth for 2000

Race/ethnic group	Median Net Worth
Latino/a	$9,750
African Americans	$7,500
Whites	$79,400

Source: U.S. Bureau of the Census. 2003c. *Net worth and asset ownership of households: 1998–2000.* Household Economic Studies, P70–88. Prepared by Shawna Orzechowski, and Peter Sepielli. Bureau of the Census, Washington, D.C. (Note: Asians and Pacific Islanders median net worth was not incorporated into this study.)

As Census Bureau analysts point out, "[w]hen...considered alone, income—the resources a household or person receives from a job, transfer program, or other source—provides an incomplete picture of economic well-being. Only when wealth or net worth—the difference between assets and liabilities—a person or household has at any given time is considered in conjunction with income does a better understanding of economic health and well-being emerge" (Bureau of the Census. 2003c, 1). In fact, the net worth data show the persistence of economic inequality along racial and ethnic lines. Although Latinos/as and African Americans also experienced increases in net worth, in 2000, "White households in every income quintile had significantly higher levels of median net worth than their Black and Hispanic counterparts.... Between 1998 and 2000, the median net worth of non-Hispanic White households jumped by over $8,000" (12).

The severity of the socioeconomic emergency existing in Latino/a communities was spelled out in a recent article on the health of Latino/a children in the *Journal of the American Medical Association*:

> Latino children...are 13 times more likely than whites to be infected by tuberculosis.... In 1999, 20% of Latino youth reported considering suicide, compared to 15% of black and 18% of white youth.... A half million Latino children have asthma; two thirds of them are Puerto Rican.... Children of migrant Latino farm-workers are particularly at risk for suboptimal health and use of services.... Latino youth by far have the highest school dropout rate in the nation, 29%, compared with 13% for blacks and 7% for whites. Although 36% of Latino

children live in poverty, only 26% attend Head Start programs.... Latinos are underrepresented at every level of the health care professions.... Latinos are more likely to be uninsured (27%) than any other ethnic group of US children. (Flores et al. 2002, 83–88)

A closer look at specific health problems reveals other very alarming facts about the condition of Latinos/as in the United States. For instance, Latino boys and Latina girls are the most overweight of any racial or ethnic group of children in the United States, correlating with a precipitous rise in diabetes among Latino/a children (Flores et al. 2002, 86). Cross-border health statistics are also a major concern. One study comparing Mexican American school children and their cross-border counterparts for depression and suicide on the Texas border with Mexico "revealed that 48% of Mexican American students scored above the critical level for depression on a standardized scale compared with 39% of Mexican youths, and 23% of US [Mexican American] adolescents reported current suicidal ideation compared to 12% of Mexican students" (87). Hence, Latino/a children on the U.S. side of the border with Mexico were at even greater risk for depression and suicide than Mexican youths. Because "Latinos are the largest minority group of children in the (11.6 million) United States" (82), the crisis they face now can have severe consequences, not just for their future, but for the entire United States.

Although persons of Cuban origin in the United States generally exhibit higher socioeconomic indicators than those present in most other Latino/a groups, it is becoming increasingly clear that more recent Cuban arrivals fall into socioeconomic patterns matching those of most other Latinos/as. Unlike the first wave of those who left Cuba soon after the 1959 revolution who were mostly from Cuba's economic elite, later arrivals, particularly those since the Mariel exodus in 1980, were more likely to be Black and working class. As Sylvia Pedraza points out (1996, 275), "when we consider Cubans by their race, we can see that while only 14 percent of White Cubans fall below the poverty line, 35 percent of Black Cubans and 23 percent of racially mixed Cubans fall below the poverty line—figures that compare most closely to the poverty rates among Black Americans and Puerto Ricans in the United States."

Moreover, other problems, such as residential segregation, compound the difficulties Latinos/as face in obtaining equality of opportunity and advancement (Walker et al. 2004, 76–78). Recent census data reveal extremely high levels of group isolation and a marked increase in residential segregation over the last decade, with Latinos/as in cities such as New York among the groups experiencing the most separation (Scott 2001, B1). An analysis by the Mumford Center at the University at Albany in New York (2001, 1) found that an average White person in a U.S. metropolitan region "lives in a neighborhood that is 80% white and only 7% black." For equal distribution to occur between Whites and Latinos/as nationally, 51.5% of either Latinos/as or Whites would have to relocate (Mumford Center 2002, 7). Mexicans, Dominicans, Central Americans and Puerto Ricans, most particularly, tend to live in highly segregated communities (7). The physical separation along racial and ethnic lines thwarts contact and understanding among communities, exacerbating an already volatile situation in a society susceptible to prejudice and discrimination.

PREJUDICE AND POPULAR IMAGES: HAVE LATINOS/AS REALLY MADE IT?

As Madison Avenue and media outlets increasingly depict Latino/a images, food, and music—from salsa dancing to Jennifer Lopez—as all the rage, it may appear incongruous that Latinos/as would still be considered the objects of negative, racialized stereotypes and discrimination. But as Professor Arlene Dávila finds (2001, 217), it is still true that "U.S. minorities [including Latinos/as] are all subject to stereotyping as low income, unskilled, uneducated crime-ridden, unemployed, and, in some cases, as perpetual foreigners, and…they are always required to prove their worth and compensate for their image." In her study of the current trend to market the "Latino" image, Dávila further explains that:

> If Latinas are hot, does this mean that someone who is not "making it" is experiencing individual failure not social inequality? If the consumption indexes of blacks and Latinas are supposedly growing exponentially, does this mean that poverty, unemployment, or steady employment are no longer issues? After all, the people who are consuming must be making money; should we then care if they do so by holding three jobs, by working at the periphery of the informal economy? Or should we care that their income still lags behind that of whites? If the household incomes of Asian Americans are above the U.S. average, who cares if they are channeled into some professions, absent from others, or if their success comes at the cost of a greater human investment than whites make? Ultimately these questions bring to the fore that marketing discourse is not without political and economic repercussions. It prioritizes consumption over income, and spending over employment or economic parity, veiling the ongoing segmentation between those with "real" jobs and income, and those who lack it. (Dávila 2001, 235)

Indeed, Dávila challenges us to examine whether popular Latino/a images are simply geared to reap large corporate profits while creating the image for U.S. Whites of the "ideal," non-threatening, successful Latino or Latina—à la Ricky Martin—after whom Latinos/as are supposed model themselves (234–36). Of course, as the previous discussion about current socioeconomic conditions illustrates, the opportunities for upward mobility in Latino/a communities are very fleeting.

While many Latinos/as may be cognizant of the reality of discrimination, many—including those who have had a significant presence in the United States for some time—find the effects of discrimination in the United States nonetheless disconcerting and destabilizing. Based on research focused on Puerto Ricans, sociologist Joseph F. Healey observes:

> In the racially dichotomized U.S. culture [of Black and White], many Puerto Ricans feel they have no clear place. They are genuinely puzzled when they first encounter prejudice and discrimination based on skin color and are uncertain about their own identity and self-image. The racial perceptions of the dominant culture can be threatening to Puerto Ricans to the extent that they are victimized by the same web of discrimination and disadvantage that affects African Americans. There are still clear disadvantages to being classified as black in U.S. society. Institutionalized racial barriers can be extremely formidable, and in the case of Puerto Ricans, they may combine with cultural and linguistic differences to sharply limit opportunities and mobility. (2003, 371)

A New York Times/CBS poll suggests that because Puerto Ricans have been in the United States longer than some other Latino/a groups, they are less likely to be optimistic about their life circumstances in the United States (Navarro and Connelly 2003, B1, B4). While Latin American newcomers escaping abject poverty and other economic, social, or political hardships and persecutions are likely to be optimistic about starting a new life in the world's wealthiest country, they are often not prepared to confront the types of discrimination experienced by Latinos/as in the United States.

RESPONSES TO INEQUALITIES AND INJUSTICES

In its historical context, the Latino/a experience with discrimination reveals a long trajectory of overcoming formidable legal barriers as well as political and social limitations. As African Americans, Native Americans, and Asian Americans have done over decades, Latinos/as responded to discrimination and unjust treatment by organizing efforts to protect and expand rights that should have been accorded them. Their response often took the form of grassroots organizing, as in the efforts of César Chávez and the United Farm Workers to unionize and protect exploited laborers of the 1960s and 1970s (Acuña 2000, 351–56). Other Latinos/as embraced more radical concepts for creating social, economic, and political change for Latinos/as, as in the Chicano movement's Brown Berets on the West Coast (Haney López 2003) or the Puerto Ricans activists in the Midwest and East who organized the Young Lords (Torres and Velázquez 1998).

As discrimination frequently has sought not only to marginalize but to undermine a sense of identity, self-esteem, and ethnic solidarity, many Latino/a organizing efforts in Latino/a communities past and present have made the reaffirmation of identity and culture an integral part of their mission. Latino/a communities gave rise to leaders, such as Bert Corona and Antonia Pantoja— who inspired pride and unity and contributed to advancements in such areas as labor rights, education, civil rights, and politics for Chicanos and Puerto Ricans (see García 1994; Pantoja 2002).

The specific means through which change was to be effectuated also took many forms. Marches, sit-ins, protest rallies as well as community outreach and education projects were undertaken to bring attention to the problems faced by Latino/a communities. Legal battles and various kinds of political activism, both within the established political party system or on a more ad hoc community level, have been indispensable tools in the effort to bringing about improvements in the lives of Latinos/as. In view of the social, economic and political realities Latinos/as have faced, it follows that Latinos/as would be active in the civil rights movements of the 1960s and 1970s and beyond (Gonzalez 2000; Healey 2003).

In spite of the best efforts of the past, Latino/a communities continue to confront inequalities and discrimination in areas, such as education, housing, and employment. To address issues of inequality and injustices, Latinos/as have focused on affecting political, economic, and social change through such means as legislative reform and legal actions. Legal and legislative efforts were often grounded in or complementary to community-based struggles. In the fight for bilingual education, affirmative action, and voting rights over the years, the courts have been one of the most important venues for setbacks or victories for Latinos/as (Perea et al. 2000; Delgado and Stefancic 1998).

Since 1968, the Mexican American Legal Defense and Education Fund (MALDEF) has been a leading civil rights, legal advocacy, and educational outreach organization for Latinos/as in the United States. It has taken on many of the most pressing issues involving voting rights, immigrant rights, and discrimination in employment and education. In recent years, nativist sentiments have found expression through the Official English movement and legislation targeted at restricting immigrants' rights.[5] California's propositions 187, 209, and 227—legislative initiatives calculated to end the provision of basic health and educational services to undocumented persons, affirmative action programs, and bilingual education, respectively—represent a backlash to the civil rights gains of the 1960s and 1970s (Acuña 2000, 452–56; Perea 1997a). In response, Latino/a communities have galvanized opposition to these legislative measures, and organizations, such as MALDEF, have been at the forefront of many of the legal challenges to protect the rights of immigrants and Latinos/as in general.

MALDEF was among the nonprofit legal organizations that successfully negotiated the final settlement in which Governor Gray Davis and the state of California officially agreed to dismiss their appeal of the district court's decision in the case of *Gregorio T. v. Wilson*, 54 F.3d 599 (9th Cir. 1995). Through this settlement, nearly all of California's Proposition 187 provisions denying education, health care, and other social services to the state's undocumented immigrants were struck down. This legal victory also helped to preserve the right of immigrant children to public education in accordance with the U.S. Supreme Court's decision in *Plyler v. Doe*, 457 U.S. 202 (1982). The *Plyler* decision held that the Equal Protection Clause of the Constitution's Fourteenth Amendment prohibits states from denying a public education to undocumented children, and it rejected, *inter alia*, the argument that such services impose a "special burden" on the state (226–30).

Puerto Ricans also formed their own legal organization to fight for equal opportunity in the United States. Since the 1970s, the Puerto Rican Legal Defense and Education Fund (PRLDEF) has fought in U.S. courts to realize civil rights in housing, education, and voting for Puerto Ricans and other Latino/a groups. PRLDEF represented Aspira, a nonprofit organization founded to advance educational opportunities for Latinos/as, in securing the landmark 1974 Aspira consent decree, entitling Spanish-speaking Latino/a children to receive

---

5. The term "nativist" is used in reference to "nativism," which, as described by Perea (1997a, 1), embodies "a preference for those deemed natives; simultaneous and intense opposition to those deemed strangers, foreigners." Nativism views White U.S. citizens as "real" Americans and casts non-Whites as representing that which is non-native and "un-American" (1). Deeply rooted in U.S. history and society, nativism's resurgence in recent years most often targets Latinos/as and Asians as persons who are foreign and "illegal" (2).

bilingual education programs in New York. Yet in spite of the success of their legal advocacy, the arduous task of enforcing compliance of the consent decree has been typical of the difficulties that Latinos/as face sustaining rights won over the long term. Indeed, PRLDEF was forced to institute further legal action to hold the New York City Board of Education in contempt for failing to fulfill its responsibilities under the consent decree (*Aspira of New York, Inc., et al. v. Board of Education of the City of New York, et al.,* 423 F. Supp. 647 (S.D.N.Y. 1976)).

On the question of discrimination within the criminal justice system, Latino/ communities remain active in pursuing change and challenging racial profiling and laws, including draconian drug laws and mandatory sentencing laws that have been associated with the high rates of Latino/a incarceration (Villarruel et al. 2002). A recent project sponsored by Building Blocks for Youth places special emphasis on working with Latina and Latino youth and families in addressing bias in the criminal justice system (73–75). This project promotes a multifaceted approach to reach and organize Latino/a communities, emphasizing strategies for increasing and improving bilingual services within the justice system; advocacy to end racial and gang profiling; legislative reform to repeal or amend laws that have a disproportionate impact on Latinos/as, such as certain drug laws and "three-strike laws"; and enhancing family and community involvement in monitoring the criminal justice system for bias and abuse against Latinos/as (27–80).[6]

CONCLUSION

The similarities in the experiences of people of color with issues of discrimination have led to the theoretical conclusion that continuity exists in the colonization or conquest of certain groups in the United States. Foremost in advancing this theory has been Robert Blauner (1972), who viewed Latinos/as,

---

6. "Three-strikes laws," in which a third criminal offense automatically results in a severe prison sentence, have not been proven to be effective against crime. A recent study by the Justice Policy Institute shows that other states without three-strikes law have experienced a greater decline in crime when compared to California's "Three Strikes and You're Out" law, one of the strictest three-strike laws in place for more than ten years (Ehlers, Schiraldi, and Ziedenberg 2004, 14–21). Rather than reduce crime, the three-strikes law has led to the disproportionate incarceration of Latinos/as and African Americans (11–13). In California, the "Latino incarceration rate for a third strike (17 per 100,000 Latino residents) is *45 percent higher* than the third strike incarceration rate for Whites (12 per 100,000 White residents)" (emphasis in the original) (11).

Native Americans, African Americans and Asian Americans as "colonized minority groups" who have endured a process of colonization, conquest, or other forms of exploitation and domination not experienced by other groups who came to the United States under circumstances that were more voluntary. Other social scientists have underscored that Latinos/as—along with African Americans, Native Americans and Asians—have continued to fall prey to the existing ethnocentrism, competition, and power dynamic within the United States culminating in their disadvantaged or "minority" status in relation to the dominant White society (Noel, 1968). But whether one subscribes to these theories or not to explain the current condition of Latinos/as in the United States, the unequal treatment of Latinos/as in the United States is unquestionable. From the Treaty of Guadalupe-Hidalgo and the Treaty of Paris to the rise of contemporary anti-immigrant and anti-bilingual movements, most Latinos/as have been affected by a long series of events that have sought to dehumanize them and de-legitimized their rights to political, social, and economic advancement in relation to the dominant society.

Although the United States has seen a progression away from some of the most virulent forms of oppression, including slavery and *de jure* segregation, prejudice and discrimination have remained a part of the Latino/a experience in the United States (Healey 2003; Schaefer 2004). Media images of Latinos/as continue to be stereotypically negative (Berg 2002; Delgado and Stefancic 1992) or rare (Hoffman 2003). The plethora of negative images of Latinos and Latinas in U.S. films—as the stereotypical "bandito" in Westerns or the incorrigible inner-city drug-user or criminal—have been difficult to overcome and still resonate in Hollywood and throughout U.S. society (Berg 2002, 270). The power of misrepresentations in the news and entertainment media assures that Latinos/as are likely to remain objects of prejudice and discrimination into the future.

Specifically with respect to the criminal justice system, criminologists Samuel Walker, Miriam Delone, and Cassia C. Spohn find in their "analysis of race and crime in the United States...that those who conclude that 'the criminal justice system is not racist' are misinformed...the U.S. criminal justice system has never been, and is not now, color-blind" (2004, 359).[7] As other scholars have also shown (Delgado and Stefancic 1998; Perea et al. 2000; Haney López 2003; Mirandé 1987), this conclusion holds true for Latinos/as, not only in the area of criminal justice, but in virtually all aspects of U.S. society. Understanding that racial and ethnic bias persists, the question becomes

---

7. Specifically, Walker et al. (2004) refute the assertions of William Wilbanks (1987).

one of how to create a more just society for all. With more than one in eight people in the United States being of Latin American descent and with that proportion growing (Bureau of the Census 2002b, 1), it is more urgent than ever that access to justice and equality be made available for Latinos/as and other people of color. If not, Latinos/as run the risk of being permanently condemned to marginalization, discrimination, and injustice.

CHAPTER 4

LATINOS/AS AND THE U.S. JUSTICE SYSTEM: BOTH PRESENT AND ABSENT IN THE SYSTEM

Beyond the problems Latinos/as face within the justice system that were identified previously, this chapter probes more directly into issues concerning the quality of justice afforded to Latinos/as in the United States. This examination not only looks into Latino/a representation among the incarcerated, but it also considers the impact that the lack of meaningful Latino/a representation has on all levels of the justice system's administration and implementation. The significance of a presence of Latino/a professionals within the justice system is discussed in view of the potential to enhance the system's ability to afford greater equality and access to justice.

To further the discussion about the Latino/a experience of the justice system, this chapter contains a case study of one group actively engaged in the criminal justice system, the Latino Officers Association (LOA). While the presentation of this group's position here does not purport to be representative of all Latinos/as in law enforcement, the perspective of LOA represents a contemporary wave of Latino/a activism and advocacy within the justice system. LOA speaks for a sizable and visible group among Latinos/as inside law enforcement agencies. As such, their stance on and their insights into the justice system become invaluable in broadening our understanding and addressing the pressing concerns of Latino/a communities in the administration of justice. Their views allow us to reflect on the ways law enforcement currently functions and assist in envisioning ways that may make the justice system more effective and just.

LATINOS/AS AND OVERREPRESENTATION IN THE CRIMINAL JUSTICE SYSTEM

Statistics routinely describe the alarming racial and ethnic disparity that exists in incarceration rates in the United States. The United States is considered to be the country with the highest rate of incarceration in the world. The Bureau of Justice Statistics reported that by 2002 at year's end 2,166,260 persons were incarcerated in the United States (2003d, 1). Stated differently, one in every 143 U.S. residents was in prison or in jail (2). Factoring in U.S. census data for 2000, Human Rights Watch (2002) indicates that "[o]ut of a total population of 1,976,019 incarcerated in adult facilities, 1,239,946 or 63 percent are black or Latino, though these groups combined constitute only 25 percent of the national population" (1). In 2002, of a total of 1,291,326 sentenced prisoners under state or federal jurisdiction, 235,000 were Latino and 15,000 were Latina, with Latino men representing 18.1 percent of prisoners under state or federal incarceration (Bureau of Justice Statistics 2003d, 9). Indeed, Latinos/as represent "the fastest growing group being imprisoned, increasing from 10.9% of all State and Federal inmates in 1985 to 15.6 percent in 2001" (Sentencing Project 2003, 1).

A closer look at the incarceration rates of Latinos/as exposes an even more disturbing picture:

- In ten states, Latino men are incarcerated at rates between five and nine times greater than those of white men.
- In eight states, Latina women are incarcerated at rates that are between four and seven times greater than those of white women.
- In four states, Hispanic youths under age eighteen are incarcerated in adult facilities at rates between seven and seventeen times greater than those of white youth. (Human Rights Watch 2002, 2)

At first glance, these statistics can lead one to conclude that Latinos/as are simply committing more crimes than Whites. However, contrary to the impression left by incarceration data, empirical evidence increasingly suggests that the considerable disparities in race and ethnicity are not just due to the incidence of crime in communities of color but result from discrimination as it functions within the justice system. Disparities, of course, do not prove *per se* that discrimination occurs within the justice system. But when controlling for numerous factors other than discrimination that may account for disparities, discrimination most often surfaces as a key factor explaining the differences found between people of color and Whites within the criminal justice system. As shown in the previous chapter, when accounting for differences in crime rates in communities (Spitzer 1999, x) or different levels of disrespect for police (Walker et al. 2004, 111), the only factor left that accounts for the disparities in treatment in the justice system appears to be discrimination.

Specifically regarding the disproportionate rate of incarceration of Latinos/as, common misperceptions about Latinos/as and crime emerge as significant in contributing to the overrepresentation of Latinos/as in prison populations. As shown in a variety of studies (such as, Office of National Drug Control Policy 2003; Hagan and Palloni 1999), Latinos/as are not necessarily any more prone to illicit drug activity than Whites nor are Latino/a immigrants inclined more than any other group to engage in criminal conduct. Nevertheless, Latinos/as are most visibly overrepresented in federal prisons among those convicted of drug- and immigration-related offenses (Walker et al. 2004, 301).

Latinos/as and Drugs

Although fear of violent crime has been a primary reason for adopting stronger measures to incarcerate criminals over the last decade, more than half of the prison population consists of nonviolent drug offenders (Human Rights Watch 2003, 1). The Bureau of Justice Statistics (2003b) finds specifically that, instead of the vast majority of inmates being violent criminals, only 49 percent of state prisoners are serving sentences for violent crimes (1). The "get-tough" strategy commonly referred to as the "war on drugs" is now "the single greatest force behind the growth of the prison population" (Human Rights Watch 2003, 1). It is a strategy that has been increasingly recognized as a "war" being fought almost entirely in Latino/a and African-American communities, based largely on an assumption that communities of color bear most of the responsibility for drug-related crime in the country (Cole 2001; Donziger 1996; Human Rights Watch 2003; Walker et al. 2004).

However, as pointed out in Chapter Three, Latinos/as are no more inclined to engage in illegal drug activity than Whites. In fact, the White House's own Office of National Drug Control Policy (2003, 1) cites the 2002 National Survey on Drug Use and Health to show that 54 percent of Whites report having used illicit drugs over a lifetime, followed by African Americans at 43.8 percent. As for Latinos/as, "[t]he lowest rate of lifetime illicit drug use was among Hispanics (38.9%) and Asians (25.6%)" (1). In addition, the Office of National Drug Control Policy finds that "[o]f 12th graders, whites tended to have the highest rates of use for a number of drugs, including inhalants, hallu-

1986). Research has also shown that of persons presumed to be innocent before trial, Latinos/as are less likely to be released on bail (Walker et al. 2004, 154–62). Although the lack of financial resources to make bail certainly accounts, in part, for pretrial detentions, researchers have also concluded that race and ethnicity have also been known to influence many judges' bail decisions (162). Given these circumstances, Latinos/as are more vulnerable than Whites to being denied bail, which in turn is reflected in the disproportionate rates of incarceration.

Similar to the myths about Latino/a drug use or Latino/a immigrant crime, the belief that Whites are more likely to be victimized by a person of color is also false. Data for 2000 indicate that the Latino/a rate of victimization for all forms of violent crimes totaled 27.9 per 1000 while White victimization was 26.5 per 1000 (Bureau of Justice Statistics 2002, 2). The 2002 National Crime Victimization Survey of the Bureau of Justice Statistics reports that of all persons young African American males are most likely to be victims of violence (Bureau of Justice Statistics 2003b). "Hispanics and non-Hispanics were victims of violence at similar rates during 2002, with one exception: Hispanics were more likely than non-Hispanics to be victims of aggravated assault" (8). As for hate crimes, FBI statistics reveal that African Americans and Latinos/as are most commonly the victims of hate crime along with Asians and persons identified as being of "mixed race" (Walker et al. 2004, 53).

LATINOS/AS AND UNDER-REPRESENTATION IN THE JUSTICE SYSTEM

Regrettably, the deep-seated concerns about Latinos/as in association with crime tend to overshadow the need for Latinos/as to become part of the justice system as lawyers, judges, jurors, and other professionals, lending their skills and services to make the system more effective and equitable. Given the disproportionate Latino/a presence within the prison system, the absence of Latina and Latino professionals in the legal process becomes even more conspicuous. Moreover, a system based on the principle of trial by one's peers should also address problems linked to the difficulties Latinos/as face being chosen as jurors.

The Lack of Latina/o Lawyers and Judges

In addition to the statistics mentioned above, other studies identify Latinos/as as having high rates of involvement in the judicial system, either as defendants or plaintiffs (Moore and Pachon 1985; Reynoso 2000; Falcón 2002, 2). In stark contrast, however, the number of Latina and Latino attorneys and judges in the United States remains extremely low. The American Bar Association (ABA) Commission on Racial and Ethnic Diversity in the Profession reports that in 1999 only 5.7 percent of all those enrolled in law school nationwide were Latino/a while African Americans were 7.4 percent, Asians were 6.3 percent, and Native Americans were less than 1 percent (Chambliss 2000, 3). For 1998, people of color made up 7 percent of all lawyers and only 3 percent of all partners in law firms (1, 9). More specifically, only 2.8 percent of all lawyers are Latino/a while Whites comprise 92.6 percent (*U.S. News and World Report* 2003).

The ABA also contends that increasing the number of people of color entering the legal profession has been hindered by the efforts in recent years to abolish affirmative action (Chambliss 2000, 2–3). After many years of controversy, the U.S. Supreme Court in 2003 ruled in favor of affirmative action programs similar to that of the University of Michigan Law School in the case of *Grutter v. Bollinger*, 539 U.S. 306 (2003). But this important victory in favor of diversity notwithstanding, the attacks against affirmative action over the last decade have been proven to have set back law school enrollment of people of color, especially in states that banned affirmative action (Chambliss 2000, 1).

The scarcity of people of color is so acute that even the ABA concedes that the legal profession has one of the lowest levels of representation of people of color among all professions:

> Minority representation among lawyers lags well behind minority representation in most other professions. In 1998, African Americans and Hispanics made up 12.5 percent of all professionals, including 14.3 percent of accountants, 9.7 percent of physicians, 9.4 percent of college and university teachers, and 7.9 percent of engineers—but only 7 percent of lawyers. The professions with lower levels of minority representation were dentists (4.8 percent) and natural scientists (6.9 percent). (Chambliss 2000, 2)

In a recent study sponsored by the Puerto Rican Legal Defense and Education Fund, Angelo Falcón (2002) reports that the degree of Latino under-representation in the judiciary is extraordinarily high, and he projects an almost insurmountable gap for the future, given the ever-increasing Latino/a population. Using disparity ratios to examine levels of representation, Falcón finds a significant gap between the percentage of Latinos/as in the population and Latinos/as on the bench:

The percentage of Hispanic-Americans holding federal judgeships was 3.7 percent in 2000, compared to 3.8 percent of those holding state judgeships.... Dividing these percentages by the Hispanic percentage of the total U.S. population (12.5 percent) yields Hispanic judgeship disparity ratios of -70.4 percent at the federal level and -69.7 percent at the state level. (3)

Raising grave concerns about fairness in the judicial system, Falcón warns that if current trends persist an even larger disparity would result, with the percentage of judges only growing slightly over time. "[B]y the year 2050 (when the Census conservatively projects the Hispanic-American population to reach 24.3 percent of the total population), the number of Hispanic-American judges would have grown to 4.7 percent in the federal courts and 5.3 percent in the state courts" (4).

Whether or not the judicial system would function more fairly simply with an increase in the numbers of Latino/a judges may be open to some debate. With regard to African American judges, some scholars view African American judges as more capable of understanding poor defendants and the experience of communities of color, resulting in decisions that may be more conducive to fairness (Welch, Combs, and Gruhl 1988). Other scholars have found few differences between White judges and African American judges in sentencing decisions (Engle 1971; Uhlman 1978; Spohn 1990; Spears 1999).

However, in a study comparing White judges and Latino/a judges, Holmes, Hosch, Daudistel, Perez, and Graves (1993) found that Latino/a judges sentenced White and Latino/a offenders alike, but White judges levied harsher sentences on Latinos/as. Thus, this study suggests that Latino/a judges produce fairer results than White judges. Interestingly, the researchers rationalize that "Anglo judges are not so much discriminating against Hispanic defendants as they are favoring members of their ethnic group" (502). Of course, if White judges are treating groups unequally based on race or ethnicity, they would, by definition, be acting in a discriminatory manner.

Many scholars readily acknowledge that prejudice and discrimination persist in today's society are manifested in ways that are more subtle and indirect, with Whites tending to regard their behavior and attitudes as untainted by prejudice (Healey 2003, 123–54). How Latinos/as in the courts have been treated has also been found to reflect nuanced forms of prejudice and discrimination.

In his study of Chicano cases in Los Angeles in the late 1960s and 1970s, Professor Ian F. Haney López (2003, 6) argues that simply acknowledging that race is a social construct is not enough. Instead, he posits that it is important to understand what makes racism operational. He views racism functioning

as a form of common sense—informing and engendering discriminatory behavior and "rendering such behavior as normal and legitimate" (7). In de-
scribing discrimination experienced by Chicanos in Los Angeles courts, Haney
López explains:

> Called upon to pick grand juries from a cross-section of Los Angeles
> county, the judges…consistently nominated their friends and neigh-
> bors…insisted that they desired only to pick qualified persons for the
> grand jury. But as became clear in their testimony, patterns of social,
> educational, residential, and workplace segregation ensured that the
> judges had few Mexican acquaintances, save perhaps their gardeners,
> and that they regarded Mexicans as unqualified to serve on the grand
> jury. The judges assumed that persons like themselves—white, older,
> affluent, and male, or married to someone like that—deserve that
> honor. For the judges, it was simply indisputable that people like
> themselves were dependable, competent, and qualified, meriting not
> only a seat on the grand jury but the esteem accorded friends. Like-
> wise, it was common knowledge to the judges that Mexicans were,
> well, inferior. Intentional discrimination was unnecessary. To system-
> atically exclude Mexicans from the Los Angeles grand jury, the judges
> only had to rely on what seemed to them common sense. (7–8)

Placed in this context, Haney López asserts that the normative aspects of discriminatory behavior continue to play a major part in society today (7).

In this same vein, the legal profession and the justice system tends to norm
and homogenize certain behavior. Judges, regardless of race, are influenced
by the system and are probably not likely to rule much differently than the
norm found within the institution that has selected them—a court system
that tends to be conservative and that tends to reinforce the middle- and
upper-class values and experiences of those who predominate in the judiciary
(Uhlman 1978, 893; Walker et al. 2004, 237–38). Indeed, to buck the system
can come at a great cost for a person of color who is a professional within the
justice system (Wright 1987).

Nevertheless, federal appellate court judge Sonia Sotomayor (2002) provides an important perspective on the importance of Latina and Latino representation within the judiciary. She reminds us that the experience and understanding that many venerated jurists brought to the bench, such as Oliver
Wendell Holmes and Benjamin Cardozo—judges who voted on cases up-
holding gender and race discrimination—are not usually brought into question. As a Latina member of the judiciary, Judge Sotomayor maintains that
Latina and Latino judges must retain their identity and be able to use their ex-

perience and background, not to curry favor for their own, but to make the system fair for all: "[W]e who judge must not deny the differences resulting from experience or heritage but attempt…continuously to judge when those opinions, sympathies and prejudices are appropriate" (92).

Latino/a Representation on Juries

The right to a jury of one's peers is a fundamental principle of U.S. law. But it has also been the case for many years that people of color have had to face all-White juries (see Cole 1999; Haney López 2003; Walker et al. 2004). *Hernandez v. Texas*, 347 U.S. 475 (1954), stands as a testament to the historical exclusion of Latinos/as from juries. Today, potential Latino/a jurors still encounter barriers to serving on a juries. Their proficiency in a second language (Spanish), rather than being deemed an asset, may be treated as a liability that leads to their exclusion from a jury.

In *Hernandez v. New York*, 500 U.S. 352 (1991), the U.S. Supreme Court in a six-to-three decision held that a criminal defendant's Fourteenth Amendment rights to equal protection were not violated when a prosecutor exercised a peremptory challenge excluding potential Latino/a jurors who understood Spanish on the basis that they might not accept the court interpreter's version as the final arbiter in the case.[3] The defendant had argued that the elimination of potential Latino/a jurors violated his right to a trial by his peers in violation of his constitutional rights. But the majority in *Hernandez* explained that the prosecutor's reason for excluding Latino/a jurors was "race-neutral" because anyone, regardless of race, may be fluent in a language other than English (361–62).

The court in *Hernandez v. New York* dodges the most obvious issue in the case: the overwhelming number of the persons in the jury pool who speak Spanish in a city like New York are going to be Latina or Latino and their ex-

---

3. In *Batson v. Kentucky*, 476 U.S. 79 (1986), the U.S. Supreme Court held that the use of a peremptory challenge (the exclusion of a potential juror without the need to show cause) is permissible except in cases of race-based exclusions which violate the Constitution's Fourteenth Amendment Equal Protection Clause. As Del Valle notes (2003, 196), the Supreme Court in *Hernandez* did not give serious consideration of the "sociological link between race and language" critical to understanding how language would violate the equal protection rights of Latinos/as. She explains that the *Hernandez* Court looked narrowly at the issue of race, relying on *Batson*, and applied an intent standard that focused on the "subjective intent" of the prosecutor, rather than a disparate impact standard, which would have more been appropriate given the impact peremptory challenge have on excluding Latino/a jurors (196–98).

clusion through the peremptory challenge process would have an adverse impact on the make up of juries, particularly in cases where the defendant is Latino/a. The flawed reasoning of the majority opinion in *Hernandez* is exposed in Justice Stevens's dissent:

> First, the [prosecutor's] justification [for the use of the peremptory challenge] would inevitably result in a disproportionate disqualification of Spanish-speaking venirepersons [prospective jurors]. An explanation that is "race neutral" on its face is nonetheless unacceptable if it is merely a proxy for a discriminatory practice. Second, the prosecutor's concern could easily have been accommodated by less drastic means. As is the practice in many jurisdictions, the jury could have been instructed that the official translation alone is evidence; bilingual jurors could have been instructed to bring to the attention of the judge any disagreements they might have with the translation so that any disputes could be resolved by the court. See, *e.g., United States v. Perez*, 658 F.2d 654, 662–663 (CA9 1981). Third, if the prosecutor's concern was valid and substantiated by the record, it would have supported a challenge for cause. The fact that the prosecutor did not make any challenge...should disqualify him from advancing the concern as a justification for a peremptory challenge. (*Hernandez v. New York*, 500 U.S. 352, 379 (1991))

Justice Stevens further posits that the use of peremptory challenges to disqualify Spanish-speaking venirepersons is completely unnecessary: "An even more effective solution would be to employ a translator, who is the only person who hears the witness' words and who simultaneously translates them into English, thus permitting the jury to hear only the official translation" (379n2).

As the law stands today, potential Latino/a jurors may be disproportionately rejected through the use of peremptory challenges virtually anytime a prosecutor claims that he or she feels that a bilingual person would not abide by the court's official translation (Méndez 1993). In fact, in the *Hernandez* trial, prospective jurors with Latino/a surnames were systematically excluded from the jury, and no Latinos/as served on the jury (Del Valle 2003, 190–91). The decision in *Hernandez* has been singled out as one example of the U.S. justice system's inability to properly handle the discrimination that bilingual Latinos/as encounter (Méndez 1993; Del Valle 2003).

Latinos/as in Law Enforcement

Increasing Latino/a representation in the administration of judicial and law enforcement processes can only be regarded as a partial solution. It is evident that to be effective Latina and Latino participation in the justice system must also be meaningful. In line with the view expressed by Judge Sotomayor, the cultural knowledge and experience of Latino/a judges, lawyers, law enforcement personnel and jurors can be utilized to advance an effective and fair system of justice throughout the system, from local police precincts to the highest courts in the land. But this can only be made a reality if the opportunities to do so are opened.

Historically, the first obstacle communities of color have had to overcome was the fact that careers in law enforcement were closed largely because of racial and ethnic discrimination. Progress toward equal opportunities for employment in law enforcement began only after legal action was taken by civil rights organizations. It was the Puerto Rican Legal Defense and Education Fund's lawsuit against the City of New York and the New York Police Department (NYPD), for example, that brought down the barriers for Latino/a officers seeking promotions. The suit successfully challenged non-job related examinations that had a disparate impact on the ability of Latino/a offices to move up in the ranks within the department (*Hispanic Society of the New York City Police Department, et al. v. New York City Police Department*, 42 Fair Empl. Prac. Cas. (BNA) 905, 40 Empl. Prac. Dec. (CCH) P36, 385 (S.D.N.Y. 1986), *aff'd*, 806 F.2d 1147 (2d Cir. 1986)).

Although nationally the percentage of Latinos/as city police officers rose from 5.2 percent in 1990 to 8.3 percent in 2000 (Bureau of Justice Statistics 2003a, 4), Latinos/as generally are still underrepresented in many cities. Underrepresentation is especially marked in the upper ranks of the police, particularly from the rank of sergeant on up, with Latina women "almost completely unrepresented in the rank of sergeant and above" (Walker et al. 2004, 134).

Augmenting the number of police officers of color, while often cited as a remedy for strained police-community relations, falls short of a satisfactory remedy for the deeply entrenched problems of bias in law enforcement and problems related to a police culture predisposed to shield officers from accountability in cases of misconduct or excessive use of force.

Consistent with certain studies on judges mentioned earlier, having people of color represented among police officers does not necessarily result in changes in police behavior. No significant differences in policing patterns have been recorded in the ways that police officers of color do their jobs as compared to White officers in research involving the use of deadly force (Fyfe 1981) or in arrest patterns (Black 1980). These results seem to show that the officers of color are not likely to veer away from well-established patterns of behavior within the police force. Familiar practices and behaviors engrained in police culture appear likely to be replicated by officers of color. Having few persons of color in supervisory and decision-making positions able or willing to break with traditional patterns and practices, it stands to reason that officers of color would be less inclined to and capable of establishing new modes of working with or viewing the communities they serve.

Perhaps the aspect of police culture most resistant to change has been the unwritten "code of silence," in which officers refuse to provide honest testimony to protect their colleagues from allegations of wrongdoing (see Amnesty International 1998; Human Rights Watch 1998). Accounts of instances where an officer fails to observe the code of silence show that such behavior can exact a heavy price. Such was the case involving Latina police officer Daisy Boria of the New York City Police Department (NYPD). Officer Boria, who witnessed the death of Anthony Báez at the hands of a White police officer who used a chokehold prohibited under department rules, testified about what she witnessed regarding police perjury and obstruction of justice in the Báez case (Weiser 1998, B1). For her honesty, Boria was reportedly harassed, left without back up in dangerous situations by her fellow officers, and eventually forced to resign (Gonzalez 1996, 21). This instance serves as a cruel lesson for those Latino/a officers who defy the code of silence that rigorously protects its ranks even in egregious cases of misconduct and abuse.

Activism in Law Enforcement: The Latino Officers Association

Aside from contract disputes, rarely do police officers organize opposition to policies and practices within their own police departments. However, the one consistent exception over the years has been the organized efforts by African American and Latino/a officers, who have often challenged discriminatory department policies and practices. Indeed, as in the court case cited above, the Hispanic Society of the New York City Police Department was a lead organization in the early lawsuits that helped open opportunities for Latinos and Latinas in the department. In recent years, the emergence of the Latino Officers Association (LOA) has sparked new activism among Latino and Latina officers in the New York City Police Department. Its expansion into a national entity has given rise to a new name, the National Latino Officers Association.

Founded in 1996, LOA immediately attracted headlines as a Latino/a advocacy group that successfully challenged in federal court the City and the NYPD's attempts to block the group from marching in parades wearing their uniforms (Weiser 1999b, B5). LOA has also backed numerous discrimination cases against the City and the NYPD on behalf of Latino/a officers. In addition to class action-oriented litigation, LOA has supported individual cases, as in the case of William L. Acosta who filed suit against New York City for having been wrongfully dismissed from the police force in retaliation for uncovering police corruption (*New York Times* 1999, B7).

One of LOA's largest lawsuits involved the disproportionate number of disciplinary cases against officers of color within the NYPD. In 1997, when NYPD internal police data for 1996 revealed that 31.7 percent of the force were police officers of color, but that 54.8 percent of all departmental disciplinary charges were against officers of color, LOA and an African American officers group filed a complaint with the federal Equal Employment Opportunity Commission (*New York Times* 1997, B4). A lawsuit was subsequently filed in 1999, charging that Latino/a and African American officers are more harshly disciplined than White officers (Weiser 1999a, B3). On February 1, 2004, the National Latino Officers Association announced that New York City agreed to settle for $26.8 million the lawsuit filed against the New York City Police Department, former mayor Rudolph W. Giuliani, and former Police Commissioner Howard Safir (Moynihan 2004, 33). While the city admitted no wrongdoing, the settlement requires the City to pay compensation to Latino/a and African American officers who experienced discriminatory treatment, including hostile work conditions and reprisals (33). In addition, changes to the department's disciplinary process and compliance monitoring are included in the settlement (Pérez 2004, A12). At its press conference, the LOA proclaimed that after a four-year court battle this settlement served as an acknowledgement of the type of internal discrimination and retaliation that has existed in the NYPD (Moynihan 2004, 33).

The spokesperson and executive director of the National Latino Officers Association is 43-year-old Anthony Miranda, a retired NYPD sergeant who served 20 years on the force. Born to Puerto Rican parents, Miranda grew up in New York's Bedford Stuyvesant community in Brooklyn, where he still resides. Passionate and outspoken, Miranda states that the organization's mission is to promote racial and ethnic tolerance and equality and to end all forms of discrimination, sexual harassment, and retaliation against people of color in law enforcement agencies. To that end, Miranda asserts that LOA has successfully supported a series of legal actions. Its accomplishments have spurred on the organization's growth to thousands of members, and its membership not only includes police officers, but law enforcement agents in corrections, probation, customs, hospitals, and other agencies. According to Miranda, LOA has established chapters outside of New York in places such as Florida, Maryland, Alaska, and Puerto Rico (Miranda 2002).

Its achievements notwithstanding, Miranda sees much that still needs to change from the perspective of Latinos and Latinas in law enforcement. In response to the issue of increasing Latino/a representation in law enforcement, he emphasizes that expanding the number of Latino/a officers alone does not instantly result in a police force that is sufficiently sensitive and fair toward Latino/a communities. As Miranda describes, police training promotes the idea that one's sense of self should revolve exclusively around the police force over one's own family ties and cultural identity:

> At the academy, you go through what I call a 'brainwashing period,' when they get you to stop identifying with anything else that you had outside the police department. The mentality they teach you: there's 'us' and there's 'them.' Nobody else is going to be there for you except for us. You have to depend on us. We're the 'Blue,' and that's how we identify and you get the whole blue wall of silence thing that comes up. (Miranda 2002)

Miranda further explains that after intense and rigorous physical training, Latino/a police officers are exposed to ideas that have an enormous psychological impact. Miranda describes that officers in training are told:

> 'we have to stick together'... 'these officers have gotten killed in the line of duty, and you have to understand how officers are in danger all of the time, and you're going to be a target, and people are always going to be looking at us,' and that type of thing. So you grow into that identity that you have to stick together. You have to depend on each other. You can't depend on somebody outside of our group. And that is when you start losing your people of color and the impact that they can have. That starts off with an intense six months and then you're off to your field training period, which is probably another six months to another year. (Miranda 2002)

Speaking from his experiences and that of other members of LOA, Miranda asserts that success in law enforcement depends greatly on how well one adapts to the police culture:

> You want to get this job and want to be successful, and you want to go home and say I did something. So you're going to strive to adhere to as much of their rules because you want to be successful. We're driven by a desire to be successful in what we do, so when we get in there, we're going to give it all. And in order for me to be a part of it, I have to be in it. That's when we start adapting those mentali-

ties—a very limited perception of things—and you lose contact with your friends, and your neighbors and the people that you use to play basketball with or the people that you went to college with. And they'll do that. You're going to lose your friends, get a new group. (Miranda 2002)

As part of the pressure he felt to conform to the police culture, Miranda recounts that while he was on the force he was chastised by White officers for continuing to live in the Bedford-Stuyvesant community, a neighborhood that has for decades consisted largely of people of color. He notes that many White officers in the NYPD do not live in the city and "have never seen or interacted with Hispanics or Black people.... They used to ask me why I still live in Bedford-Stuyvesant. Why don't I move out? Because, I don't have to.... Why am I still in Bedford-Stuyvesant with all these things going on? This is where I grew up. I feel comfortable. I'm not scared" (Miranda 2002). Consistent with Sergeant Miranda's claim that the residency of officers matters, the New York City Civilian Complaint Review Board (2003, 70) reports that of the officers against whom allegations of brutality or other misconduct were *substantiated* during the period of January to June of 2003, 52.8 percent were non–New York City residents.

The New York Chapter of the Latino Officers Association has been especially vocal in cases of police misconduct and brutality. It has been forthright in support of families of victims of police violence, including the family of Anthony Báez. Miranda avows that police misconduct operates in the larger context of racial profiling and police practices that specifically single out Latino/a neighborhoods and communities of color for arrests.

The unwritten rule, according to Miranda, is to "get the numbers"—that is, arrests—in areas where African Americans and Latinos/as live because it is assumed that "we're the ones [Latinos/as] committing the crimes, which is not the case." He asserts that throughout his career this assumption was present within the precinct house as much as it was on the streets. Miranda states that it is taken as a given "that most cops that get disciplined happen to be people of color" because it is believed that they are the most deserving of discipline in as much as communities of color are targeted because it is thought that they commit most of the crime (Miranda 2002).

However, in his experience, Miranda says, the perception that people of color were mostly responsible for crime was mistaken, noting that wherever police officers were assigned that is where arrests were made: "When I worked in a predominately White community, then I would be arresting White people." Miranda insists that, in spite of the many claims by the department that a quota system does not exist, quotas do exist, informally and unofficially, to selectively "get the numbers" from the areas of the precinct where people of color live. He distinctly recalls being ordered by his superiors to conduct arrests in certain predominantly Latino/a or African neighborhoods: "In this neighborhood, we want numbers. Whereas, if we ended up on Avenue U and Avenue X, down that side, we were told you can't give out any summonses" (Miranda 2002).

Miranda and other officers confirm that racial profiling has often been practiced within the department. As an example of racial and ethnic profiling, Miranda claims he was stopped for no reason by fellow officers while driving his car (Miranda 2002). Another Latino officer, who preferred to be identified only as Police Officer David (2002), stated that in 2001 alone he was stopped four times while driving, asserting that fitting the racial/ethnic profile could be the only explanation for being stopped.

Reinforcing Miranda's contention that Latino/a officers are discouraged from relating to their own community, Officer David related an experience in which he was disparaged by another officer for engaging in conversation with a "perp" (a Latino male) while on duty. He stated that it is not unusual to hear officers casually refer to young Latino males on the streets as "perps" (perpetrators), even when they are not under arrest or suspicion. According to Officer David, baggy pants and a baseball cap are usually sufficient for a Latino male to be labeled a "perp" (Police Officer David 2002).

The NYPD, as do many other law enforcement agencies, contests the assertion that its practice is to target people and communities of color. Police departments typically argue that they deploy officers to areas where they have received the most complaints. But in an extensive study of racial profiling Professor David A. Harris notes that "police do not get reports on all crime, and for those not reported police will make no arrests" (2002, 76). Professor Harris (2002, 76) cites the 1999 National Crime Victimization Survey which shows that

> victims of violent offenses did not report these crimes to the police *more than half of the time—54.3 percent.* Almost three-quarters of all sexual assaults, more than a third of all robberies, and more than 40 percent of all aggravated assaults go unreported; almost 75 percent of all purse snatchings and nearly half of all household burglaries never make it into police files.

Professor Harris recognizes, of course, that police departments regularly receive complaints about drugs and crime that occur on the streets and in neighborhoods. But he also explains that the great bulk of drug activity, including the transport of larger quantities of drugs by couriers, goes unreported, unseen, and undetected. Police officers may have *general knowledge* of drug activity, its locations, or the people involved. But this tells them little about any specific patterns or instances of offending. Weapons possession offenses work much the same way.... So if police want to enforce laws against illegal guns, they must seek out the offenders—that is, they must go find these otherwise hidden activities. (77)

Harris also cautions against the use of incarceration rates as an indicator of who is actually committing crime, noting that "incarceration rates measure not crime but the activity of people and institutions responsible for determining criminal sentences—primarily legislatures (the bodies that make the law that determines sentences) and judges (the people who do the actual sentencing)" (78). Consistent with former Police Sergeant Miranda's experience, Harris finds that statistics that show a disproportionate number of drug-related arrests of African Americans, for instance, reflect the "decisions made by someone in the police department—the chief, lieutenants, street-level supervisors, or even the individual officer themselves—to concentrate enforcement activity on these individuals" (78).

Professor Harris explains that the assertion by police officials that Latinos/as and African Americans are stopped more often than Whites because the police "go where crime is" is not borne out by the best data currently available. An examination of data of hit rates—that is, "the rates at which police actually find contraband or other evidence of crime when they perform stops and searches"—repeatedly show that Latinos/as and African Americans were disproportionately stopped even though Whites were in fact more often found with contraband or otherwise engaged in criminal conduct (79). Indeed, hit rates from Maryland, New Jersey, North Carolina, and New York all reveal the same pattern (79–82). Hit data from New Jersey, as an example, showed that even though police targeted African Americans and Latinos/as for stops at a higher rate, Whites who were stopped "were *almost twice* as likely to be found with contraband as blacks, and *five times* as likely to be found with contraband as Latinos—clearly not what the advocates of racial profiling would predict" (80).

Moreover, although Latinos/as and Africans Americans are disproportionately stopped by customs agents at airports (43 percent in 1998), the Custom Service's own data for 1998 reveals that the hit rates for White passengers was actually higher at 6.7 percent than for African Americans at 6.2 percent. For Latinos/as, who are specifically and most frequently profiled as drug couriers, the hit rate was the lowest at 2.8 percent (Harris 2002, 84).

In view of this information about racial profiling, LOA has been quite sensitive to the subtle ways in which profiling occurs. An especially trying aspect of policing for Miranda and LOA members has been the common practice of identifying a suspect solely as "Hispanic" with very few, if any, other details or descriptive information: "What does a Puerto Rican look like? When they start putting these descriptions out like that, using that terminology, there's no justification for that. So, they say a male, Hispanic, 5'9." What does a male Hispanic look like?" (Miranda 2002).

Miranda and the LOA have raised numerous concerns about racial and ethnic bias throughout the justice system, including instances of racial and ethnic prejudice directed at Latino/a officers. He cites instances when Latino officers were placed on wanted posters and when racial and ethnic slurs were used in police stations:

> LOA did a whole big thing on the wanted posters, because they started putting the names of Latino cops on the wanted posters…in the precincts. 'It was a joke.' But it wasn't a joke to us. So we have been fighting them on a number of issues just like the racial profiling, the slurs that go on in the commands…they're so comfortable in doing it to us, and we're in uniform. And that's why I used to tell officers, you know, sometimes people say it's a joke. Don't let it be a joke, because that's how they think about you. (Miranda 2002)

LOA has also been concerned with the treatment of Latina women officers in different agencies and has lent support to Latinas who have filed discrimination claims. Miranda declares that Latina women officers are often treated unfairly and are given the worst assignments. Miranda complains the attitude that " '[t]hey shouldn't be here' " is not uncommon among male officers (Miranda 2002).

Miranda and LOA find the type of sensitivity and racial/ethnic diversity training offered to police officers to be superficial and ineffective. For this reason, they find it critical for Latino/a officers to stay in touch with who they are and where they come from:

> In terms of changing the mentality, we just have to be stronger, as people, and we cannot afford to have separation in Latino law enforcement and in our Latino communities, and that's part of what we [LOA] push. We stress that in the new officers. And the old officers who are already indoctrinated, re-acclimate yourself to your family, and every time you see them out there doing something make believe that's your brother or sister, that's potentially your family member

CHAPTER 5

A TALE OF TWO CITIES: LATINOS/AS IN LOS ANGELES AND NEW YORK

In a press release announcing that the Latino/a population had reached an "all-time high of 38.8 million" in June 2003, the U.S. Census Bureau (2003e) described Latinos/as as "young, diverse, [and] urban." Los Angeles and New York City are two cities that in many ways represent the dynamic population that makes up the Latino/a presence in the United States. Latinos/as in both cities, indeed, are young, diverse, and urban. The various Latino/a groups who reside in these two major metropolitan areas come from very dissimilar regions of Latin America—Mexico, the Caribbean, and Central and South America—and bring with them differences in culture, language, history, and traditions.

At the same time, Latinos/as also share much in common. In Los Angeles and New York, as elsewhere in the United States, economic and social marginalization characterizes much of what the vast number of Latinos/as experience. Their ability to garner adequate local and state government assistance in response to their community needs is often complicated and a source of frustration and disappointment. Their relations with law enforcement as well are typically strained. Both cities are divided economically, with Latinos/as primarily inhabiting the areas of these cities that are most underserved by public services and deprived of basic health care, education, housing, and jobs. In both cases, Latinos/as are part of those groups most affected by poverty, economic inequality, and residential segregation and most entangled in controversies predicated upon their desire for fair and equal justice in their interactions with the police and the judicial system. Both cities share a long history of ethnic and racial tensions. Both cities have been marred by police scandals, corruption, and misconduct—problems that have affected adversely people of color and Latinos/as, in particular.

This chapter takes a look at the experience of Latinos/as in their struggle for economic and social justice in Los Angeles and New York. It is the story of communities striving to make better lives under circumstances that continually fall short of the mythical "American dream." It is also a story of perseverance and activism in response to conditions that Latinos/as face in these cities. Highlighted in this chapter are the lives of two contemporary members of the Latino/a communities—Alex Sánchez in Los Angeles and Iris Báez in New York—and their struggles for justice. Alex Sánchez and Iris Báez—two individuals of different age groups and national origins—call our attention to some of the most pressing questions about justice that Latinos/as face in their daily lives.

Los Angeles and New York City

In 2000, New York City and Los Angeles had the largest Latino/a populations in the United States—New York with 2,160,554 Latinos/as and Los Angeles with 1,719,073 Latinos/as (Bureau of the Census 2001b, 7, table 3). Both cities have Latino/a communities that generally live under highly segregated circumstances. Both cities also continue to experience new waves of immigrants from Latin America and have Latino/a populations that are relatively young.

Nationally, the largest concentration of Latinos/as reside in urban centers, and of all urban areas, the highest concentration of Latinos/as live in East Los Angeles where 96.8 percent of the population (120,000) is Latino/a (Bureau of the Census 2001b, 7).[1] As in East Los Angeles, New York City has had and continues to exhibit very high levels of residential segregation, with Latino/a communities among the groups most isolated from Whites in New York (Scott 2001, B1, B5).

In addition to living largely separated from Whites, Latino/a communities in both cities continue to experience an influx of new groups from Latin America. Indeed, in Los Angeles, where the largest group of Latinos/as are of Mexican descent, and in New York City, where Puerto Ricans still make up the single largest Latino/a group, new immigrants from Latin America have been steadily settling into the *barrios* of these respective cities. In the Washington Heights/Inwood section of Manhattan, for instance, by the 1990's, almost one out of every two persons were of Dominican descent and "78 percent of all new immigrants who settled in the neighborhood came from the Dominican Republic" (Hernández 2002, 112). Along with Dominicans, new immigrants from Mexico have been arriving in New York City and settling in

---

1. The cities of El Paso and San Antonio, Texas, also had majority Latino/a populations, with 76.6 percent and 58.7 percent, respectively (Bureau of the Census 2001b, 7).

places such as East Harlem (*El Barrio*), a longstanding Puerto Rican neighborhood. With a population estimated at 200,000, Mexicans are now the third-largest Latino/a group in New York City after Puerto Ricans and Dominicans (Feuer 2003, B1). Similarly, Los Angeles has seen noticeable increases in new immigrants, including arrivals from Central America. Nationally, the largest group of Central Americans is Salvadoran, comprising 655,000 persons or 1.9 percent of the total Latino/a population in 2000 (Bureau of the Census 2001b, 2).

These new arrivals settle in communities that are poor and exceedingly underserved and are often where other Latinos/as already live. The natural consequence of this is a perennial "fight over crumbs"—that is, Latino/a groups find themselves pitted against each other in competition over limited resources and services in such areas as employment, education, business opportunities, housing, health care, and other public services. As the results of a study by the Urban Institute show (2002, 1), "[d]espite their strong attachment to the labor force, many immigrants in Los Angeles County and New York City are experiencing a substantial unmet need for health care, food assistance, and other social services." The Urban Institute also found that "[p]overty rates for immigrant families are more than twice as high as rates for native citizen families in California and New York state" and that "[i]mmigrants tend to have lower incomes despite high labor force attachment, largely because they are more likely than native citizens to work in low wage jobs" (2).

Factors that are internal and external to Latin American countries help explain recent migratory patterns (see Hernández 2002, 25–26). Inside the United States, U.S. business enterprises continue to act as a force attracting immigrants from Latin America desperate for jobs. In spite of the movement of many industries outside the United States in the past decade, Los Angeles and New York still remain centers of commercial and industrial activity that lure workers from Latin America. Both cities still play an especially pivotal role in the U.S. apparel industry, an industry notorious for its exploitation of Latino/a and Asian immigrant laborers (Gereffi, Spener, and Bair 2002).

Among New York City's Latino/a sweatshop workers, Dominicans predominate (Palpacuer 2002, 61). In Los Angeles, Mexican and Central American workers are most commonly exploited as cheap labor (Kessler 2002, 75). Notwithstanding campaigns to rid these cities of sweatshops, including the Department of Labor's "No Sweat Initiative," the illegal practice of hiring workers to work under substandard conditions and below the minimum wage continues to thrive as employers count on immigrant workers to be unwilling to unionize for fear of retaliation or termination (90).

Outside the United States, economic turmoil and despair cast a long shadow over most of Latin America, causing many workers to flee in the hope of finding jobs elsewhere. Countries in Central America have been particularly hard hit, unable to compete in an unfair global market place in which the world's richest nations—the United States, Japan, and the developed nations of Europe—subsidize their farmers and maintain protective tariffs on agricultural products (see *New York Times* 2003d). The U.S. government spends $19 million annually in financial support for U.S. agri-businesses that, in turn, dump their surplus grain on the world market, hurting farmers in developing countries unable to compete with cheaper U.S. grain (Pollan 2003, 41–48).

The failure of globalization and free trade to remedy the economic plight of Latin American countries has left many Latin Americans with few choices other than to leave their homelands in search of employment in the United States. Working people in countries such as El Salvador have grown desperate, unable to weather economic hard times. Falling coffee prices in 2003 caused by a worldwide surplus of coffee beans sparked a surge in migration out of El Salvador. Many Salvadorans and other Latin Americans, who have found themselves without a livelihood, risk their lives to make the dangerous trek through the Sonora Desert to reach the United States (Hadden 2003b).

Latino/a populations have also tended to be relatively young compared to the rest of the U.S. population. In 2000, thirty-five percent of Latinos were under the age of 18, in contrast to 25.7 percent nationally (Bureau of the Census 2001b, 7). The median age for Latinos/as in the United States was 25.9 years, as compared to 35.3 years for the whole U.S. population (7).[2] As a result, adolescent Latinos/as, whose families fled war and/or poverty in Central America, have been joining the ranks of marginalized youth finding a sense of identity and family in street gangs both in the United States and in Central American countries such as El Salvador, Guatemala, and Honduras.

In a report from El Salvador aired on *National Public Radio*, young Salvadoran gang members who called a press conference held in 2003 provided their perspective on the current situation facing youths in their country:

> We, the saddest children in the world, were never children. We never had toys, kisses or hugs. The most important thing has always been

---

2. The U.S. Bureau of the Census reported in 2001 that "Mexicans had a median age of 24.2 years, Puerto Ricans 27.3 years, Central Americans 29.2 years, Dominicans 29.5 years, South Americans 33.1 years, Spaniards 36.4 years, Cubans 40.7 years, and all other Hispanics had a median age of 24.7 years" (2001b, 7).

to survive in this crazy, savage and disorderly world. Why bother learning to read and write when our parents sacrificed us for the illusion of a better life, fleeing the country. (Hadden 2003a)

Their economic predicament and the effects of decades of internal armed conflicts also lead many Central American youths to travel north to live in cities, such as Los Angeles. Once in the United States, the financial, social, familial, and cultural dislocation they encounter cause many of them to turn to street organizations in search of cohesion, self-worth, identity, and dignity (see Kontos, Brotherton and Barrios 2003).

In the 1990s, with the worst of the Central American wars over, many youths were deported back to their homelands, including youths who had adopted gang lifestyles. Central American societies have proven intolerant of gangs, adopting harsh laws that specifically targeting youths gangs. In Honduras, for example, a young person can be sentenced for up to 12 years for merely having a gang tattoo and similar crackdowns on youths are underway in El Salvador and Guatemala (Hadden 2003a). Thus, Latino/a youths report feeling trapped between two worlds: marginalized in the United States and equally unwelcome in their countries of origin (see, e.g., DeCesare 2003).

POLICE-LATINO/A COMMUNITY RELATIONS IN BOTH CITIES

In 1988, twenty years after race riots broke out in major U.S. cities, such as Los Angeles and New York, and twenty years after the Kerner Commission's finding that racism and inequality were dividing the country, it was assessed that discrimination and inequality was worsening an already difficult economic and social situation (National Advisory Commission on Civil Disorder [1968] 1988; Harris and Wilkins 1988). Now, thirty-six years since the Kerner Report, both Los Angeles and New York City can still be considered as cities reflecting two separate and unequal societies, where the schism in society is not simply between Blacks and Whites, but more generally between people of color and Whites. Discrimination, segregation, "frustrated hopes," the "legitimization of violence," and "powerlessness"—terms used by the Kerner Commission to identify the basic causes for the disturbances of the 1960s in places such as Los Angeles and New York (National Advisory Commission on Civil Disorder [1968] 1988)—are words that, in many ways, are still applicable to the circumstances under which many Latinos/as, African Americans, and other people of color live within U.S. society.

Frustration with longstanding inequality and discrimination among Latinos/as has been cited as a major factor in the sizeable Latino/a participation in the 1992 Los Angeles uprising following the Rodney King verdict. As a result of this expression of Latino/a disillusionment, 49 percent of the damage caused was in Latino/a communities, and a majority of those arrested in the 1992 Los Angeles disturbances were Latino/a (Martínez 1993, 469; Pastor 1993). It is not coincidental that Latino/a dissatisfaction would be registered over a case largely considered a travesty of justice since it appeared to communities of color that White police officers would once again walk free after committing a heinous act of brutality. The 1968 Kerner Commission report singled out the perception of "the existence of police brutality and corruption, and of a 'double standard' of justice and protection" (National Advisory Commission on Civil Disorder. [1968] 1988, 206)—a conclusion that many Latinos/as and people of color hold to be true today. The dissatisfaction among people of color with the double standard of justice they experience in the justice system is present in the many reports examining police-community tensions in Los Angeles and around the country in recent years (see, e.g., Amnesty International 1998; Human Rights Watch 1998). Citing a *NY1* local television news poll in 1997, Human Rights Watch (1998, 275) reported that 81 percent of African Americans and 73 percent of Latinos/as in New York City indicated that police brutality was a severe problem.

In Los Angeles, the 1943 zoot-suit riots—in which police officers in combination with White military servicemen rampaged through the Latino/a *barrio* for several days, brutalizing Mexican Americans and other people of color—remain emblematic of the extended history of strained relations between the police and Latino/a communities (see Escobar 1999). Strained relations continue today, as the police and law enforcement establishment are criticized persistently for their tactics, corruption, and brutality in both Los Angeles and New York.

New York City and Los Angeles, without question, have long histories of police misconduct and abuse that have directly affected Latinos/as and other people of color. In both cities, investigative commissions have repeatedly linked corruption with brutality (Chevingny 1995; Human Rights Watch 1998). In New York, the 1972 Knapp Commission and the 1993–1994 Mollen Commission examined issues of excessive use of force and corruption following revelations of major police scandals, and both called for major reforms in the NYPD.

Indeed, the link between police corruption and brutality in New York City policing could not have been established more clearly than through the commission testimony presented by NYPD officers Bernard Cawley and Michael

Dowd. Officer Bernard Cawley, nicknamed "The Mechanic," whose job it was to "tune people up," testified: "We'd just beat people in general...to show who was in charge" (quoted in Human Rights Watch 1998, 268). Officer Dowd represented the extent to which the police department had become so corrupted that brutality was tolerated and even considered a necessary part of the job if an officer wanted to be accepted. In his testimony, Dowd acknowledged that "[Brutality] is a form of acceptance. It's not just simply giving a beating. It's [sic] the other officers begin to accept you more" (quoted in Human Rights Watch 1998, 273). Crawley and Dowd presented evidence that this behavior was endemic, testifying to "hundreds of acts of brutality they engaged in; yet apparently no fellow officer had filed a complaint about either of them" (273–74).

Scandals continue to mar the reputation of the NYPD. The "quality of life" and "zero tolerance" tactics adopted by Mayor Rudolph Giuliani, so highly acclaimed at first, exacerbated racial tension and brought on numerous protests and claims of discrimination as the number of innocent people of color killed at the hands of White police officers climbed. The 1999 case of the African immigrant Amadou Diallo killed in a hail of 41 bullets outside his Bronx home by members of the now infamous Street Crimes Unit and the 1997 case of Abner Louima who was tortured and sodomized with a stick by police officers in a Brooklyn precinct house were among the cases that received national attention and helped galvanize a movement calling for an end to police violence against communities of color (see McArdle and Erzen 2001; Human Rights Watch 1998; Amnesty International 1998).

Other cases revealed a pattern of police violence directed at other communities of color. The 1995 shooting death of a sixteen-year-old Chinese boy Yong Xin Huang and the 1994 chokehold death of Anthony Báez were among the cases in the Asian and Latino/a communities that aroused opposition to Mayor Rudolph Giuliani and NYPD (McArdle and Erzen 2001).

Following the precipitous rise in cases of alleged police brutality, the Street Crimes Unit—the specialized unit that engaged in stop-and-frisk tactics in search of guns or drugs and that was often implicated in brutality cases—was dismantled. Nevertheless, stops-and-frisks practices have not ended, but instead, those duties were transferred to the NYPD's Anti-Crime Units. Additionally, although the events of September 11, 2001 have drawn much attention away from problems in police-community relations, controversies surrounding deployment of police and their tactics in communities of color have not subsided. They continue to be raised by the Latino Officers Association and by numerous community-based organizations in communities of color in New York City (McArdle and Erzen 2001).

In Los Angeles, the videotaped beating of Rodney King by police officers served as the impetus for an investigation by the Independent Commission on the Los Angeles Police Department, referred to as the Christopher Commission. As in New York's Mollen Commission findings, the Christopher Commission reported that police violence had also become the norm throughout the department. According to the Commission, race was inexorably tied to the unlawful and excessive use of force against persons of color because "an officer's prejudice towards the suspect's race may lead to the use of excessive force" (Independent Commission on the Los Angeles Police Department 1991, 69). The Christopher Commission also discovered a pattern of police conduct tied to the "code of silence," the unwritten vow of secrecy responsible for inhibiting the proper investigation and prosecution of police abuse and excessive force cases (170). Unfortunately, as with the inquiries into corruption and brutality in New York, the heightened awareness of the crisis in law enforcement in Los Angeles did not provide the fundamental changes in the police culture needed to prevent future corruption and scandals.

Like the controversies that tarnished the reputation of the NYPD's Street Crimes Unit, the corrupt and brutal police tactics by the LAPD's CRASH or Community Resources Against Street Hoodlums unit, eventually led to its dissolution. The CRASH unit, which focused its operations in the section of town known as Rampart, left the LAPD under a cloud of disgrace and controversy. The infamous Rampart CRASH scandal shocked Los Angeles and the nation with revelations that while engaging in "[p]olice work targeting predominantly Latinos/as and Latino/a 'suspected gang members' in Los Angeles...[it] framed thousands of innocent people by planting evidence on them, committed perjury in court to gain convictions, and physically brutalized innocent youth and adults" (Villarruel et al. 2002, 64). Police brutality was shown to be linked to illegal conduct, including drug-related activities, on the part of police officers (Cannon 2000).

As news of the CRASH scandal broke, the corrupt activities of the police within Latino/a communities was unmistakable. It was disclosed that an officer planted false evidence on a Latino man who was left paralyzed and wrongfully charged and convicted (Cannon 2000, 32; see also Chemerinsky et al. 2000). At the center of the Rampart CRASH scandal was a Latino police officer, Rafael Pérez, a Puerto Rican, who at his sentencing characterized his actions as having become "consumed by the 'us-against-them ethos of the overzealous cop' after he transferred to Rampart Crash" (Cannon 2000, 32).

Disturbingly, CRASH became a mirror image of the unlawful "hoodlums" that it was supposed to have been placing under control. Its members brandished gang-styled patches and logos, and its motto, "We intimidate those who intimidate others," was proudly hung over on the unit's door (Cannon 2000, 32). In his testimony Pérez revealed that the CRASH culture and behavior was encouraged and protected by his own supervisors who "specifically instructed him to lie on police reports in order to have a more successful prosecution" (Chimerinsky 2001, 637n183).

Most significantly, it is apparent from the Rampart CRASH scandal that it is not just the LAPD that bears responsibility, but the entire criminal justice system. In interviews for a *New York Times Magazine* article, several Los Angeles county judges admitted readily to presiding in cases where they suspected police officers of committing perjury, and one judge conceded that:

> It's said that we need to change the police culture.... But we have to change the judicial culture too. The judicial culture is hostile to the defense. You'll hear judges talking at lunch about some stupid thing a defense attorney did—they rarely talk that way about a prosecutor. I don't think they're aware how biased they sound. (Cannon 2000, 32)

The CRASH unit debacle brings to the fore the ease with which the criminal justice system obtains convictions of Latinos/as youths. Particularly when the arresting officer is Latino/a or a person of color, the system can pretend not to be biased against certain racial or ethnic groups and thereby buffer itself from criticism.

In Los Angeles, the heightened fear of gang-related crime and violence has contributed to the enactment of a series of laws that are increasingly being viewed as exacerbating stereotypes against Latinos/as and leading to unfair and discriminatory results. In a joint report by the Institute for Children, Youth, and Families of Michigan State University and the organization Building Blocks for Youth assessed California's anti-gang efforts:

> Anti-gang laws, such as California's ballot initiative, Proposition 21, have converted a broad range of youth offenses, including misdemeanors, into adult felonies.... In practice, anti-gang laws have caused significant numbers of Latino/a youth across the country—only some of whom are actually members of gangs—to receive harsh treatment by police, detention facilities staff, prosecutors and the courts.... Under California's Proposition 21, by merely alleging that an offense is 'gang-related,' prosecutors may have the power to file charges against a youth as young as 14 years old directly in adult court, without the generally required 'fitness' hearing before a judge (Cal. Pen. Code § 186.22(b); Cal. Wef. & Inst. Code § 707 (d)(2)). (Villarruel et al. 2002, 62)

sources are needed to supervise criminal justice agencies to prevent unlawful abuses (see Amnesty International 1998; Human Rights Watch 1998; Villarruel et al. 2002; Donziger 1996).

An additional remedy available in cases of police brutality is a civil action under the 1871 Ku Klux Klan Act, commonly referred to as Section 1983 litigation for the section where it is found in the federal code (42 U.S.C.A. §1983). Section 1983 civil rights actions have been used to recover monetary damages from municipalities in many instances, but they also often fall short of affording an opportunity for redress for everyone affected by police violence or abuse. As Harvard law professor Randall Kennedy maintains (1997, 121), these lawsuits frequently do not serve as a useful alternative for persons because of the expense, delay, and legal intricacies involved. As a result, it is conceivable that many Latinos/as and people of color do not mount legal actions because of the time, effort, and complexities involved in such litigation.

It is also questionable whether such civil rights lawsuits are truly effective at holding local police departments and governments accountable. Despite the fact that in 1998 New York City spent a record $40 million to settle police misconduct claims (Flynn, 1999, B1), many doubt that such huge sums have provoked fundamental change in the city and its police department. Hefty monetary damages paid to victims are so common that local municipalities seem to absorb the expanse simply as part of the cost of doing business, rather than seeing them as an urgent call for change.

In reference to the situation in Los Angeles, New York University law professor Paul Chevingny comments that "[p]olice brutality litigation has become a cottage industry" (1995, 52). He points out that, in spite of the abundance of cases brought, law enforcement agencies have proven to be resilient against change. In fact, in 1992 New York City's police union, the Patrolman's Benevolent Association, sponsored an angry protest rally against reforms designed to better manage police corruption and abuse (64–65). Chevingny notes that officers yelled out racial slurs, leading the police commissioner at the time to conclude that there were "serious questions about the department's willingness and ability to police itself" (65). Thus, even in police abuse cases that are effectively litigated through the courts, achieving fundamental change in police conduct and policies still appears to be a distant goal.

ACTIVISM, PROTESTS, AND RESISTANCE

The long trajectory of discrimination and prejudice against Latinas and Latinos in Los Angeles and New York has given rise to a shared history of activism, protest, and resistance. From the zoot suit—worn by Latinos as a symbol of identity and defiance in the 1940s (Escobar 1999)—to the formation of the earliest organizations that addressed unfair treatment of Mexican Americans, to the militancy of young Chicanos and Puerto Ricans in the 1960s and 1970s, to the immigrant rights movement of the present, Latinos/as have understood the significance of organizing opposition to oppression, inequality, and injustice. Responding to the need for services and equal rights, the G.I. Forum of the 1940s and later the League of United Latin American Citizens (LULAC) were precursors of many other organizations that came afterwards. In fact, LULAC was instrumental in supporting the earliest court battles to desegregate schools, including the case of *Mendez, et al. v. Westminster School District*, 64 F. Supp. 544 (1946) (Gómez Quiñones 1990, 63).

By the 1960s, the frustration with the continued oppression of Mexican farm workers and the continuing injustices and deprivations experienced among all Latinos/as nationwide prompted new kinds of activism, self-awareness, and militancy. César Chávez and the United Farm Workers of America ignited a struggle to defend Mexican agricultural workers and brought national attention to the plight of laborers who worked under inhuman conditions. Groups with more radical agendas also formed in the 1960s, calling Latino/a youths and students to action. In Los Angeles and the West Coast, the Brown Berets and the United Mexican American Students (UMAS), developed an agenda for political change through their many organizing activities (Gómez Quiñones 1990, 101–153). They also struggled with questions of race and identity in the face of the dominant White society that had effectively racialized Mexican Americans as non-White "others" who were, therefore, not entitled to equality and justice as real "Americans" (see Haney López 2003). The need to assert racial and cultural identity in the face of racism pushed many Mexican American youths to gravitate to Chicanismo, "a politically charged *Mexicanidad*" (Gómez Quiñones 1990, 104).

In Chicago, New York, and other parts of the East Coast, Puerto Rican youths and students became active in such groups as the Young Lords in response to the forms of discrimination Puerto Rican communities faced in housing, schools, and health care, and the need to address the issues of Puerto Rican identity in view of Puerto Rico's ongoing colonial status with the United States (Morales 1998; Meléndez 2003). Both the Chicano and Puerto Rican movements in the 1970s clashed with law enforcement and were subject to the FBI's counter intelligent operations (COINTELPRO), which sought to disrupt nationalist movements in communities of color regardless of whether their activities were constitutionally protected under freedom of expression and association (see, e.g., Haney López 2003, 34; Morales 1998).

On the legal front, the Mexican American Legal Defense and Education Fund—with national and regional offices in Los Angeles, Sacramento, Chicago, Washington, D.C., San Antonio, and Houston—and the Puerto Rican Legal Defense and Education Fund in New York City are law and advocacy groups that have worked to safeguard the rights of Latinos/as in the courts. Over the years, other civil rights groups have also served as legal advocates for the rights of Latinos/as, including the Center for Constitutional Rights, the American Civil Liberties Union Foundation of Southern California, the New York Civil Liberties Union, and other public interest legal groups. A myriad of private attorneys—Latinos/as and non-Latinos/as—nationwide have also been instrumental in protecting Latino/a rights and access to justice.

Latino/a Activism Today

Latino/a activism today takes many forms. One very prominent effort is to protect the rights of immigrants and to offer solutions to the plight of Latino/a immigrants who work and contribute to the United States, but still remain isolated, exploited, and marginalized as "aliens." The 2003 Immigrant Workers Freedom Ride across the United States, reminiscent of the Freedom Rides for African American civil rights of the 1960s, brought together numerous community-based groups, labor unions, and churches of various religious denominations, including the Catholic Church, in a call for an end to the harassment and exploitation of immigrants and a granting of legal status to immigrants from many different countries upon whose work and services the United States depends economically (Greenhouse 2003a, 33).

The backbone of social change for Latino/a communities, however, has been the activism of community-based groups and Latino/a communities themselves. Many community-based projects have formed over the years that work daily to organize, protect, and educate Latinos/as on a broad spectrum of issues such as workers' rights, immigrants' rights, literacy, police misconduct, and education. Organizations such as the Instituto de Educación Popular del Sur de California and the Asociación Tepeyac de New York work with many Latino/a immigrants, providing needed advocacy and services to their constituents. Police Watch and the Coalition against Police Abuse in California as well as the National Congress of Puerto Rican Rights (now commonly referred to as the Justice Committee) and other groups in New York have played significant roles in responding to the issue of police brutality in Latino/a communities. Indeed, community-based organizing, education, and mobilization have been central to the gains that have been made.

Characteristic of Latino/a activism is its emergence from the events that have directly touched the lives of Latino/a community members. What follows are the stories of two activists: In Los Angeles, Alex Sánchez, a Salvadoran, former gang member, helps to lead a group created to assist Latino/a youths out of the gang lifestyle. In New York, Iris Báez, whose son Anthony was killed by a police officer in 1994, has become an advocate and activist for Latino/a communities after the tragedy that befell her family.

Alex Sánchez

Founded in 1996, Homies Unidos, a non-profit gang violence prevention and intervention organization, provides crisis intervention and support for transnational, gang-affected families in San Salvador, El Salvador and Los Angeles, California. In Los Angeles, Homies Unidos works closely with street gang members, creating alternatives to violence and drugs by making available access to alternative education, leadership development, health education programs, and the building of self-esteem. One of its founders is a former gang member, Alex Sánchez. His early life story has become one that is all too common in the city of Los Angeles. It is the story of families from Central America fleeing the seemingly endless and brutal armed conflicts in their countries during the 1980s. Los Angeles was one of the main destinations for Salvadorans seeking to escape the horror that engulfed their homeland.

Under the banner of the anti-communist Cold War effort, the U.S. government spent billions of taxpayer dollars to support governments favorable to U.S. interests in places such as El Salvador and Guatemala. In turn, Central America was rendered a bloody battlefield, where right-wing death squads razed villages, massacred innocent civilians, and even U.S. priests and nuns were targeted for politically-motivated killings (LaFeber 1993; LeoGrande 1998).

The Salvadoran Peace Accords of 1992—ostensibly marking an end to the war—and the wave of anti-immigrant sentiment sweeping the United States at the time led to thousands of Salvadorans being deported back to El Salvador. After decades of war, El Salvador was a country left in economic and social ruin. With numerous broken families and the social fabric of society in decay, death squad activity, drugs, and gang rivalry and violence reemerged (DeCesare 2003).

Alex Sánchez was among the youths caught in between the war in El Salvador and the harsh realities of Los Angeles street life. An impetus for establishing Homies Unidos, initially founded in El Salvador, was his interest in addressing the transnational character of the problem. Sánchez explains that upon their return to El Salvador, gang members from the United States became role models for youths who, after the war, had little hope for the future and even fewer role models to look up to:

> All of a sudden they see these guys coming down there all tough macho, bigger, you know, because the way they were bred here, I guess,…we're going down there and to see the skinny kids over there with big bellies…and these kids are out there running loose, they analyzed us when we got down there. They saw us and…they idolized us and they did everything that we did. They wanted to get tattoos… they wanted to get into the gangs…they started copying everything that we did. (Sánchez 2001)

Sánchez has come across similar patterns in Guatemala, Honduras, and Nicaragua, where disaffected youth from these war-torn nations have sought refuge in the gang lifestyle, either in the United States or in their countries of origin. Throughout Central America and in the United States, these youths have found themselves subject to harassment, intimidation, and, eventually, imprisonment at the hands of the authorities. In Central America today, the remnants of the right-wing death squads of the 1980s now prey on youth gangs, such as the Eighteenth Street gang or the Mara Salvatruchas (MS) gang (DeCesare 2003). Sánchez himself explains that if he had been deported back to El Salvador, it was certain he would have been killed:

> If I were to be sent to my country I was facing death. I had been outspoken about the death squads, I had been about the…gangs really killing each other down there,…I had been outspoken…talking about the LAPD. So I was speaking out against a lot of people, you know, which put me in a situation where I could have gotten killed. …I had enemies down there already that were coming over to my auntie's place and asking for me. (Sánchez 2001)

As described above, death squads who kept surveillance on his aunt's home were among the enemies that Sánchez faced. With the support of former U.S. Senator Tom Hayden, a campaign to garner national and international support and attention for Alex Sánchez was successful in preventing his deportation, based on the imminent danger of persecution awaiting him in El Salvador. His cause now is the work of Homies Unidos.

Spearheading the coordination of Homies Unidos today are Salvadoran-born Silvia Beltran, a former staff member to Sen. Hayden and the Executive Director of Homies Unidos, and Alex Sánchez, who serves as Homies Unidos's Program Director. Their focus, as explained by Sánchez, is to convey a message about alternatives to the gang lifestyle, not by simply lecturing to Latino/a youths and gang members, but through education (Sánchez 2001). Their program encompasses these specific areas: violence prevention and intervention, creating alternative educational opportunities, strengthening families, artistic expression, and health care education. Thus, the program provides participants with the tools to improve their lives by helping them advance educationally, by tapping into their creativity and potential, and by learning how to lead healthy and productive lives. Homies Unidos's educational programs have expanded under the Epiphany Project, a project encompassing a variety of skills and self-development components, including personal coping skills, health awareness, leadership, and other educational programs.

While many have come to believe that Homies Unidos is a beacon of hope in the sea of neglected *barrios* in Los Angeles, others have remained skeptical and often hostile toward the group's work. The Los Angeles police have often been cited as treating Homies Unidos as a criminal enterprise, rather than a source for constructive change and peace (Rappleye 2000). Homies Unidos, nevertheless, has persevered, growing in importance and in its impact on the problems of youth alienation and gang violence (Hayden 2000, B11).

Iris Báez

Since his death at the hands of a New York City police officer, Anthony Báez has become symbolic of the problem of police brutality in Latino/a communities. Angered by a football that accidentally hit a police car as Anthony and his brothers played in the street, New York City Police Officer Francis Livoti used a chokehold, prohibited under department regulations, killing Anthony Báez in 1994 (McArdle 2001). Even though the judge recognized that the police department engaged in "a nest of perjury," officer Livoti was acquitted at trial in state court (Human Rights Watch 1998, 290). International human rights organizations that studied this case have concluded that it represents an unmistakable case of police racism and brutality (Human Rights Watch 1998; Amnesty International 1998). Left to contend with what was widely considered a travesty of justice was Anthony's mother, Iris Báez.

Born in 1942 in Ponce, Puerto Rico, Mrs. Báez came to New York at an early age, where she lived and raised six of her own children and adopted another six. She is a woman who has worked all her life—as a home attendant, as a teachers aide, and a medical assistant in several hospitals. She was active in the local Parents Teachers Association (PTA) in the Bronx and had even become PTA president. From her perspective, until 1994 her life had not been affected directly by discrimination:

I didn't know what racism was until, really, this happened. Though before I saw it, but I didn't know what that was.... So I didn't know there was a problem. I didn't know what I was, as a Latina, running into.... Why do they treat you different? I never really focused on those issues. I...worked, I brought my kids home, made sure they were okay. And my husband, you know, and I, we did everything like we were supposed to, you know, and we go to church and that's it. (Báez 2002)

She recalls that the day that her husband was called to go to Union Hospital, where he received the news that their son Anthony was dead, there was still uncertainty about the magnitude of the problem. It was only after the autopsy results and the disclosure of evidence at trial that Mrs. Báez came to fully appreciate that a heinous offense had been committed against her son.

After the initial dismissal of the cases against Officer Livoti in state court, the testimony of Latina Police Officer Daisy Boria proved to be crucial in a subsequent federal court case for civil damages. It was through these court proceedings that it was disclosed that Livoti had a history of brutality complaints. Livoti "had been subject of at least eleven brutality complaints over an eleven-year period" (Human Rights Watch 1998, 290). The trial convinced Iris Báez that her son's death was linked to racial and ethnic discrimination: "it was because my son was Latino. They said, 'no, don't put race into this right now.' But I say that was part of it, because afterwards, I started finding out stuff about Lavoti. Livoti didn't get along with Latinos" (Báez 2002).

The federal civil case against the City and NYPD resulted in a damage award of three million dollars, which Mrs. Báez has used to establish a foundation in her son's name. The Anthony Báez Foundation provides her with the basis for continuing to work in support of others affected by police misconduct and abuse. She has also participated in the formation of Parents Against Police Brutality, a community organizing and support group for family members whose children have died or have suffered from encounters with New York City police officers (Hsiao 2001; Johnson 2003, 292).

Her son's death created a sense of awareness of her community's relationship to the law and law enforcement not present before. She finds solace that her son's case "gave the people something to say: 'Hey, we've got to put a stop to this—this abuse in the neighborhood'.... When I used to walk around, everybody used to come out and tell me: 'You know that cop, that cop did this to me.' So I'd say: 'Why didn't you do something?' You know, maybe if we would have stop them back then, he would have never murdered my son!" (Báez 2002).

Like Alex Sánchez, her life and understanding of the larger society were transformed—a transformation that led her to work for social change. In 2002, Iris Báez ran for District Leader for the 86th District in the Bronx. Though unsuccessful in her bid for political office, she remains committed to a life of community service.

Conclusion

Los Angeles and New York City exemplify the diversity of Latinos and Latinas in the United States from Mexico, the Caribbean, and Central and South America. They are also representative of the past and future struggles, hopes and aspirations of Latinas and Latinos. The stark realities of discrimination, residential segregation, and political and economic marginalization are readily discernible today. Present-day social deprivation and dislocation experienced by Latinos/as are rooted in the colonial conquests of the past and the colonial and neocolonial relationship maintained between the United States and the Latin American countries from which Latino/a migration derives. Prejudices and stereotypes of the past manifest themselves in the policies and practices of the present that preserve the image of Latinos/as as "foreign," even if they are U.S. citizens. Latino/a youth, in particular, are viewed with suspicion—too often perceived by the dominant White society as potential criminals, not as young people with potential.

Tragically, for most Latinas and Latinos the promise of escaping the poverty and despair of their respective homelands in the hope of a better life in the United States never materializes. Many Latino/a youths find themselves in search of identity, caught between the homelands their parents left and a new society which is often not welcoming and sometimes overtly hostile. Many Latino/a youth, like Alex Sánchez, have sought to find their own sense of self within the collective bonds they create for themselves in the form of street organizations, commonly referred to as gangs (Kontos, Brotherton, and Barrios 2003; Bourgois 1995). While gang-related violence and crime is, indeed, a major concern, it behooves us to be cautious not to label all youth of color on the street as gang members. As Walker, Spohn, and DeLone warn (2004), myths about gangs abound. Stereotypes that all gangs are involved in illicit drug activity, that they are only located in large urban areas, and that gangs exist only among youth of color are popular misperceptions that ignore the complexity of this phenomenon (54–59).

Efforts to improve the lives of our society's youths should also not be summarily dismissed in favor of a narrow focus on incarcerating as many gang members as possible. As with Alex Sánchez, many other young Latinos and Latinas that have tried to change their own personal circumstance and have taken the initiative to work within their communities and among Latino/a youth in constructive ways. Ironically, Sánchez describes his work and the work of Homies Unidos as focusing heavily on education—one of the basic public services most neglected in Latino/a communities. The work of Homies Unidos, thus, entails making up for that which the greater society has consistently placed as a low priority: the education of children in the United States, and especially those in poor communities of color.

Like Alex Sánchez, Iris Báez is also worried about the future. At 63, her concern is not about her own future, but the future of other Latino and Latina youths. It is a concern fixed on preventing another tragic and needless death by a police officer whose biases are expressed through violence. Iris Baez's personal loss was due to the insensitivity and illegal operations of a law enforcement agent, something that has become all too frequent in cities like New York City and Los Angeles. To her credit, Iris Baez did not allow the loss of her son to remain simply a personal tragedy. The events that led to and followed her son's death transformed her life. They made her more aware of the world around her; they politicized her and gave her life a different purpose: to serve the community and others.

The lives of both Alex Sánchez and Iris Báez are now dedicated to issues related to justice. As Alex expresses it, he struggles with a society that has sought to criminalize youths and immigrants through its laws and its legal system: "All these laws that are just against the youth. You know, they're criminalizing everybody. They're criminalizing the youth, they're criminalizing the immigrants, they're criminalizing just about anything that they don't want in this country anymore" (Sánchez 2001). The rejection of Latinos/as as rightful members of U.S. society and the dehumanizing effect of unjust and discriminatory treatment is an experience that generations of Latinos/as in Los Angeles, New York City, and many other parts of the United States recount. It is also part of a larger narrative of resistance and social change.

Alex Sánchez analogizes his work to that of planting seeds: "You've got these seeds and...and maybe it won't happen the next week or maybe it won't happen that year, but that seed is there and it will grow" (Sánchez 2001). In their own ways and in their own work, both Alex Sánchez and Iris Báez seek to plant seeds—seeds of change for a more just society and seeds of hope for future Latino/a youth and communities in the United States.

CHAPTER 6

A CULTURE-BASED APPROACH TO WORKING WITH LATINO/A COMMUNITIES: A CASE STUDY

Reaffirmation of culture and identity has been integral to Latino/a responses to marginalization and disempowerment. Just as racism and forms of colonial oppression have aided the United States in maintaining its dominance over Latin America, within the U.S. domestic context control over Latinos/as in the United States has been exercised by institutions that reinforce the racialized, structural inequalities that sustain Latinos/as as a subordinate group. Indeed, the racialized and unequal treatment of Latinos/as mirrors colonial modes of domination that Latin Americans have experienced abroad.

This chapter addresses the common problems faced by Latino/a youth and families in their efforts to negotiate structural inequalities in the provision of basic health care, education, and other human needs and services that impede their attainment of full and equal human rights in the United States. It looks at strengthening the cultural identity and ethnic solidarity within Latino/a communities as a model for reversing the effects of marginalization, racialization, and disempowerment. To this end, this chapter's main focus is a project designed to address these problems, using a culture-based approach to working with Latino/a youths and families.[1]

Palenque—a program established at John Jay College of Criminal Justice— aims to decolonize on personal and collective levels by addressing the problems of alienation and disempowerment frequently observed among Latino/a

---

1. I extend my appreciation to Prof. Luis Barrios of the Puerto Rican/Latin American Studies Department of John Jay College of Criminal Justice for his dedication and vital contributions in conceptualizing and implementing the John Jay College-Family Life Center/*Palenque* described in this chapter.

youths and families. Low self-esteem is a recurring indicator among the participants in the program, as the youths and families are chosen on the basis of being considered "at risk" of finding themselves mired in social problems. Inverting the popular notions about at risk youth and families, *Palenque* views the lack of community services and the neglect of public institutions as institutions at risk which then adversely affect youth and families. *Palenque* focuses on the many positive elements of Latino/a families and culture as a means of building self-confidence and achievement. Its culturally-oriented approach fills the void among Latino/a youths and families who typically experience an absence of respect for and protection of their human rights both within the criminal justice system and in attaining equal access or opportunities in other areas of daily life, such as education or housing. In a society where Latino/a cultural identities and social and linguistic attributes are often devalued, the validation of culture, heritage, and traditions within Latino/a families becomes an essential part of working with Latino/a communities. Professor Luis Barrios and this author, both from the Puerto Rican/Latin American Studies Department at John Jay College of Criminal Justice, serve, respectively, as the program's principal investigator/director and co-principal investigator/summer program coordinator. It is from this hands-on research perspective that this chapter is written, highlighting three years of the program's operation (2000–2003).

Reaffirming Culture and Identity

The history of Latino/a community-based initiatives to organize and mobilize for social change in the United States has typically involved a process of reengaging with cultural roots and reaffirming a sense of self and of identity within the culture. Indeed, the rejoinder to the prevailing White/Black racial paradigm facing many Mexicans in the United States in the 1960s and 1970s was to embrace "Brown" as part of a self-aware Chicano identity grounded in the culture and history of *La Raza* (see, e.g., McWilliams 1990, 285–308; Haney López 2003). Music, art, language, theatre, and literature have and continue to be expressions of cultural reaffirmation and a means of organizing within communities (see McWilliams 1990, 297–304). Indeed, *Teatro Campesino* used theater as an important organizing tool for the Chicana/o movement of the 1960s and 1970s (see Broyles-González 1994). Among Puerto Ricans in the United States from the 1960s to the present, reconnecting to their music and cultural identity has played an important part in the process of developing their understanding of Puerto Rico's colonial status or the destructive effects of the U.S. Navy's bombing of the island of Vieques, Puerto Rico (see Meléndez 2003).

Palenque follows in this long tradition of reestablishing and reaffirming cultural awareness and identity among Latinos/as by incorporating cultural elements throughout its curriculum. Formally known as the John Jay College-Family Life Center (JJC-FLC), *Palenque* is a project of the Puerto Rican/Latin American Studies Department of John Jay College of Criminal Justice. Founded in 2000, *Palenque* operates during the academic year and the summer, promoting Latino/a cultural identity as a means of reducing violence in the lives of urban youths and their families. The program's name, *Palenque*, was the term that self-liberated slaves (*Cimarrones*) in the Caribbean used to identify zones that they created to protect their personal and collective identities. *Palenque* is as an alternative to traditional approaches that seek merely to keep youth off the streets and out of trouble. As such, it is designed to create a safe haven, similar symbolically to that created by *Cimarrones* for their own protection. Within this safe space, *Palenque* provides a wide range of academic, cultural, career, and personal and family development activities that emphasize the community's cultural knowledge and ethnic solidarity while addressing problems of alienation, low self-esteem, and marginalization among Latino/a youth and families.

Drawing from Paulo Freire's work with the poor and oppressed (1994), *Palenque* attempts to make the young people more conscious of their world and aims to transform and empower them. Freire pointed to a problem present among the most disadvantaged in society: the internalization of the judgment of those who are dominant in that society (24). He noted that

> [s]o often do they hear that they are good for nothing, know nothing and are incapable of learning anything—that they are sick, lazy, and unproductive—that in the end they become convinced of their own unfitness. (45)

Moreover, Freire considered "the fundamental theme of our epoch to be that of *domination*—which implies its opposite, the theme of *liberation*, as the objective to be achieved" (84). The data results showing low self-esteem among the *Palenque* participants is consistent with findings that Latinos/as and other youths of color experience cultural alienation and marginalization, requiring intervention for empowerment (Freire 1994; see also Cummins 1993). Indeed, Freire held that "intervention in reality" was basic—that is, learning to think critically and understand the world in which one lives is an essential part of becoming empowered and thereby able to transform and improve one's life circumstances (Freire 1994, 90).

Palenque's focus on strengthening cultural identity and forging greater ethnic and cultural solidarity among the youths and their families is also grounded in research that indicates that traditional Latino/a cultural values and norms appear to deter delinquency and other socially counterproductive behavior (Rodriguez 1996; see also Hagan and Palloni 1999). A recent study focusing on Latino/a homicide rates in five major U.S. cities—Chicago, El Paso, Houston, Miami, and San Diego—reveals that strong social networks within Latino/a communities help deter criminal activity (Martinez, Jr. 2002). These findings reinforce the call for greater "cultural competency" within public institutions (Villarruel et al. 2002) and greater efforts to work with Latino/a youths within their cultural contexts (Koss-Chioino and Vargas 1999). Thus, *Palenque's* culture-based approach, while having addressed a population of largely Dominican youths, has implications for assisting other Latinos/as and can be adapted to various specific cultural needs.

Palenque's methods and goals also find support in international human rights standards intended to protect minority group rights; economic, social, and cultural rights; and linguistic human rights (see, e.g., Skutnabb-Kangas and Phillipson 1995).[2] It is an approach that is culturally relevant and specifically designed to provide tools for empowering Latino/a youths and families. This method is compatible with international human rights goals geared to the social, cultural, and economic advancement of all sectors of any given society. Considering the marginality and social dislocation experienced by Latino/a communities, it is an approach that is appropriate to the situation of Latinos/as in the United States.

PALENQUE AND THE WASHINGTON HEIGHTS/INWOOD COMMUNITY

The target area for *Palenque* is the Washington Heights/Inwood area (Community District 12), a high-density urban neighborhood located in Manhattan. At any given time, the program participants consist of a cohort of 30 to 40 youths who are commonly categorized as "at risk" because of the lack of educational, health or other basic services available in their neighborhood and

---

2. The term human rights, as used in this chapter, encompasses the broadest concepts of economic, social, and cultural rights recognized internationally in addition to the political and civil rights commonly acknowledged under U.S. law. The use of international human rights law, norms, and principles in the context of Latinos/as in the United States is further explored in Chapter Seven.

their vulnerability to being exposed to or involved in violence while living in their community (Hernández and Torres-Saillant 1996). The project attracted Latino/a participants who are primarily, but not exclusively, new arrivals from the Dominican Republic who have settled in the area and are among the largest, youngest, and most disadvantaged groups in New York City.

In world history, nations engaged in imperial conquests have usually imposed their own cultural norms to dominate other peoples at the expense of native identity and culture. In response to such domination, different forms of resistance have typically taken shape as a means of countering the impact of cultural imperialism (Said 1993; Memmi [1965] 1991; Fanon [1963] 1986). Within Latino/a communities in the United States, a similar phenomenon has been observed as Latinos/as have clashed with assimilationist modes of addressing Latino/a cultural differences (see Chapman 2002, 179–84). This has especially been the case in the area of Washington Heights/Inwood, a community where many come from the Dominican Republic, a country repeatedly invaded by the United States and subject to U.S. hegemonic power and influence. The dominant-subordinate relations between the United States and the Dominican Republic are often replicated in the relationship between Dominicans and other Latinos/as in the Washington Heights/Inwood area and the public institutions in that community which have for too long failed to meet the most basic needs of the people of that community.

The Washington Heights/Inwood area can be characterized as a poor, working-class community, consisting primarily of Dominican immigrants (Hernández 2002, 112–17; Grasmuck and Pessar 1991), with a growing population of immigrants from Mexico (Smith 1996, 65). The area is a vibrant ethnic enclave, with streets and avenues lined with thousands of businesses that provide cultural goods, services, and job opportunities (Grasmuck and Pessar 1996) while, at the same time, many of its residents strive to overcome poverty and marginalization (Hernández 2002, 117–19).

Poverty rates in the area are reported at over 80 percent, and it is also the area with the largest number of children receiving public assistance in Manhattan, the fourth largest in New York City (Citizens' Committee for Children 2000). Schools in the district (District Six) are overcrowded and characterized by severely deficient educational facilities or resources. The long-term implications of a substandard education are alarming. Longitudinal research points to the importance of school achievement as a critical risk factor for child and youth violence (Hirschi and Hindelang 1977; Eron and Huesmann 1990). As a result, students who are low achievers will be more likely to start skipping school or drop out altogether. Patterson, Reid, and Dishion (1997) find that truants usually begin to hang out with each other when not attending school,

Development Center, provide support in the areas of individual and family counseling, crisis intervention, and other services when needed.

The program focuses on five specific developmental areas in its curriculum:

Academic development: This component incorporates a variety of activities that promote greater interest in and improved attitudes toward schooling. Given the harsh conditions of overcrowding, unqualified teachers, lack of resources and other problems that plague the New York City public schools, most of the program participants experience high levels of alienation within the educational process. To address this problem, *Palenque* uses innovative, nontraditional approaches, including a computer-based mathematics instruction program that was effective in keeping the participants engaged in an academic activity they would typically reject. Computers were also used to create web pages that promote peaceful resolutions to disputes and tension. Other academically-oriented activities included poetry writing, where Latino/a poets and writers assist the participants in creating their own poetry, which, in turn, enhances their writing and language skills.

Personal Development: Conflict resolution and problem-solving workshops have been conducted by the City University of New York Dispute Resolution Consortium and/or the *Palenque* staff. These workshops include weekly life skills training workshops on a wide range of areas, including motivation, self-discipline; frustration tolerance; habits and attitudes; decision-making; problem-solving; and peer influences. The poetry workshops, in relation to personal development, provide another forum for the development of critical thinking and awareness of themselves in relation to their environment and community. In addition, participants have held meetings with police officers from their own community to discuss each other's role in producing and preventing violence in the community.

Cultural Development: The *Palenque* participants have engaged in a variety of Latino/a cultural activities in the areas of music, dance, and painting. For instance, the summer 2001 participants were taught the art of Dominican-style ceremonial mask-making. Through these classes, the youths learned how culture varied by region and the socio-political meanings reflected in the colors and designs of the masks. The participants also learned how to paint their own works of art, to appreciate various forms of Latino/Dominican music, and to understand how various forms of Caribbean music—merengue, bachata, salsa, classic, rap, reggae, rock, hip-hop, modern, and others—are linked to history and culture. These workshops helped promote socio-cultural awareness and pride in their families and their community.

Career Development: The *Palenque* staff have offered photography workshops to present the youths with a concrete example of a career option. The youths were given a 35-millimeter, disposable camera and chose assignments related to the conditions within their neighborhood. Their photographs, for instance, captured the symbols or evidence of violence in the community as well as the struggles of everyday life. Deadlines and other requirements were established to help them develop work skills, including meeting deadlines, managing time and resources, and working with others.

Recreational Enrichment: A recreational component—that includes playing dominoes, basketball, and dancing—has been integrated into the program to teach the youths how to abide by rules, work collectively, improve concentration and memory, and in some instances, as with dominoes, help enhance mathematical skills.

Each of the program's components cover many issues in every session, providing for enriching discussions that advance personal, educational, and developmental objectives. For instance, poetry sessions encompass multiple levels of personal development—including constructive discussions about sex, love, gender roles, and relationships—while engaging in academic development activities that assist the participants in improving their grammar, spelling, vocabulary, and writing skills in both English and Spanish. The variety of culture-based components have provided the occasion for each participant to choose areas in which they are able to excel and generate interest among the participants in activities not usually attractive to youths.

PALENQUE'S IMPACT ON LATINO/A YOUTHS

Assessing *Palenque's* impact has been accomplished through an array of quantitative and qualitative data gathered throughout the academic year and the summer program. To measure academic development through quantitative means, the Wide Range Achievement Test, Third Edition (WRAT-3) and the School Bonding Index-Revised (SBI-R) have been administered. To gauge personal, cultural, and career development, the program has used the Youth Self-Report Inventory (YSR), the Multigroup Ethnic Identity Measure (MEIM), and the Career Maturity Inventory (CMI). Finally, the participants complete the Violence Risk Assessment Inventory (VRAI) to assess the level of violent behavior in the lives of youth participants. Over the three years (2000–2003), the academic year participants and the summer participants, separately, were given pre-and post-tests to measure change in the participants. Control groups were similarly tested for comparison.

Qualitative data have also been collected. Life history interviews, photos, poems, drawings, paintings, and field observations have been conducted on all participants, focusing on various themes, such as community violence, immigration history, educational history, employment history, experiences with delinquency, conflict resolution, relationships with parents, and ethnic identity. Field observations have centered on recording classroom interaction and dialogues between youths and police officers. Other data of a qualitative nature include the participants' writing projects, photographs, paintings, and other art work.

In the relatively short period in which the funder's guidelines[3] required the program to work with 30 to 40 youths—Mondays through Thursdays for four to seven weeks during the summer and after school Mondays through Thursdays from 4:00 p.m. to 8:00 p.m. during the academic year—it was predictable that some results of the quantitative tests would be mixed, with some youth still requiring greater improvement in such areas as academics and self-esteem. In addition, the quantitative instruments required by the funding source did not always produce the most valid and reliable results. For instance, the tests were written in English, a language in which some participants were not proficient. Test results also suggested the need for greater long-term cultural reaffirmation to improve self-esteem, in addition to the need for a study spanning a longer period of time in which to observe the participants' progress. While there remain areas requiring improvement, the program has succeeded in meeting its overall goals, evidence of which was most visible in the qualitative data.

It must be noted that since the first year of the program (2000–2001) did not emphasize culture, there was greater reliance on traditional methods of quantifying progress. The program's initial inability to effectively engage the participants required the shift to a culturally-oriented approach based on the work of Prof. Luis Barrios (Barrios 1998; Kontos, Brotherton, and Barrios 2003). The refocusing of the program to include culture as a central theme and the inclusion of qualitative measurements has dramatically enhanced the program's effectiveness and reinforced the thesis that culture matters. The program's components, thus, have begun to more successfully reach the youths on multiple levels—personal, academic, social, and developmental—in ways not easily measured by the quantitative tests.

The most compelling evidence of the program's success is present from a variety of qualitative data gathered, including journal entries, photographs,

---

3. Funding for *Palenque*/John Jay College-Family life Center (2000–2003) was provided by the Family and Community Violence Prevention (FCVP) Program of Central State University, Wilberforce, Ohio, which administers funds from the Office of Minority Health, Department of Health and Human Services.

poems, life histories, post-program interviews, and focus groups. Academically, non-traditional academic approaches, such as the specialized computer-based math instruction, increased the overall enthusiasm and motivation of the summer participants toward academic achievement. Summer 2001 participants, for instance, reported math to be one of the activities that they most enjoyed.

Many elements of the program in combination have produced positive results. The cultural-orientation plus the program's efforts to expose the youths to a college environment and to worlds beyond their community have provided an enriching experience for the program participants. The completed artistic works produced by the youths—including photographs, poetry, and paintings—have been publicly exhibited each year at John Jay College of Criminal Justice and at other locations, including *La Casa de La Cultura Dominicana*, a cultural center in the Washington Heights community, and *El Museo del Barrio*. These exhibits have reinforced positive self-perceptions and enhanced the participants' sense of accomplishment. Moreover, components within *Palenque*'s academic development curriculum which foster a positive cultural and linguistic identity (e.g., through poetry writing in the students' native Spanish) are consistent with calls for greater language diversity in schools attended by Latino/a children (Delpit 1995). Additional positive results were garnered through the use of John Jay College student mentors who served as examples of persons from similar backgrounds pursuing educational and career options unfamiliar to many of the youths and their families.

Numerous participant reactions solicited from the participants also show a remarkable improvement in attitude and academic performance. Formerly reserved youths exuded confidence in being able to interact in the classroom. Below, for example, are two former participants' comments after returning to school in the fall of 2004:

> What I learned was to have guts; to say what's on my mind in front of everybody [in the group], not to hold anything back…that's helping me in school, like in my class participation rate. Now I participate more. (15-year-old male, Summer 2003 participant)

> I learned how to communicate better, to have self-esteem; I learned to listen better, like, it [the program] helped me in English class. I thought English was boring but now I listen more. It helped [me with] my listening skills. (17-year-old male, Summer 2003 participant)

Our qualitative findings also confirm that the conflict resolution/peer mediation workshops have been successful in helping participants recognize anger; accept and manage it in constructive ways; and articulate negative emotions that the youths have identified as having been previously unrecognized or normalized in everyday life. The participants' journal entries indicate success in having learned skills to cope with conflict in their daily lives and in their communities, and they articulate the interrelation between personal anger with the structural oppression and exclusion experienced in school or in other aspects of their lives. Among the entries common in their journals are notes of a particular session in which strategies to deal with conflicts were discussed. One participant's outline was typical of most of the youths' written notations:

"J.", male, 14 years old:[4]
Alternatives to violence
- Resolving conflicts
- Negotiation for win/win situation
- Listening to each other
- (not imposing your ideas)
- Need patience in order to listen/to resolve conflict
- Seek peaceful solution to violence or negative situation
- There are always two sides to a story
Negotiation process
- Use mediator if possible
- Go to a neutral place where both parties feel safe
- Both parties must want to resolve situation
- Listen, Listen, Listen
- Help deciper [sic] fact from gossip

However, the most telling of the positive results were the journal entries that expressed how well they learned and that articulated the ways they could incorporate the lesson in their personal lives, as the following examples show:

"I.," female, 14 years old:
The way that I'm going to use the alternatives to violence and the negotion [sic] process is by listening more because most of the time I really don't listen to what people have to say I just asume [sic] that I'm right and there [sic] wrong and today I learned that that is not correct.

---

4. To preserve the participants' confidentiality on personal work product, the participants' names have been withheld.

"J.," female, 15 years old:
I feel that I can use this in my life in any future confrontations that I may have. Also discussing negotiation between people and gangs leads me to learn that not everything is what you think. I learned that assumptions can cause a lot of issues and looking at both sides is a key struggle.

"I.," female, 16 years old:
I want to use this in my life in the way that when I'm stuck in a conflict I can find a better way to solve without violence. I also want to take this [sic] skills and knowledge to improve the way I think about certain things. Besides this is a good learning experience that I can carry throughout myself and motivated to successed [sic] in the future.

Of course, the harsh realities of life for these youths have found expression in the many works of the youths. Painting, photographs, and poems have often touched on the problems of police brutality, rape, and other forms of violence. However, *Palenque's* curriculum has focused on positive messages, encouraging the participants to be proactive in promoting peace as a response to the negative depictions of their community as marred by violence.[5] In fact, "keeping the peace" was the motto created and adopted by the summer 2003 participants. Discussions on conflict resolution and about how to "keep the peace" were subsequently reflected in the many forms of artistic expression the participants engaged in throughout the program that summer. Below are two of many examples of poetry that articulate their thoughts on the topic:

What Eye See
by Brain Heredia,[6] age 16

Life through my unique eyes
I see the true lies
Violence, and the people who would light you up like fireflies
They don't be seeing what life is worth
You wanna keep killing yourself, go back to birth

---

5. Other programs have also taken steps to move youth toward positive and peaceful solutions. Homies Unidos in Los Angeles is one such example, where "peace" is emphasized as a central theme in its work.

6. Consent was obtained to publish the poems of the participants whose names appear in this chapter. These poems were also displayed and presented publicly as a way for participants to contribute to each other and to the community.

suggests that even non-Dominican participants in *Palenque* (such as Haitian and Ecuadorian youths) benefited from this approach since they were able to relate to and participate in cultural activities, such as music and art.

Palenque's goals reaffirm the idea that culture matters and promote personal and collective identities within Latino/a communities as integral to a multi-faceted approach to assisting Latino/a communities in view of the harsh historical and present-day realities of Latinos/as in the United States (see Barrios 1998; Kontos et al. 2003). The program's approach is also consistent with a series of established and developing norms and principles of international human rights law that seek to protect the rights of all persons to their culture, language, heritage and identity as fundamental rights for those persons who do not constitute a majority of the population. Many countries in the world recognize these protections as legitimate with respect to excluded or marginalized groups in their own countries and for the general advancement of entire societies (see, e.g., Skutnabb-Kangas and Phillipson 1995). A discussion of the intersection between the culture-based model presented here and norms and principles of international human rights law is more extensively addressed in the next chapter.

CONCLUSION

Past and current injustices demand responses that validate the existence of Latinos/as as human beings—persons whose social, cultural, and economic well being are deserving of respect and protection in addition to promoting equality of civil and political rights. The culture-based approach of *Palenque* is one of many methodologies that can be employed to address injustices experienced by Latinos/as at a grassroots, community level. It does not seek to create only a diversion for Latino/a youths, but to help empower them through the use of their own cultural knowledge and solidarity. Empowerment remains a critical need in all Latino/a communities. A cultural experience that creates a critical consciousness among the participants about the society in which they live—including an awareness of the dynamics of race, class, and gender that affect their lives—can help transform and mobilize them to change their realities for their own individual as well as their community's collective advancement.

Palenque offers a model that reaffirms Latino/a culture, linguistic heritage, and identity among Latino/a youth and families—a model that has the potential to improve the status of Latinos/as in relation to the rest of U.S. society. It is a program that also serves as an example of an effective university-community partnership that brings together talent and resources from the community. The qualitative data results show that Latino/a youth understand that society sends them a clear message: they are the recipients of the worst schools, educational instruction, health care, and other social services in the society, and they are the subjects of discrimination based on race and ethnicity, as manifested by their treatment within the legal system, the lack of basic social services, and the poor conditions in their communities. As evidenced by our data and experience with the participants in the *Palenque* program, Latino/a youth receive a loud message that "they are less than" in the context of U.S. society. It, therefore, is inconceivable that Latino/a youth and families will ever be able to advance in the United States without first addressing the conditions that reinforce low self-esteem and marginalization. However, the lesson to be drawn from *Palenque* is that, when given the opportunity and the tools to excel, Latino/a youth hold great promise. Like all young people, Latino/a youth aspire to a better future. Their sense, and the reality, that a better life is remote presents a seemingly insurmountable obstacle in their paths. Thus, breaking down barriers is the quintessential challenge that must be faced. *Palenque* attempts to meet that challenge.

Palenque's preliminary success makes it worthy of additional study, as do other programs with similar goals, strategies, curricula, and focus. The non-traditional approach to teaching academic subjects, coupled with an environment that accepts and reaffirms the participants' cultural background has yielded promising initial results that bode well for the continued success of programs such as this. *Palenque* offers an approach to working with Latino/a communities that reinforces the essential qualities basic to all humanity: culture, language, and identity. It addresses economic, social and cultural conditions acknowledged under international human rights law standards, an area that will be discussed in the next chapter.

CHAPTER 7

INTERNATIONAL HUMAN RIGHTS STANDARDS AND LATINO/A COMMUNITIES IN THE UNITED STATES

The culture-based model presented in the previous chapter finds support in international human right standards that are consonant with the idea of cultural rights as part of human rights. Forms of cultural domination and marginalization as experienced by Latinos/as in the United States require the implementation of strategies that advance the promotion of equality and justice. International human rights laws and principles provide guidance on issues of cultural domination and marginalization on both international and domestic fronts. Adherence to international standards would not only help resolve problems related to U.S. foreign policies toward Latin America and Latin Americans, but international human rights principles and standards on economic, social, and cultural rights also provide direction on how to address the condition of Latinos/as in the United States.

This chapter highlights aspects of international human rights laws and principles that may help effectuate positive changes for Latino/a communities in the United States and enhance their ability to gain equality and justice. Moreover, the benefits of recognizing and implementing international human rights laws and principles in the United States—particularly calling for an expansion of economic, social, and cultural rights—would have positive ramifications for the broader U.S. society by augmenting opportunities and rights for everyone.

CULTURAL SUBORDINATION IN INTERNATIONAL AND U.S. DOMESTIC CONTEXTS

A variety of mechanisms—military, economic, political, social, and cultural—have been employed to subordinate Latin America to and Latin Americans in the United States. As described by Smith (2000, 6), the United States today "wields unilateral hegemony." Over time, the subordination of Latin American identity and culture has been as important as the use of U.S. military, economic, and political might in establishing and maintaining U.S. control and domination. Implicit in the racialization of Latin Americans as "other" to justify U.S. conquests and domination of the hemisphere is the notion that Latin Americans lack any redeeming cultural, religious, or linguistic traditions. U.S. policies and practices toward Latin America not only presume U.S. cultural as well as racial superiority but also affect social and cultural changes that disempower and dominate Latin American societies.

In the Latin American context, Puerto Rico serves as an example of the methods used to dominate social and cultural life. U.S. policies and practices in Puerto Rico regarding language and religion in the aftermath of the U.S. war with Spain in 1898 are especially illustrative of the subordination of the language and culture of Latin American peoples. From 1898 to 1948, the United States unilaterally imposed the use of the English language as the only language of instruction in public schools in Puerto Rico, banning Spanish, the native language of Puerto Rico, in the educational process of Puerto Rican children. A 1929 study by the International Institute of Teachers College, Columbia University revealed a school dropout rate in Puerto Rico of more than 80 percent among students as a result of this imposed language policy, and in examining the effects of this policy, scholars have found that the impact is still being felt today (Zentella 1999, 158). Similarly, with the U.S. military intervention in 1898 came a concerted effort by the U.S. military and U.S. religious organizations to "Americanize" Puerto Ricans by promoting Protestantism— a religion considered by the North American victors of the war with Spain to be a more "modern" or "enlightened" religion than Catholicism and, therefore, superior (Díaz-Stevens 1996, 156–61).

As with the colonial conquest of Puerto Rico, the Spanish language in the territories wrested by the United States following the U.S.-Mexican War of 1846–1848—such as California and New Mexico—was also systematically suppressed (Hernandez-Chávez 1995, 146–48). Indeed, the widespread use of Spanish in New Mexico became a factor in delaying statehood for this former part of Mexico. Only when the English language became dominant and the Anglo-American population exceeded the number of Mexicans was state-hood granted to New Mexico, a process that took sixty-four years (147).

In later years, the imposition of U.S. views and cultural values took other forms. In the early 1940s, the U.S. government under President Franklin Delano Roosevelt established the Office of the Coordinator of Inter-American Affairs (OCIAA), an agency headed by Nelson Rockefeller calculated to disseminate pro-U.S. positions and information to counteract a growing fear of Nazi influence in Latin America (Smith 2000, 80–83). As part of this endeavor, Hollywood's cooperation was solicited in the production of films to be distributed in Latin America that presented the United States in a favorable light. The U.S. State Department reported the success of the OCIAA in a memorandum of 1942, concluding that "[i]t was the greatest outpouring of propagandistic material by a state ever" (quoted in Smith 2000, 83).

Throughout contemporary Latin America, U.S. corporate interests continue to project their cultural, linguistic, and commercial ideas and standards. Ariel Dorfman and Armand Mattelart (1984), in a now famous work entitled *How to read Donald Duck: Imperialist ideology in the Disney comic*, drew attention to the impact of Disney, Coca Cola, and other powerful U.S. companies in fostering dependence on the consumption of U.S. products and a cultural atmosphere in Latin America favorable to the continued exploitation of Latin America for the benefit of U.S. commercial and corporate interests. The result, as Dorfman and Mattelart assert, has been the stifling of economic development and improvements in the social conditions of most Latin Americans. Hence, Dorfman and Mattelart's book became a central document in the study of "cultural imperialism" in the 1980s (Holden and Zolov 2000, 272)—a term used in reference to the many direct and indirect ways in which the United States has used its power to influence and dominate Latin American and other societies through commerce and the media to impose and disseminate its own language, values, ideas, beliefs, and views to advance U.S. policy goals and business interests (see Tomlinson 1991).

As discussed previously in this volume, racialized, structural inequalities, and marginalization are replicated through many institutions of U.S. society, such as education, housing, healthcare, and criminal justice, which reflect the norms prevalent in the dominant culture. The application of a culture-based approach to addressing the problems faced by Latino/a communities in the United States is derived from an understanding of the ways in which Latinos/as are affected by the dominant perspectives that position Latinos/as as "less than" within the society, which in turn leads to disempowerment and alienation. For this reason, a culture-based approach, such as that taken by *Palenque*, emphasizes the community's cultural knowledge and ethnic solidarity to address problems of alienation, low self-esteem, and marginalization among Latino/a youth and families. But it is essential to know that this approach does so with the understanding that the economic, social, and cultural contexts in which Latinos/as live functions in ways that undermine equality, justice, and progress for many Latinos/as.

A key dimension of *Palenque* is its ability to address the problems of marginalization, alienation, and disempowerment among Latino/a youths and families by providing a type of personal and collective decolonization relevant to the U.S. context. *Palenque* helps participants and their families in the process of exercising a form of self-determination, analogous—though not strictly identical—to the principle found in international law that recognizes the right of "peoples" to "freely pursue their economic, social and cultural development" (United Nations 1960, para. 2; United Nations 1966a, art. 1; United Nations 1966b, art. 1; see Appendices B and C).

Under international law, "peoples" are those who can exercise full rights to determine their own political status, including their right to establish an independent nation, as well as the right to complete determination of their economic, social, and cultural development (see United Nations 1960; Appendix B; see also, Cassese 1996). It is not argued here that Latino/a communities in the United States are entitled to rights as "peoples" to establish an independent nations, as defined in international law, but rather, that they comprise a group entitled to minority rights under international law (see United Nations 1992; Appendix D). Nevertheless, as set forth by Robert Blauner (1972), the experience of Latinos/as, along with other groups such as Native Americans, African Americans, and Asians, has been compared to that of groups that have been subject to imperial conquests and control and, thus, treated as "colonized minority groups" within the United States, as opposed to European immigrants who relocated to the United States on a more voluntary basis.

While some have critiqued Blauner's theory as too limited in its approach to the issue of race in the United States because of its reliance on a nation-based paradigm, it nevertheless provides a useful framework, particularly for explaining the experience of Latino/a groups in the United States (see Omi and Winant 1994, 46–47). The conquest of Puerto Rico and its continuing colonial status; the conquests of Mexican territories; U.S. interventions and occupations of Caribbean and Central American countries, such as the Dominican Republic and Nicaragua; and the economic hegemony that the United States maintains over Latin America all speak to forms of colonialism relevant in shaping the Latino/a experience in the United States.

Certainly one of the most abhorrent facets of colonialism is its tendency to deny peoples not merely their right to political self-determination, but also to usurp the ability of peoples to determine their own economic, social, and cultural development. Indeed, seizing control over the culture and identity of those in colonial or neocolonial situations has been identified as an indispensable goal of colonialism in order to maintain peoples under subjugation (Césaire 2000; Fanon [1963] 1986; Memmi [1965] 1991; Ngũgĩ 1986). Comparable to the need to address the economic, social, and cultural impact of colonialism and neo-colonialism on the peoples of Latin America, Latino/a communities confront impediments that prevent them from pursuing their own political, economic, social, and cultural improvement. Faced with failing schools, poor housing and health care, and lack of employment, Latino/a communities endure hardships that tend to reinforce the idea that Latinos/as are "less than" and, therefore, un-deserving of the most basic of human needs and opportunities.

Palenque seeks to make attainable a form of decolonization that provides youths and families with the tools to gain control over their individual and collective right to determine their future. It is a program that begins to attend to the issues of culture and identity that are at the heart of the problems of low self-esteem that many Latino/a youths experience. It mirrors the decolo-nization process that, on an international level, addresses the need to dis-mantle institutions that subvert the culture and identity of those affected. *Palenque* assists Latino/a youths and their families in regaining and reaffirm-ing their own cultural, social, and economic development through its educa-tional and career development components. Its culturally-oriented approach attempts to fill a void among Latino/a youths and families who typically ex-perience an absence of respect for and protection of their Latino/a cultural identities aa well as their social and linguistic attributes.

Palenque's goals reaffirm that culture matters, particularly in working with people who experience high levels of alienation in society (Barrios 1998; Kon-tos et al. 2003). Its methods mirror legal rights paradigms found in interna-tional human rights standards intended to protect minority group rights, eco-nomic, social, and cultural rights, and linguistic human rights (see Skutnabb-Kangas and Phillipson 1995). It is consistent within an international human rights framework that acknowledges as legitimate the right of persons who do not constitute a majority of the population to maintain their own cul-ture, language, heritage, and identity as basic to the human rights of all per-sons. The protection of these rights should not simply be viewed a matter of respecting excluded or marginalized groups in their own countries, but an es-sential part of providing for the overall well-being and advancement of the whole society (see Goldewijk, Baspineiro, and Carbonari 2002).

Although often maligned in the United States, bilingual education, for in-stance, is an integral part of the educational system of many countries around the world as a matter of right. Countries—including Norway, England, the

Netherlands, Sweden, Australia, Mexico, and China—help insure equal educational opportunity for linguistic minority groups through bilingual education programs that recognize the right of all persons to an education (Krashen 1999). In turn, these programs have been shown to be successful in assisting students acquire the national language while subjects are taught in their native tongue (22–48). Such educational systems are premised on the basic concept that bilingual educational programs are not only pedagogically valuable, but that they also serve the greater good by advancing the education of all the people living within their countries and that preserving the rights of linguistic minority groups to retain their cultural identity is a right that is basic to the dignity of all persons.

International Recognition of Economic, Social, and Cultural Rights

Early in the twentieth century, the League of Nations recognized the importance of protecting the rights of ethnic, linguistic, and religious minorities in the post-World War I period. Various ethnic, linguistic, and religious minority groups were threatened by changes in the political configuration of states after the war, and as a consequence, an effort to protect their rights was initiated (Buergenthal, Shelton, and Stewart 2002, 10; Sohn and Buergenthal 1974, 213). These efforts culminated in the development of special treaties for the protection of the human rights of ethnic minorities (see Hannum 1990, 50–55; Buergenthal, Shelton, and Stewart 2002, 11; Lauren 1998, 95).

Since its inception in 1945, the United Nations has made the development of international standards for the protection of human rights a central part of its mission. To that end, human rights principles and norms developed over the years have been codified to require states to respect and enforce various human rights provisions. Within the U.N. system for the protection and promotion of human rights, the International Bill of Human Rights is a central component. The International Bill of Human Rights consists of the Universal Declaration of Human Rights (United Nations 1948; Appendix A), the International Covenant on Economic, Social and Cultural Rights (United Nations 1966b; Appendix C), and the International Covenant on Civil and Political Rights (United Nations 1966a) and its two optional protocols.[1]

---

1. The two protocols to the International Covenant on Civil and Political Rights of 1966 include the Optional Protocol to the International Covenant on Civil and Political Rights

In consideration of the fact that the human dignity of all persons rests not just on their ability to exercise civil and political rights, the United Nations has made clear that human rights protections extend to a broad array of economic, social, and cultural rights:

> International human rights law has been designed to protect the full range of human rights required for people to have a full, free, safe, secure and healthy life. The right to live a dignified life can never be attained unless all basic necessities of life—work, food, housing, health care, education and culture—are adequately and equitably available to everyone. Based squarely on this fundamental principle of the global human rights system, international human rights law has established individual and group rights relating to the civil, cultural, economic, political and social spheres. (United Nations 1991) [an unpaginated electronic work]

Most importantly, the United Nations has emphasized that economic, social, and cultural rights are not secondary to civil and political rights, but stand on equal footing, as stated in paragraph 1 of the United Nations General Assembly resolution 32/130 of 16 December 1977:

> (a) All human rights and fundamental freedoms are indivisible and interdependent; equal attention and urgent consideration should be given to the implementation, promotion and protection of both civil and political, and economic, social and cultural rights;
> (b) The full realization of civil and political rights without the enjoyment of economic, social and cultural rights is impossible; the achievement of lasting progress in the implementation of human rights is dependent upon sound and effective national and international policies of economic and social development, as recognized by the Proclamation of Teheran of 1968. (United Nations 1977)

The United States is obligated to comply with a number of human rights conventions that it has ratified, including the International Covenant on Civil and Political Rights (United Nations 1966a), the Convention against Torture and Other Cruel, Inhuman or Degrading Treatment or Punishment (United Nations 1984), the International Convention on the Elimination of All Forms of Racial Discrimination (United Nations 1966c), and the Convention Relat-

---

of 1966 and the Second Optional Protocol to the International Covenant on Civil and Political Rights of 1989, aiming at the abolition of the death penalty (United Nations 1994).

of Latinos/as in the United States. Below is a summary of the significance of international human rights to Latinos/as and matters of justice in such areas as discrimination, immigrants' rights, Latina women, criminal justice, the death penalty, and economic and social rights:

Discrimination

The International Convention on the Elimination of All Forms of Racial Discrimination (United Nations 1966c), ratified by the United States in 1994, obligates the U.S. government to eradicate discrimination. The Convention defines "racial discrimination" as "any distinction, exclusion, restriction or preference based on race, colour, descent, or national or ethnic origin which has the purpose or effect of nullifying or impairing the recognition, enjoyment or exercise, on an equal footing, of human rights and fundamental freedoms in the political, economic, social, cultural or any other field of public life" (art. 1, para. 1). The Convention not only requires that State Parties take action to prohibit and enact appropriate action to eliminate racial discrimination (art. 2), it also calls for "special measures to be taken for the sole purpose of securing adequate advancement of certain racial or ethnic groups or individuals requiring such protection as may be necessary" (art. 4).

The implications of an effective use of the International Convention on the Elimination of All Forms of Racial Discrimination for Latino/a communities may be far reaching. The Convention is designed to address discrimination against persons based on national or ethnic origin and to have an impact on the larger issues of economic, social and cultural matters. Its application has also been viewed by human rights organizations as vital to addressing the problem of discrimination within the judicial system in the United States and, in particular, racial discrimination by law enforcement personnel (see, e.g., Amnesty International 1998; Human Rights Watch 1998).

Immigrants' Rights

Despite the many misconceptions about immigrants as a burden on the U.S. economy and society, most immigrants to the United States are in the country legally; documented and undocumented immigrants alike make significant contributions to government revenues; and immigrants make significant contributions to the growth of the economy. For instance, 84 percent of all immigrants in New York—the state with the largest foreign-born population—are legal (Passel and Clark 1998, 2). These immigrants include naturalized citizens, documented permanent residents, and refugees. Urban Institute analysts who have studied New York's immigrant population have also found that "legal immigrants pay roughly the same percentage of their income in taxes as natives do—about 30 percent" (2). Undocumented immigrants were also found to make sizable contributions in the form of federal, state, and local taxes—including Social Security, residential property, general sales and unemployment taxes—and while the percentage of their income going to pay taxes is lower (15 percent), that is attributable in part to their lower wages and lower tax brackets (5).

Moreover, the Bureau of Labor Statistics' *Monthly Labor Review* reports that "[f]oreign-born workers have come to play an increasingly important role in the U.S. economy; between 1996 and 2000, they constituted nearly half of the net increase in the U.S. labor force" (Mosisa 2002, 3). In fact, contrary to popular misconceptions of foreign-born persons in the United States, "white, non-Hispanics" had a lower labor force participation rate "than any other race/ethnic group" (6).

The true facts about immigrants notwithstanding, misperceptions and discrimination against immigrants persist in the United States. Bias crimes, as in the attacks against Latino day-laborers and the firebombing of the home of a Latino/a immigrant family in Farmingville, New York, exemplify the level of hostility and violence to which anti-immigrant sentiment can rise (Gootman 2003, B1). The value of implementing and enforcing international human rights principles and laws for Latinos/as generally—and especially vulnerable communities, such as Latino/a immigrants—has gained increased importance. In addition to anti-discrimination provisions in human rights treaties and principles, other human rights documents specifically address the human rights issues of immigrants and migrant workers.

The International Convention on the Protection of the Rights of All Migrant Workers and Members of their Families calls for the protection of the health, safety, and well-being of all migrant workers and their families, including the provision of fair and equal conditions of employment, freedom from slavery or servitude and child labor, and other basic rights and treatment (United Nations 1990; Appendix G). Implementation of these guidelines along with the enforcement of national laws can help promote protections for many Latino/a workers in the United States. In light of California's Proposition 187 and similar legislative attempts to curtail basic health, education and other public services to immigrants, legal scholars have sought to use international human rights law to promote standards that protect immigrants from legislative actions and policies that seek to blame immigrants for the economic woes of states, such as California (see Hernández-Truyol 1997).

Consistent with international standards are the types of measures that protect the human rights of immigrant workers from exploitation by U.S. companies seeking workers from Latin America as a cheap source of labor. Trafficking in human beings has become an industry onto itself, one that preys on immigrants desperately seeking jobs in the United States, often with deadly consequences. In May and June of 2003 charges were brought against approximately 100 persons accused of participating in a smuggling ring that brought Latin American immigrants into the United States (Zernike 2003, A18). The indictments were initiated after 19 of 74 immigrants from Mexico and Central America were found dead, apparently of suffocation, in a crowded truck (A18).

Nevertheless, trafficking in human beings has become a lucrative business in the United States. In October 2003, federal agents in 21 states raided 60 stores of the world's largest retailer, Wal-Mart, which had been illegally employing undocumented workers (Greenhouse 2003b, A1). It was also disclosed that undocumented workers were exploited in violation of labor laws, and as a result, the Mexican American Legal Defense and Education Fund filed suit in 2003 against Wal-Mart for paying workers below the minimum wage and for failing to pay overtime (A1).

Trafficking in human beings has been identified and condemned by the United Nations as a contemporary form of slavery and is prohibited under international human rights law, including the International Covenant on Civil and Political Rights (United Nations 1966a, art. 8). Greater awareness and enforcement of these and other international standards, such as those that protect workers rights under the International Labor Organization (ILO), could provide broader safeguards for immigrant and migrant workers.

Sensible strategies that provide immigrant workers with protections are possible. For instance, farmers in Napa County in California, who run a $4 billion wine industry primarily using immigrant labor, have begun to tax themselves to provide humane living conditions for their workers and to support legislative efforts to legalize farm workers (Sánchez 2003). These steps are being taken in view of the fact that these immigrant workers benefit the U.S. economy and that it is only just that the plight of immigrant laborers be ameliorated.

In contrast, however, recent proposals for a new guest-worker program in the United States raises legitimate concerns about the exploitation of laborers from Mexico. Such a program may replicate the worst exploitative practices of the infamous *Bracero* Program (1942–1964) and would be contrary to the protection of the human rights of migrants under international standards. The Mexican Labor Program, or the *Bracero* Program as it has become known, was an agreement entered into between the United States and Mexico, ostensibly to assuage a labor shortage in the United States during World War II. Mexico, for its part, consented to sign an agreement for a temporary guest-worker program to protect its citizens from abuse and discrimination. The accord specified that immigrant workers from Mexico would receive decent standards of health care, wages, housing, food, and other conditions and treatment. But, as Gilbert Paul Carrasco notes, the rights and protections built into the agreement were ignored by both the U.S. government and the U.S. agricultural industry:

> The upshot of the *Bracero* Program was that the U.S. government provided [U.S.] growers with cheap labor.... *Braceros* across the country were compelled to endure poor food, excessive charges for board, substandard housing, discrimination, physical mistreatment, inappropriate deductions from their wages, and exposure to pesticides and other dangerous chemicals. (1997, 195)

Considering this track record with guest-worker programs in the United States, it is imperative that the protection of immigrants and immigrant workers be advanced and enforced consistent with international human rights standards.

The Rights of Latinas

The advancement of women's rights has been a focal point of concern and action in the United States since women have and continue to face economic, social, and political inequalities and discrimination. In this regard, Latinas have not been an exception, and indeed, they often endure inequalities and discrimination even more severe than those experienced by White women.

The socioeconomic condition of Latinas has been exceptionally alarming. In comparing school-age Latinas with African American and White girls, Latinas are the most likely to drop out of school (Canedy 2001). The Census Bureau confirms that 26 percent of Latinas leave school without a diploma, compared to a drop-out rate of 13 percent among African American girls and 6.9 percent among White girls (1). Among all students, only Latino boys drop out at a higher rate, with 31 percent Latino boys dropping out compared to 12.1 percent of African American boys and 7.7 percent of White boys (1). Vulnerability to mixed cultural messages and the lack of viable career prospects are among the factors that the American Institute for Research and other prominent observers attribute to this disturbing trend among Latinas. As Rosanna Rosado, publisher of the Spanish-language newspaper *El Diario-*

La Prensa, explains, too few options and opportunities are available to Latinas, and consequently, at age "12 or 13 you pretty much realize you're not going to be Jennifer and if you're not going to be Jennifer Lopez then what is there?" (24).

Within the criminal justice system, the situation of Latinas in prison is similarly disconcerting, as evidenced by the statistics compiled in a report by the Sentencing Project:

- In state prisons and jails Hispanic females are incarcerated at almost twice the rate of white females (117 persons to 63 persons per 100,000 [persons in the] population).
- Hispanic women are three times as likely to go to prison in their lifetime as compared to white women (1.5% vs. 0.5%).
- In the U.S. general population, 9.7% of women are Hispanic. In the U.S. prison population, 15% of women state prisoners and 32% of women Federal prisoners are Hispanic.
- Between 1990 and 1996, the number of Hispanic female prisoners rose 71%.
- In New York, Hispanic women are 14% of the state's prison population but constitute 44% of women sentenced to prison for drug offenses. (2003, 2)

Undoubtedly, these disturbing statistics speak to the need to address the economic, social, and cultural conditions that Latinas face in the United States. In addition to the implementation of the aforementioned human rights provisions, the Convention on the Elimination of all Forms of Discrimination against Women (CEDAW) provides specific human rights protections for women (United Nations 1979b; Appendix F). CEDAW requires State Parties to prohibit discrimination against women and to take measures, including legislative action, to advance the rights of women in all areas of political, economic, social, and cultural life (arts. 1, 3, and 5). All aspects of family, work, security, education, and health and safety, in which women have been subject to unequal treatment, are addressed by the Convention. The benefits for Latinas, whose particular economic and social circumstances leave them susceptible to inequities and discrimination, would likely be profound if CEDAW were to be ratified and enforced in the United States.

Language Rights in Courts

The issue of language rights in the United States—especially the question of bilingual education—remains an area of much debate in the United States

(Crawford 1992). In spite of the strong, if not overwhelming, scholarly evidence about the soundness of bilingual education (see Romaine [1989] 1992; Krashen 1996; Krashen 1999; Crawford 2000; Cummins 2000), the controversy about bilingualism in schools continues. Unfortunately, anti-immigrant sentiments, xenophobia, and ethnic/racial hatred feed misconceptions about bilingualism and bilingual education (see, e.g., Crawford 2000; Cummins 2000). In stark contrast, the use of native language instruction in schools and multilingualism in many parts of the world is common, having gained acceptance as valuable both pedagogically and as a matter of human rights (Skutnabb-Kangas and Phillipson 1995; Kontra et al. 1999; Skutnabb-Kangas 2000).

Indeed, the merits of programs that meet the needs of non-English speaking persons in the United States have not gone unrecognized. As a matter of law, U.S. Supreme Court decisions still stand as precedents in support of the basic concept of bilingual education for children whose native language is not English (see *Meyers v. Nebraska*, 262 U.S. 390 (1923); *Lau v. Nichols*, 414 U.S. 563 (1974)). Moreover, a substantial body of research conducted in the United States about bilingual education, including studies sponsored by the federal government, speaks to the effectiveness of bilingual education programs when properly organized and funded (Del Valle 2003, 223–224; see also Romaine [1989] 1992; Krashen 1996; Krashen 1999; Crawford 2000; Cummins 2000).[3]

Controversies about bilingual education notwithstanding, it would seem only reasonable for courts to protect persons whose language is not English from being convicted simply because that they did not understand the charges, the testimony, or the legal proceedings against them. But in fact, no Supreme Court decision has recognized a constitutional right to an interpreter in court; no national standards for interpreters in state courts exist; and courts have regularly refused to recognize a constitutional right to an interpreter in civil or administrative proceedings (Piatt 1990). Taken together, these present formidable obstacles to equal justice for many Latinos/as.

The Court Interpreters Act, 28 U.S.C. § 1827 (1994), does extend the right to an interpreter within the federal court system, but it also requires astute

---

3. A longitudinal study of bilingual education conducted at the request of the federal government by J. David Ramirez found that bilingual education had positive results, supporting the theory posited by Jim Cummins that development of the first language increases the development of the second (Del Valle 2003, 223). Other extensive studies support the validity of long-term developmental bilingual programs for language-minority children, including that of Drs. Virginia Collier and Wayne Thomas (224).

and persistent advocacy on the part of legal counsel to insure full and proper discharge of this right (Piatt 1990). Given the difficulty that a poor, limited-English Latina or Latino is likely to have in securing adequate counsel, this federal right is not a sure safeguard.

Problems also arise even in state courts that provide for assistance for those who speak a language other than English. Although the Second Circuit Court of Appeals in 1970 in *United States ex rel. Negron v. New York*, 434 F.2d 386 (2d Cir. 1970), held that non-English-speaking defendants had a right to simultaneous interpreters at the government's expense, in cases where a defendant's lawyer can interpret, courts have placed the burden of translating on the attorney, presenting obstacles for both the attorney whose advocacy may be impaired and the client whose case may suffer from not having a simultaneous translation. In other instances where an interpreter is provided, attorneys may still have to insist on a simultaneous translation (Piatt 1990).

With respect to interpreter services for witnesses, witnesses are not necessarily provided interpreters even when an interpreter is requested. Legal scholars point to the case of *Gonzalez v. United States*, 33 F. 3d 1047 (9th Cir. 1994), as an example of where the denial of an interpreter may have caused the defendant to plead guilty inadvertently (Méndez 1997; Del Valle 2003). A reading of the court transcript in the *Gonzalez* case ostensibly shows a witness with limited English proficiency confused by the questions asked by the judge, yet the guilty plea was upheld on appeal (Méndez 1997). In *Gonzalez*, in spite of a request for a certified court appointed interpreter the court denied the request and ruled that Gonzalez's wife could assist as an interpreter, even though there was no proof that she could translate accurately and impartially, as required by the Court Interpreters Act (93).

The results of the *Gonzalez* case appear to support the assertion of some legal scholars that courts commonly take a cavalier and ethnocentric approach in cases involving Latinos/as (see, e.g., Haney López 2003; Bender 2003). Examples of inconsistently applied or nonexistent standards for the use of interpreters stand as a testament for the need to establish nationwide guidelines that address the linguistic and cultural needs of a diverse population. In this respect, international human rights principles may serve as a model for the development and implementation of appropriate safeguards for language minority groups in the United States.

It is also important to account for the linguistic variations that exist among Latinos/as in the provision of bilingual services. Latinos/as generally share certain cultural characteristics, but they should not be assumed to have identical linguistic needs, particularly within the criminal justice context. The meaning of words and the use of expressions in Spanish vary from one Latin American country to another in ways that may be significant in a court proceeding. Therefore, culturally competent and appropriate services, such as qualified bilingual interpreters familiar with the linguistic differences between persons of specific Latin American countries, should play a part in taking appropriate measures to produce a system that adequately addresses the linguistic needs of all persons who enter into the judicial process. In fact, researchers and policy reform advocates alike have reported on the detrimental effects of not providing culturally competent services in the criminal justice system, prompting urgent calls for the creation of such services (see Villarruel et al. 2002).

Criminal Justice

International human rights groups have campaigned strongly for expanded use of international human rights standards to help secure accountability in police misconduct and brutality cases in the United States (Amnesty International 1998; Human Rights Watch 1998). In response to the many cases of the excessive use of police force in Latino/a and African American communities, international human rights groups have supported the implementation of international standards of conduct for law enforcement officials to improve the situation of police misconduct, especially the rules found in the Code of Conduct for Law Enforcement Officials (United Nations 1979a). The provision of the Code that is most basic to protecting human rights maintains that "[l]aw enforcement officials may use force only when strictly necessary and to the extent required for the performance of their duty" (art. 3).

Additional guidance to law enforcement personnel is found under article 5 of the Code, which instructs law enforcement agents that "[n]o law enforcement official may inflict, instigate or tolerate any act of torture or other cruel, inhuman or degrading treatment or punishment, nor may any law enforcement official invoke superior orders or exceptional circumstances such as a state of war, threat to national security, internal political instability or any other public emergency as a justification of torture or other cruel, inhuman or degrading treatment or punishment." This provision has drawn particular attention in recent years with the highly publicized case of Abner Louima, the Haitian immigrant who was sodomized with a stick by a police office in a Brooklyn police station in 1997.

As a matter of international law, torture or cruel, inhuman or degrading treatment or punishment is prohibited pursuant to many international human rights treaties, including the International Covenant on Civil and Political

Rights (United Nations 1966a, art. 7) and the Convention against Torture and other Cruel, Inhuman or Degrading Treatment or Punishment (United Nations 1984). Having ratified both treaties, the United States is obligated to observe their provisions. Human rights groups have urged for stricter adherence to the requirements of these treaties in order to provide additional protection to communities of color, including Latino/a communities, from police violence (see Johnson 2003, 293).

The Death Penalty

The United States is the only industrialized nation that maintains and supports the institution of capital punishment. The world community has widely adopted a policy to abolish the death penalty as a matter of fundamental human rights. Human rights groups not only condemn the U.S. government's reluctance to end capital punishment, but denounce its disproportionate effect on people of color. The racial impact of the death penalty has been widely documented, with Whites representing 48 percent of all death row inmates and all others representing 52 percent of death row inmates, including African Americans at 42 percent, Latino/s at 8 percent, and "others" as 3 percent in 1990 (Amnesty International 1998, 111). Although Latinos/as are not affected to the extent African Americans are, there is still reason for concern. Race continues to loom large in how the death penalty is applied (Amnesty International 2003). As history shows, whenever the race variable becomes an issue, Latinos/as have usually been affected. Moreover, as Amnesty International reports (2003), there are a significant number of documented death penalty cases involving Latinos where race appears to have been a decisive factor.

One indicator of racial and ethnic bias in the criminal justice system's handling of death penalty cases is the data that show that the race of the victims in almost all capital punishment cases tends to be White. From 1976 to 1990, 83 percent of the victims in capital cases were White while only 12 percent were African American and 4 percent were Latino/a. However, for the same period only 50 percent of murder victims were White (Amnesty International 1998, 111). Thus, a person of color was more likely to be sentenced to death for killing a White person than a White person for killing a person of color.

Another significant issue that has gained considerable attention in recent years is the mounting number of persons on death row proven to have been wrongly convicted and sentenced to death. With the rise in the use of DNA tests and other methods to prove their innocence, an ever-increasing number of death row inmates have gone free. From 1973 to 1998, approximately 75 people sentenced to death were found to be innocent (Amnesty International

1998, 118). Moreover, a number of states have looked into the possibility of imposing moratoriums on the death penalty as the number persons on death row who are found to be innocent grows. In fact, Governor George Ryan, a Republican from Illinois, not only took the dramatic step of imposing a moratorium after 13 individuals sentenced to death were found innocent, but he also commuted sentences of all death row inmates in January 2003 based in large part on the racially discriminatory impact of the capital punishment process. In doing so, Governor Ryan not only singled out the fact that over two thirds of the death row inmates were African American, he pointed out that at least 35 of them had been sentenced to death by all-White juries (Amnesty International 2003).

The growing body of evidence linking racial and ethnic bias to the death penalty process coupled with the history of racial and ethnic bias against Latinos/as within the U.S. criminal justice system and the ever-increasing number of Latinos/as imprisoned by the criminal system should make capital punishment an issue of enormous concern for Latino/a communities. The death penalty becomes another area within the justice system that exposes Latinos/as to unfair and unequal treatment.

Adding to the perils faced by Latinos/as with regard to the death penalty, there have been many instances in which the United States has been willing to defy international law in order to try and execute persons from Latin America. Amnesty International (1998) and other human rights groups have repeatedly condemned the actions of the U.S. government for violating the Vienna Convention on Consular Relations, a treaty that the United Sates is obligated to observe. In 1998, in defiance of a decision by the International Court of Justice, the United States allowed the execution of Ángel Francisco Breard, a Paraguayan who was never allowed to exercise rights to secure assistance from the Paraguayan consular office as provided for under Vienna Convention on Consular Relations (125). Similarly, the case of Humberto Álvarez Machaín—a Mexican citizen who was kidnapped from his country by the U.S. Drug Enforcement Agency, then tried and executed in the United States—sparked an international incident as he too had been denied the right to assistance from the Mexican consul in an egregious violation of international law (124–25).

U.S. violations of the basic sovereignty rights of Latin American countries and the Vienna Convention on Consular Relations signal a continuation of the paternalistic and condescending patterns and policies of the past. These violations demonstrate the need for the United States to make changes in its policies towards Latin America and Latin Americans. Adherence to international law standards would be an essential first step. To that end, the United

States should not only join the vast community of nations that prohibit the death penalty, it should also respect the most basic principles of international law that pertain to the equal rights and sovereignty of nations. (see, e.g., United Nations 1945, arts. 1 and 2).

ECONOMIC, SOCIAL, AND CULTURAL RIGHTS: RIGHTS FOR ALL

International human rights laws and principles protect the human rights of all members of society. These international protections extend into the realm of economic, social, and cultural rights as well as civil and political rights. As such, the International Covenant on Economic, Social and Cultural Rights seeks to insure that the right to work, to fair wages, to equality of remuneration, to adequate health care, to education, and to maintain one's linguistic and cultural heritage are protected for everyone without discrimination as to race, color, sex, language, religion, political or other opinion, national or social origin, property, birth, or other status (United Nations 1966b). The realization of these principles stands to benefit everyone since they are intended to provide a basic standard of living that would assist in preventing crime and other social problems.

Unfortunately, it is widely assumed that people of color in the United States comprise the vast majority of the poor and persons receiving public assistance in some form. Just as the culprits of crime have been racialized, so has poverty. A study of news stories by the media found that the news media often present a distorted image of the racial and ethnic make up of the poor in the United States. Professor Martin Gilens (1999) at Yale University discovered that 65 percent of television news and 62 percent of newsmagazines depicted the poor as African Americans when in reality African Americans make up only 29 percent of the poor. The study concludes that welfare and poverty have been "racialized" because public attitudes toward welfare and poverty are heavily influenced by negative stereotypes of African Americans in particular, including the perception of African Americans as lazy (70–71). Although not to the same degree as the depiction of African Americans, the study shows that Latinos/as are also negatively perceived as "lazy," and predicts that "[a]s the country's Hispanic population continues to grow, attitudes toward welfare may become as strongly associated with perceptions of Hispanics as they are now with perceptions of blacks" (71). This conclusion is consistent with the analysis of other scholars who have examined the problem of Latino/a stereotypes in the United States and have shown that "laziness" is among the most omnipresent stereotypes attributed to Latino/s (see, e.g., Bender 2003; Haney López 2003).

The persistence of stereotypes of Latino/s as "lazy" obfuscates the reality that the Whites comprise the single largest group living in poverty in the United States, according to the latest census data (Bureau of the Census 2003d, 2).[4] Welfare reform in the 1990s reduced dramatically the number of persons on public assistance, from 5 million to 2 million persons (Rainwater and Smeeding 2003, 141), but it did little to eradicate poverty. In fact, poverty rates have actually been on the rise. Poverty in the United States rose from 11.7 percent in 2001 to 12.1 percent in 2002 (Bureau of the Census 2003d, 1). Accordingly, substantial benefits would probably accrue to Whites if the United States were to embrace international human rights standards that promote economic, social, and cultural rights than any other group.

Indeed, recent studies indicate that it is increasingly difficult to argue that economic and social conditions in the United States are better than most other advanced nations. Recent census data show that about 43.6 million people (15.2 percent of the population) in the United States are without health coverage in 2002, an increase of 2.4 million (14.6 percent) from 2001 (Bureau of the Census 2003a, 1). The United States is the only developed nation without some form of universal health care, something that has long been deemed vital in many countries to the economic and social wellbeing of a nation.

In its call for universal health coverage in the United States by the year 2010, the Institute of Medicine of the National Academy of Sciences (2004b, 1) not only drew attention to the nation's appalling lack of health coverage, but pointed out that "[a]bout 18,000 unnecessary deaths occur each year because of lack of health insurance." The Institute of Medicine report further explains that:

- The number of uninsured individuals under age 65 is large, growing, and has persisted even during periods of strong economic growth.
- Uninsured children and adults do not receive the care they need; they suffer from poorer health and development, and are more likely to die early than are those with coverage.
- Even one uninsured person in a family can put the financial stability and health of the whole family at risk.
- A community's high uninsured rate can adversely affect the overall health status of the community, its health care institutions and

---

4. The Bureau of the Census (2003d, 2, table 1) indicates that 15,271,000 of persons under the category of "White, not Hispanic" fall below the poverty level while 7,997,000 of those categorized as "Hispanic (of any race)" and 8,136,000 of those categorized as "Black" fall below the poverty level.

providers, and the access of its residents to certain services. (Institute of Medicine of the National Academy of Sciences 2004a, 2)

Although the United States is the wealthiest country in the world, the United Nations Development Programme (2003, 249) reports that according to its Human Poverty Index (HPI), which measures national levels of poverty, illiteracy, unemployment, and life-expectancy, Sweden ranked first among the world's richest countries and the United States last. While Sweden has a lower per capita income, the United States, on average, has more adults who are functionally illiterate and more who are living in poverty (248–49).

In a analysis comparing the United States and 14 other developed countries of the world conducted by researchers of the Luxembourg Income Study Lee Rainwater and Timothy M. Smeeding (2003, 21), it was found that the United States has the highest percentage of children (20.3 percent) living in poverty.[5] This study also speaks to the issue of economic inequality in the United States, noting that the poor are not necessarily better off in the United States:

> A comforting belief in the United States is that while we may have more inequality than European countries, decades of economic growth have lifted even the worst-off Americans to a higher standard of living than the marginal economic classes of Europe. Rather surprisingly, this turns out not to be the case. In half of our comparison countries roughly the lowest income third of children are better off in real terms than their American peers. And in the others (except for Australia, Spain, the United Kingdom, and Italy) the children in the same rank as the poor American children who make up the bottom income child quintile are as well or better off. (48)

Rainwater and Smeeding also found that children in the United States are likely to be poorer longer and are less able to move out of poverty than in other countries they studied. In comparing the United States to Germany, they state that "[n]ot only are more children poor for a longer period of time than in Germany, but American children are much more likely than German children, if they have been economically marginal as adolescents, to also experience poverty when they grow up" (67).

---

5. Rainwater and Smeeding (2003, 21) found the United States to have the highest rate of child poverty followed by (in descending order) Italy, United Kingdom, Canada, Australia, Spain, Germany, France, the Netherlands, Switzerland, Belgium, Denmark, Norway, Finland, and Sweden.

As for the impact of immigration on poverty, their study showed roughly that "while in most (or perhaps all) countries recent arrivals have elevated child poverty rates compared with rates for natives, these differences nowhere approach those in the United States between minorities and whites. And it is not clear that the differences that do exist are likely to persist over the decades in the same way they have in the United States" (31).

The hope for children in the United States, as Rainwater and Smeeding conclude, lies in the implementation of a comprehensive plan that invests in the following societal needs: job creation (employment), parental leave, child care, child-related tax policy, child support, and education (132–41). These areas are, in fact, among the areas that pertain to economic, social, and cultural rights under international human right law.

Resolving problems of poverty and other forms of economic and social deprivation will require more than an effort to address a presumed lack of family values. Sweden, with a much lower percentage of children born into poverty than in the United States, has proportionately a larger number of children born out of wedlock (Donziger 1996, 215). Why other developed countries fare better has much to do with the social safety net that is available in those countries (Donziger 1996; Rainwater and Smeeding 2003).

Ultimately, the United States must also come to terms with the social costs of the enormous number of persons without heath insurance and with other problems related to high levels of economic inequality. Poor health and low economic status are associated with long-term problems and consequences to society in the form of social dislocation and increases in criminal behavior (see Walker et al. 2004, 65–89). Thus, it becomes incumbent on society to adopt measures that address the economic, social, and cultural rights of all persons in line with those recognized under international human rights standards. As international law scholar Louis Henkin asserts (1990, 10), a commitment to human rights implies that societies must take responsibility to meet the basic needs of all:

> We are all members of a community that benefits all. Community and communality imply obligations, and high among them is the obligation to assure basic human needs for those who cannot satisfy their own.

CONCLUSION

Having ratified several major international human rights treaties, the United States is obligated to observe and protect human rights pursuant to these international agreements and article VI of the U.S. Constitution, which requires that "all Treaties made, or which shall be made under the Authority of the United States, shall be the supreme Law of the Land." This obligation notwithstanding, the United States still lags behind most nations of the world in ratifying many human rights agreements. Although U.S. presidents have signed the International Covenant on Economic, Social and Cultural Rights, the Convention on the Elimination of all forms of Discrimination against Women, and the Convention on the Rights of the Child, there is negligible interest in the U.S. Senate for the ratification of these international instruments.

The United States has also been reticent to enforce the international human rights documents that it has ratified. The ratification of human rights treaties, such as the International Covenant on Civil and Political Rights or the Convention against Torture and Other Cruel, Inhuman or Degrading Treatment or Punishment, was accompanied by reservations that limited their application and enforceability within the United States. U.S. reservations relating to the death penalty and to cruel and unusual punishment, for instance, have been the subject of controversy and objections at the international level since such reservations have been deemed to undermine the meaning and purpose of human rights treaties. The U.N. Human Rights Committee (1994) has declared that these types of reservations are detrimental to the implementation and effectiveness of human rights treaties. Nevertheless, the Human Rights Committee's admonitions have fallen on deaf ears in the United States.

One of the major obstacles to the enforcement of international human rights law in the United States is the requirement of an enabling federal law granting jurisdiction to U.S. courts to hear cases brought pursuant to human right treaties. Indeed, even provisions of the U.N. Charter related to human rights (arts. 55 and 56) have been found to be non-self-executing (that is, lacking an enabling federal statute) and therefore unenforceable in U.S. courts (*Sei Fujii v. California*, 38 Cal.2d 718, 242 P.2d 617 (1952)).

In a some instances, gross violations of human rights so universally condemned by the world community, as in the case of torture, have been able to proceed successfully through U.S. courts as a matter falling under the Alien Tort Claims Act and customary international law (see, e.g., *Filartiga v. Peña-Irala*, 630 F.2d 876 (2d Cir. 1980)).[6] However, with the exception of the limited cases in which U.S. courts have had to confront issues of international

---

6. In *Filartiga v. Peña-Irala*, 630 F.2d 876 (2d Cir. 1980), the court relied on the Alien Tort Claims Act, 28 U.S.C. §1350 (1982), a law with origins in the Judiciary Act of 1789. Similar to the Alien Tort Claims Act, a subsequent law was passed in 1992, the Torture Victims Protection Act, 28 U.S.C. §1331 (1992), which provides the right to bring an action

human rights, the United States has failed generally to fully comply with international law, either in the courts or as a matter of government policy.

U.S. observance of international law and standards has implications for all of Latin America. Respect for the sovereignty of Latin American nations, in instances such as the Álvarez Machaín case, have an impact on matters of justice in both Mexico and the United States. Similarly, the United States is obligated to eradicate colonialism in all its forms pursuant to the world's repudiation of colonialism under the United Nations Charter and other authoritative documents, but in the case of Puerto Rico, it has refused to do so (see Trías Monge 1997; Fernandez 1994; Maldonado Denis 1972). Puerto Rico's continuing colonial status deserves immediate attention since it represents an affront to international law affecting the lives of millions of Puerto Ricans. U.S. adherence to international law and the U.N. standards delineated in the Declaration on the Granting of Independence to Colonial Countries and Peoples (United Nations 1960; Appendix B) is, therefore, paramount.

Given the potential to expand human rights for the benefit of all society, the relevance of international human rights standards become ever more salient in the United States. Similarly, major international human rights organizations, such as Amnesty International and Human Rights Watch, stress the need for the United States to comply with international standards it has already ratified and to begin to join the many other countries of the world that have expanded their concept of human rights law standards (Amnesty International, 1998; Human Rights Watch, 1998).

For Latinos/as, who suffer under the continuing deprivation of rights, these existing standards serve as a model for the protection of their rights, not in the form of preferential treatment, but as human rights principles increasingly grounded in worldwide acceptance. Increased knowledge and familiarity with international human rights principles and their applicability to local struggles can help champion respect for and the protection of cultural, linguistic, social and economic rights, opening the opportunity to advance Latino/a rights throughout the United States.

To protect the economic, social, and cultural rights of every person is to protect that which is most essential to the dignity of all human beings (Goldewijk, Baspineiro, and Carbonari 2002). As such, an expansion of the concept of human rights within the United States to include economic, social, and cultural rights does more than assist those that are marginalized in the

---

for civil damages in federal court against individuals who committed acts of torture outside the United States.

society. Based on the discussion above, larger benefits may be garnered by all sectors of society. Greater economic and social stability would also go far in reducing crime and other social problems. Thus, advocating for the implementation of broader human rights standards serves not merely to extend protection to Latino/a communities, but to further the cause for equal rights and human rights for all.

CHAPTER 8

CONCLUSION:
THE QUEST FOR JUSTICE

The past and current injustices, social and economic disadvantage, and racialization of Latinos/as in the United States discussed in this book beg the question about how best to engage in effective and meaningful action to deal with these issues. A central thesis of this book has been that a response is needed that validates the rights of Latinos/as as human beings—that is, as persons whose social, cultural, and economic wellbeing is as deserving of respect and protection as their civil and political rights. Moreover, this book posits a response that does not assist Latino/a communities exclusively, but instead raises the level of rights and protections for all persons, broadening opportunities for economic and social justice throughout society.

There are many approaches used to address the panoply of justice issues Latinos/as face in the United States. This book has mentioned many strategies used by Latinos/as over the years in their struggle against discrimination and injustice, including litigation, community advocacy and organizing, protest politics, and legislative initiatives. These tactics are as relevant today for Latino/a communities as they were in decades past. However, this book has focused purposefully on aspects of justice and rights that find resonance in the realm of international human rights law and principles. Although others have advocated for the application of international law in the U.S. context (e.g., Amnesty International 1998; Human Rights Watch 1998) and some have specifically endorsed its use to address Latino/a issues (see, e.g., Hernández-Truyol 1997, 1998), this book has placed special emphasis on the facets of international human rights that provide models for seeking justice in areas of economic, social, and cultural rights. It is this author's premise that without economic and social rights and absent the respect for cultural differences in society, equality in the areas of civil and political rights will be difficult to achieve. Economic and social disadvantage undermine the civil and political progress of a community. As such, the future advancement of Latinos/as rests on progress made toward guaranteeing economic, social, and cultural rights.

Latino/as and Justice:
Recommendations

Based on the issues discussed in this book, the following recommendations can be made:

- Considering the impact that U.S. policies on Latin America and the long and ignominious history of U.S. interventions and violations of international law in the hemisphere discussed in Chapter Two, the U.S. government should comply with its obligations under international law in all aspects of its policies toward Latin America, including the respect for the sovereignty, rights of self-determination of peoples, and all protections under international human rights law. U.S. foreign policy toward Latin America continues to have an impact on the situation of human rights for Latin Americans and Latinos/as in the United States. U.S. trade and immigration policies should be consistent with the protection of human rights, including the protection of the rights of workers in Latin America and of Latino/a immigrants in the United States. The continuing colonial status of Puerto Rico should also be resolved in conformity with international law and the right of self-determination as delineated in the Declaration on the Granting of Independence to Colonial Countries and Peoples, U.N. General Assembly resolution 1514 (XV) of 1960 (United Nations 1960; Appendix B).

- Increased public awareness of the historical and present-day discrimination against and deprivations of Latinos/as is essential in the process of taking appropriate measures to protect Latino/a human rights. Too much still remains hidden, unknown, untaught, or undiscovered about the history of Latinos/as in the United States (Perea et al. 2000). Latino/a communities remain poorly understood, particularly as it pertains to the history of colonial conquest and domination that forms the basis today for unequal colonial and neo-colonial relations between the United States and Latin America—an unequal relationship that also shapes the lives of Latinos/as in the United States. To their detriment, Latinos/as are also kept uninformed about their own history and vulnerable to existing prejudices and discrimination. Future progress is dependent on how well we can learn from the past.

- There have been many recommendations made to improve the criminal justice system for communities of color in the United States. Among the most notable in view of the issues addressed in this book have been those by the National Criminal Justice Commission (Donziger 1996). With specific focus of the problems encountered by Latina and Latino youth in the U.S. justice system, the report by Michigan State University/Building Blocks for Youth is also very important (Villarruel et al. 2002). As these and other sources point out (see, e.g., Perea et al. 2000; Haney López 2003), the elimination of racial profiling and other forms of racial and ethnic discrimination in police departments and within the legal system, including the courts, requires a deeper examination into the issue of race and ethnicity in the United States as well as a better understanding of the many Latino/a communities, their histories, culture, traditions, and aspirations. In addition, many of the changes recommended by the sources cited call for profound changes in the economic and social conditions of people of color, not simply law reform (see Villarruel et al. 2002; Donziger 1996).

- Racial profiling and other forms of illegal discriminatory treatment must be addressed, not simply on the level of the local police precinct, but as a larger effort that engages the grassroots up to the highest levels of government. Indeed, as found in a study by the Vera Institute of Justice, leadership from the top has been found to be central in preventing incidents of police misconduct and abuse (Davis and Mateu-Gelabert 1999). That example can have an even greater impact if applied wherever prejudice and discrimination take place in other societal contexts.

- Fundamental and systemic problems, such as economic and social inequality and residential segregation, must be addressed with a rigorous effort to open economic and social opportunities that remain closed to many people of color. Indeed, 50 years after the U.S. Supreme Court decision in *Brown v. Board of Education*, 347 U.S. 483 (1954), U.S. schools and society remain highly segregated by race and class. As discussed in previous chapters, Latino/a communities experience disproportionately high levels of residential segregation and economic dislocation in U.S. society; their children often attend overcrowded, poorly funded schools with under-qualified teachers; and their communities suffer from inadequate housing, health care, and employment. The prospects for economic and social opportunity, advancement, and change are ostensibly bleak. For example, in New York City—where people of color comprise a majority of the population—more than 93 percent of the Fire Department's 11,112 member force still consists of White men, according to data as recent as December 2001 (Baker 2002, B3). Moreover, in a country where the rate of child poverty surpasses that of all other developed nations (Rainwater and Smeeding 2003), a majority of U.S.-controlled corporations paid no taxes from 1996 to 2000 (General Accounting Office 2004, 2). In view of persistent economic and social inequalities in the United States, the recognition and protection of economic, social, and cultural rights, as discussed in Chapter Seven, should be made a priority. Existing international human rights instruments—including, but not limited to, the International Covenant on Economic, Social and Cultural Rights (1966b; Appendix C)—can help form the basis and serve as a guide for the extension and protection of these rights.

- Culture-based approaches, such as the example of *Palenque*, are among the many ways that injustices experienced by Latinos/as at a grassroots, community level can be addressed. The culture-based model offers the means through which Latino/a culture, linguistic heritage, and identity among Latino/a youth and families can be reaffirmed, potentially serving to improve the status of Latinos/as in relation to the rest of U.S. society. Developing norms and principles of international human rights that recognize and promote the linguistic and cultural diversity of all persons in society lend support for this culturally-oriented model and should be marshaled to promote the expansion of culture-based efforts.

- Inequalities, discrimination, and injustice, if tolerated in society, will invariably be mirrored by the legal and justice systems. Police departments and the judicial system often reflect the same problems found in society. The problems of prejudice and discrimination in U.S. society must not be overlooked, but addressed meaningfully and with the goal of achieving justice in all areas of the society. In this regard, vigorous steps must be taken to end a police culture that maintains a code of silence and other forms of corruption and misconduct. Trust within communities of color, including Latino/a communities, will not be restored absent comprehensive action to prevent and punish police brutality and misconduct. Strengthening the investigatory scope of civilian review agencies and increased accountability throughout the system must be made a reality.

- Increasing the number of Latino/a police officers should be viewed as only one step in a larger process of opening access to and acceptance of people of color in police departments. New recruits should not have to conform to a police culture that tolerates unethical practices or illegal discriminatory behavior. Moreover, there must be efforts to insure meaningful access to the highest levels of decision- and policy-making.

- Latina and Latino representation in all levels of authority and in all aspects of law and public policy should not only be given greater priority, but those Latinas and Latinos holding positions within law enforcement and other institutions that serve the public should be respected for the cultural knowledge and sensitivity that they bring to their jobs. If public institutions are to truly serve all communities effectively, representation by people of color must be meaningful.

- International human rights norms and standards that relate to law enforcement must be considered and implemented in the process of reformulating policies that will be accepting of and fair to the people of color on the police force and in Latino/a communities. International human rights norms and standards that the United States is already obligated to observe must be enforced.

- Knowledge and familiarity with international human rights principles and standards should be given precedence. Principles and standards that champion the respect for and the protection of cultural, linguistic, social, and economic rights open the possibility of advancing Latino/a rights throughout the United States. Schools, law enforcement, and the courts should be engaged in a process of learning and implementing international human rights standards, not solely in order to better serve particular groups in society, but as a way to promote greater social and economic progress for all.

- The U.S. government must enforce its existing obligations under all international human rights laws and it should also take steps to join the large number of world nations that have ratified the major human right treaties—including, but not limited to, the International Covenant on Economic, Social and Cultural Rights (1966b; Appendix C); the Convention on the Rights of the Child (1989; Appendix E), and the Convention on the Elimination of all Forms of Discrimination against Women (1979b; Appendix F). Advocacy in favor of the implementation of these standards is needed as part of a larger campaign to extend human rights protections, not simply for communities of color, including Latino/a communities, but to further the cause for equal rights and human rights for all.

LATINOS/AS IN THE POST-9/11 ERA

Changes in attitudes and the absence of some of the most blatant forms of racial and ethnic hatred and discrimination in decades past can at times give the false impression that Latinos/as and other people of color are no longer vulnerable. The tragic events of September 11, 2001, while presenting an opportunity for uniting a country, also present a considerable challenge for U.S. policymakers to create effective measures to prevent future attacks by non-state actors against U.S. citizens while preserving the protection of civil rights and liberties. Washington's response to September 11, unfortunately, may be doing less to avert future attacks and more to set in motion domestic and foreign policies and practices that undercut fundamental and universally-held civil and human rights. Governmental actions and legislative initiatives premised on fighting the so-called "war on terrorism" are already causing grave concerns about the loss of basic human rights protections for citizens and non-citizens alike. As persons whose rights of citizenship and other rights have long been circumscribed in the United States, Latinos/as are especially vulnerable to violations of their civil and human rights in the post-September 11 era. In view of past and present-day policies and practices in the United States that have consigned large sectors of Latinos/as to treatment as a racialized "other" in U.S. society, the post-September 11 period may be a harbinger of the return to some of the worst policies of the past.

The terrorist deeds of September 11, 2001, in the United States do not fall within the true definition of "acts of war" under international law, but more appropriately, they constitute crimes against humanity by non-state actors. Nevertheless, the war metaphor has been appropriated by the Bush Administration to press for restrictions on foreign and domestic human rights that may have the most immediate impact on the rights of persons in the United States who have long been the most marginalized and discriminated segments of the population, including Latinos/as.

History provides many examples of immigrants and law-abiding citizens otherwise considered as "foreign" or "others" who have fallen victim to extremist policies in times of war or emergency. One of the earliest instances was the enactment of the Alien and Sedition Act of 1798, designed to silence criticism of the U.S. government of President John Adams (Chang 2002, 2). Twentieth-century examples of governmental excess include actions taken during World War I and the World War II. In 1919, the U.S. government under the direction of Attorney General A. Mitchell Palmer rounded up more than 6,000 immigrants while searching for suspects of the bombing the attorney general's home and 556 immigrants were deported, not for their involvement in the bombing, but for their political associations (Cole and Dempsey 2002, 150). During World War II, 110,000 persons of Japanese ancestry—over two-thirds of whom were U.S. citizens—were stripped of all rights and possessions and interned in harsh detention camps for the duration of the war (Chang 2002, 39; Cole and Dempsey 2002, 150).

Latinos/as have also been affected by policies that relied on ethnic and racial profiling—policies similar to that which led to the internment of persons of Japanese descent during World War II. The Greaser Act of 1856 used racial and ethnic identifiers to enforce a purported anti-vagrancy campaign (Acuña 2000, 144). Other instances of profiling and government harassment of Latinos/as, include the targeting of Los Angeles zoot suiters in the 1940s (Escobar 1999) and the federal government's Operation Wetback in the 1950s, in which 3.7 million persons of Mexican ancestry were deported in the anti-immigrant hysteria of the time, despite many being U.S. citizens (Acuña 2000, 303–06; Mirandé 1987, 125–29; McWilliams 1990, 315–18).

The massive governmental infiltration and disruption campaign known as COINTELPRO of the 1960s and 1970s also infringed the basic rights of association and expression of Chicanos and Puerto Ricans in their advocacy efforts to secure rights for their respective communities (see, e.g., Haney López 2003; Morales 1998). Indeed, the readiness of the government to disregard basic constitutional and human rights of Latinos/as in the past resembles recent policies in New York City, Los Angeles, Chicago, New Jersey, and other parts of the United States, under which Latinos/as have been stopped based on the use of racial and ethnic criteria, as previously discussed in this volume.

Immediately following the September 11 attacks, reports of Latinos having been stopped or placed in custody began to surface, including reports of a Latino being detained by police searching for persons of Middle Eastern and Indian origin in Providence, Rhode Island (Goodstein and Niebuhr 2001, A14). Other reports came to light about any airline passengers "with dark skin or who spoke with an accent" and "any male with too much facial hair" being detained (Levy and Rashbaum 2001, A1).

Among the U.S. citizens detained as "enemy combatants," one is Puerto Rican. Since May of 2002, the government has fought to detain José Padilla, a.k.a. Abdullah al Muhajir, indefinitely without charge and without the right to counsel while alleging in the media that he is tied to a bomb plot and affiliated to a Chicago street gang (Schulhofer 2002). Many legal analysts view the government's actions in cases such as Padilla's as an assault on bedrock constitutional principles (see, e.g., Schulhofer 2002; Cole and Dempsey 2002). It is especially curious that of all the U.S. citizens who have been detained only the White U.S. citizen, John Walker Lindh, has been afforded immediate and complete rights to counsel, speedy criminal trial, and sentence (see Meek 2003, 14). One can reasonably infer from the John Walker Lindh case that the government is repeating its past practice of denying rights to those considered as "other" while sending a message that White U.S. citizens need not be concerned that their constitutional rights will be trampled upon in the "war on terror."

In the aftermath of the September 11 attacks, steps to secure the safety of persons in the United States undoubtedly were needed. Measures to bolster security at the borders, provide stronger actions to prevent money laundering, and enhancing communication among government law enforcement agencies were not unreasonable (see Cole and Dempsey 2002, 152). However, considering the ways in which Latinos/as have been racialized as the "other" and frequently perceived as criminals, new legislation passed in Washington to fight the so-called "war on terrorism" poses additional challenges for the protection of the rights of Latinos/as. The USA PATRIOT Act, for instance, broadly defines "domestic terrorism" in a manner that can potentially silence what was formerly constitutionally protected forms of dissent; it provides for infringements of privacy through its "sneak-and-peak" and other provisions allowing government access to telephone and Internet communications; it eliminates many protections for immigrants; and it can possibly render suspect many nonprofit community agencies (U.S. Public Law 107–56).

Similarly, the Homelands Security Act, promising the government "total information access," presents additional threats to the civil liberties and civil rights of groups and individuals (U.S. House 2002). These new legislative initiatives should trigger foreboding among Latinos/as since they are reminiscent of past practices of the government to unduly and illegally monitor and undermine efforts to engage in lawfully organizing activities to secure their rights in the United States. Drastic governmental proposals to fight terrorism, including attempts to authorize the use of torture in the interrogation of suspects, represent an ominous sign of the lengths to which the government is willing to go in its "war on terrorism." Little doubt is left that violations of the rights of those most vulnerable in society may likely follow.

The PATRIOT Act has been widely criticized as exceeding constitutional and civil liberties standards in ways that open the door to governmental abuse. The detention of suspects, including U.S. citizens, without charge and without legal counsel; the federal government's enhanced surveillance and monitoring mechanisms without judicial oversight; and unprecedented government secrecy are among the aspects of the PATRIOT Act considered the most perilous to constitutional and democratic principles (Leone and Anrig 2003; Schulhofer 2002; Chang 2002; Cole and Dempsey 2002). The lesson to be drawn from history and the Latino/a experience is that the protection of constitutional, civil, and human rights becomes the most crucial in times of crisis and fear. Thus, their application and enforcement are vital to protecting the rights of all people, but especially those whose rights have been violated frequently in the past, including Latinos/as.

OBSERVANCE OF INTERNATIONAL LAW AND THE PROTECTION OF HUMAN RIGHTS AND DIGNITY

As detailed in this book, the lack of observance of fundamental international laws has shaped the relationship between the United States and Latin American countries and has reinforced a long history of policies that too frequently have been paternalistic and detrimental to the advancement of human rights. These policies have also affected the ways in which Latino/a communities in the United States are viewed and treated. Today, Latinos/as remain challenged by prejudice and discrimination in U.S. society and by socioeconomic problems stemming from entrenched injustices and inequalities rooted in policies and practices that have relegated Latinos/as to a form of second-class status.

Racial profiling, drug laws and drug law enforcement policies, police brutality and misconduct, and anti-immigrant and anti-bilingual initiatives directed against Latinos/as run parallel to U.S. economic globalization strategies that replicate and reinforce U.S. domination over Latin America, its peoples and its resources. Economic exploitation, through such means as the proliferation of sweatshops or *maquiladoras* throughout Latin America, mirror past U.S. policies and practices that further poverty and despair and that result in the ongoing influx of persons from Latin America to the United States fleeing harsh conditions in their homelands. In turn, their arrival provides U.S. employers with a readily available surplus population of exploitable, low-wage workers within U.S. borders.

Given this reality, there exists a need to rethink and reframe the relationship between the United States and Latin American nations in ways that truly represent a relationship among equals as required by international law. As important is the need to reevaluate and reshape the way Latinos/as are perceived and treated in the United States. International law and, specifically, developments in international human rights, provide a framework for the respect for the political, social, economic, and cultural rights of all persons. It is a framework of rights that, if adopted in the United States, can help serve the cause of justice nationally and internationally.

For Latinos/as in the United States, the broadening of the concept of human rights to include social, economic, and cultural rights appears crucial to their quest for justice, equality, and dignity. Indeed, it has been observed that "whereas human dignity is the core and the foundation of human rights, it is through the operationalization of rights that dignity is protected" (Goldewijk 2002, 6). Thus, the Latino/a quest for justice should not be one limited to the pursuit of justice and dignity only by those who suffer from a deprivation of rights and from economic and social dislocation. It should be a quest for justice embraced by all who believe in building a more just society and in the protection of the inherent dignity of humankind.

APPENDICES

Appendix A

Universal Declaration
of Human Rights

Adopted and Proclaimed by
General Assembly Resolution 217 A (III) of
10 December 1948

Preamble

Whereas recognition of the inherent dignity and of the equal and inalienable rights of all members of the human family is the foundation of freedom, justice and peace in the world,

Whereas disregard and contempt for human rights have resulted in barbarous acts which have outraged the conscience of mankind, and the advent of a world in which human beings shall enjoy freedom of speech and belief and freedom from fear and want has been proclaimed as the highest aspiration of the common people,

Whereas it is essential, if man is not to be compelled to have recourse, as a last resort, to rebellion against tyranny and oppression, that human rights should be protected by the rule of law,

Whereas it is essential to promote the development of friendly relations between nations,

Whereas the peoples of the United Nations have in the Charter reaffirmed their faith in fundamental human rights, in the dignity and worth of the human person and in the equal rights of men and women and have determined to promote social progress and better standards of life in larger freedom,

Whereas Member States have pledged themselves to achieve, in cooperation with the United Nations, the promotion of universal respect for and observance of human rights and fundamental freedoms,

Whereas a common understanding of these rights and freedoms is of the greatest importance for the full realization of this pledge,

Now, therefore,

The General Assembly,

Proclaims this Universal Declaration of Human Rights as a common standard of achievement for all peoples and all nations, to the end that every individual and every organ of society, keeping this Declaration constantly in mind, shall strive by teaching and education to promote respect for these rights and freedoms and by progressive measures, national and international, to secure their universal and effective recognition and observance, both among the peoples of Member States themselves and among the peoples of territories under their jurisdiction.

Article 1
All human beings are born free and equal in dignity and rights. They are endowed with reason and conscience and should act towards one another in a spirit of brotherhood.

Article 2
Everyone is entitled to all the rights and freedoms set forth in this Declaration, without distinction of any kind, such as race, colour, sex, language, religion, political or other opinion, national or social origin, property, birth or other status.

Furthermore, no distinction shall be made on the basis of the political, jurisdictional or international status of the country or territory to which a person belongs, whether it be independent, trust, non-self-governing or under any other limitation of sovereignty.

Article 3
Everyone has the right to life, liberty and security of person.

Article 4
No one shall be held in slavery or servitude; slavery and the slave trade shall be prohibited in all their forms.

Article 5
No one shall be subjected to torture or to cruel, inhuman or degrading treatment or punishment.

Article 6
Everyone has the right to recognition everywhere as a person before the law.

Article 7
All are equal before the law and are entitled without any discrimination to equal protection of the law. All are entitled to equal protection against any discrimination in violation of this Declaration and against any incitement to such discrimination.

Article 8
Everyone has the right to an effective remedy by the competent national tribunals for acts violating the fundamental rights granted him by the constitution or by law.

Article 9
No one shall be subjected to arbitrary arrest, detention or exile.

Article 10
Everyone is entitled in full equality to a fair and public hearing by an independent and impartial tribunal, in the determination of his rights and obligations and of any criminal charge against him.

Article 11
1. Everyone charged with a penal offence has the right to be presumed innocent until proved guilty according to law in a public trial at which he has had all the guarantees necessary for his defence.

2. No one shall be held guilty of any penal offence on account of any act or omission which did not constitute a penal offence, under national or international law, at the time when it was committed. Nor shall a heavier penalty be imposed than the one that was applicable at the time the penal offence was committed.

Article 12
No one shall be subjected to arbitrary interference with his privacy, family, home or correspondence, nor to attacks upon his honour and reputation. Everyone has the right to the protection of the law against such interference or attacks.

Article 13
1. Everyone has the right to freedom of movement and residence within the borders of each State.

2. Everyone has the right to leave any country, including his own, and to return to his country.

Article 14

1. Everyone has the right to seek and to enjoy in other countries asylum from persecution.

2. This right may not be invoked in the case of prosecutions genuinely arising from non-political crimes or from acts contrary to the purposes and principles of the United Nations.

Article 15

1. Everyone has the right to a nationality.

2. No one shall be arbitrarily deprived of his nationality nor denied the right to change his nationality.

Article 16

1. Men and women of full age, without any limitation due to race, nationality or religion, have the right to marry and to found a family. They are entitled to equal rights as to marriage, during marriage and at its dissolution.

2. Marriage shall be entered into only with the free and full consent of the intending spouses.

3. The family is the natural and fundamental group unit of society and is entitled to protection by society and the State.

Article 17

1. Everyone has the right to own property alone as well as in association with others.

2. No one shall be arbitrarily deprived of his property.

Article 18

Everyone has the right to freedom of thought, conscience and religion; this right includes freedom to change his religion or belief, and freedom, either alone or in community with others and in public or private, to manifest his religion or belief in teaching, practice, worship and observance.

Article 19

Everyone has the right to freedom of opinion and expression; this right includes freedom to hold opinions without interference and to seek, receive and impart information and ideas through any media and regardless of frontiers.

Article 20

1. Everyone has the right to freedom of peaceful assembly and association.

2. No one may be compelled to belong to an association.

Article 21

1. Everyone has the right to take part in the government of his country, directly or through freely chosen representatives.

2. Everyone has the right to equal access to public service in his country.

3. The will of the people shall be the basis of the authority of government; this will shall be expressed in periodic and genuine elections which shall be by universal and equal suffrage and shall be held by secret vote or by equivalent free voting procedures.

Article 22

Everyone, as a member of society, has the right to social security and is entitled to realization, through national effort and international co-operation and in accordance with the organization and resources of each State, of the economic, social and cultural rights indispensable for his dignity and the free development of his personality.

Article 23

1. Everyone has the right to work, to free choice of employment, to just and favourable conditions of work and to protection against unemployment.

2. Everyone, without any discrimination, has the right to equal pay for equal work.

3. Everyone who works has the right to just and favourable remuneration ensuring for himself and his family an existence worthy of human dignity, and supplemented, if necessary, by other means of social protection.

4. Everyone has the right to form and to join trade unions for the protection of his interests.

Article 24

Everyone has the right to rest and leisure, including reasonable limitation of working hours and periodic holidays with pay.

Article 25

1. Everyone has the right to a standard of living adequate for the health and well-being of himself and of his family, including food, clothing, housing and medical care and necessary social services, and the right to security in the event of unemployment, sickness, disability, widowhood, old age or other lack of livelihood in circumstances beyond his control.

2. Motherhood and childhood are entitled to special care and assistance. All children, whether born in or out of wedlock, shall enjoy the same social protection.

Article 26

1. Everyone has the right to education. Education shall be free, at least in the elementary and fundamental stages. Elementary education shall be compulsory. Technical and professional education shall be made generally available and higher education shall be equally accessible to all on the basis of merit.

2. Education shall be directed to the full development of the human personality and to the strengthening of respect for human rights and fundamental freedoms. It shall promote understanding, tolerance and friendship among all nations, racial or religious groups, and shall further the activities of the United Nations for the maintenance of peace.

3. Parents have a prior right to choose the kind of education that shall be given to their children.

Article 27

1. Everyone has the right freely to participate in the cultural life of the community, to enjoy the arts and to share in scientific advancement and its benefits.

2. Everyone has the right to the protection of the moral and material interests resulting from any scientific, literary or artistic production of which he is the author.

Article 28

Everyone is entitled to a social and international order in which the rights and freedoms set forth in this Declaration can be fully realized.

Article 29

1. Everyone has duties to the community in which alone the free and full development of his personality is possible.

2. In the exercise of his rights and freedoms, everyone shall be subject only to such limitations as are determined by law solely for the purpose of securing due recognition and respect for the rights and freedoms of others and of meeting the just requirements of morality, public order and the general welfare in a democratic society.

3. These rights and freedoms may in no case be exercised contrary to the purposes and principles of the United Nations.

Article 30

Nothing in this Declaration may be interpreted as implying for any State, group or person any right to engage in any activity or to perform any act aimed at the destruction of any of the rights and freedoms set forth herein.

Appendix B

Declaration on the Granting of Independence to Colonial Countries and Peoples

Adopted by General Assembly Resolution 1514 (XV) of 14 December 1960

The General Assembly,

Mindful of the determination proclaimed by the peoples of the world in the Charter of the United Nations to reaffirm faith in fundamental human rights, in the dignity and worth of the human person, in the equal rights of men and women and of nations large and small and to promote social progress and better standards of life in larger freedom,

Conscious of the need for the creation of conditions of stability and well-being and peaceful and friendly relations based on respect for the principles of equal rights and self-determination of all peoples, and of universal respect for, and observance of, human rights and fundamental freedoms for all without distinction as to race, sex, language or religion,

Recognizing the passionate yearning for freedom in all dependent peoples and the decisive role of such peoples in the attainment of their independence,

Aware of the increasing conflicts resulting from the denial of or impediments in the way of the freedom of such peoples, which constitute a serious threat to world peace,

Considering the important role of the United Nations in assisting the movement for independence in Trust and Non-Self-Governing Territories,

Recognizing that the peoples of the world ardently desire the end of colonialism in all its manifestations,

Convinced that the continued existence of colonialism prevents the development of international economic co-operation, impedes the social, cultural and economic development of dependent peoples and militates against the United Nations ideal of universal peace,

Affirming that peoples may, for their own ends, freely dispose of their natural wealth and resources without prejudice to any obligations arising out of international economic co-operation, based upon the principle of mutual benefit, and international law,

Believing that the process of liberation is irresistible and irreversible and that, in order to avoid serious crises, an end must be put to colonialism and all practices of segregation and discrimination associated therewith,

Welcoming the emergence in recent years of a large number of dependent territories into freedom and independence, and recognizing the increasingly powerful trends towards freedom in such territories which have not yet attained independence,

Convinced that all peoples have an inalienable right to complete freedom, the exercise of their sovereignty and the integrity of their national territory,

Solemnly proclaims the necessity of bringing to a speedy and unconditional end colonialism in all its forms and manifestations;
And to this end Declares that:

1. The subjection of peoples to alien subjugation, domination and exploitation constitutes a denial of fundamental human rights, is contrary to the Charter of the United Nations and is an impediment to the promotion of world peace and co-operation.

2. All peoples have the right to self-determination; by virtue of that right they freely determine their political status and freely pursue their economic, social and cultural development.

3. Inadequacy of political, economic, social or educational preparedness should never serve as a pretext for delaying independence.

4. All armed action or repressive measures of all kinds directed against dependent peoples shall cease in order to enable them to exercise peacefully and freely their right to complete independence, and the integrity of their national territory shall be respected.

5. Immediate steps shall be taken, in Trust and Non-Self-Governing Territories or all other territories which have not yet attained independence, to transfer all powers to the peoples of those territories, without any conditions or reservations, in accordance with their freely expressed will and desire, without any distinction as to race, creed or colour, in order to enable them to enjoy complete independence and freedom.

6. Any attempt aimed at the partial or total disruption of the national unity and the territorial integrity of a country is incompatible with the purposes and principles of the Charter of the United Nations.

7. All States shall observe faithfully and strictly the provisions of the Charter of the United Nations, the Universal Declaration of Human Rights and the present Declaration on the basis of equality, non-interference in the internal affairs of all States, and respect for the sovereign rights of all peoples and their territorial integrity.

Article 2

1. Each State Party to the present Covenant undertakes to take steps, individually and through international assistance and cooperation, especially economic and technical, to the maximum of its available resources, with a view to achieving progressively the full realization of the rights recognized in the present Covenant by all appropriate means, including particularly the adoption of legislative measures.

2. The States Parties to the present Covenant undertake to guarantee that the rights enunciated in the present Covenant will be exercised without discrimination of any kind as to race, colour, sex, language, religion, political or other opinion, national or social origin property, birth or other status.

3. Developing countries, with due regard to human rights and their national economy, may determine to what extent they would guarantee the economic rights recognized in the present Covenant to non-nationals.

Article 3

The States Parties to the present Covenant undertake to ensure the equal right of men and women to the enjoyment of all economic, social and cultural rights set forth in the present Covenant.

Article 4

The States Parties to the present Covenant recognize that, in the enjoyment of those rights provided by the State in conformity with the present Covenant, the State may subject such rights only to such limitations as are determined by law only in so far as this may be compatible with the nature of these rights and solely for the purpose of promoting the general welfare in a democratic society.

Article 5

1. Nothing, in the present Covenant may be interpreted as implying for any State group or person any right to engage in any activity or to perform any act aimed at the destruction of any of the rights or freedoms recognized herein, or at their limitation to a greater extent than is provided for in the present Covenant.

2. No restriction upon or derogation from any of the fundamental human rights recognized or existing in any country in virtue of law, conventions, regulations or custom shall be admitted on the pretext that the present Covenant does not recognize such rights or that it recognizes them to a lesser extent.

Article 6

1. The States Parties to the present Covenant recognize the right to work, which includes the right of everyone to the opportunity to gain his living by

work which he freely chooses or accepts, and will take appropriate steps to safeguard this right.

2. The steps to be taken by a State Party to the present Covenant to achieve the full realization of this right shall include technical and vocational guidance and training programmes, policies and techniques to achieve steady economic, social and cultural development and full and productive employment under conditions safeguarding, fundamental political and economic freedoms to the individual.

Article 7

The States Parties to the present Covenant recognize the right of everyone to the enjoyment of just and favourable conditions of work which ensure, in particular:

(a) Remuneration which provides all workers, as a minimum, with:
(i) Fair wages and equal remuneration for work of equal value without distinction of any kind, in particular women being guaranteed conditions of work not inferior to those enjoyed by men, with equal pay for equal work;
(ii) A decent living for themselves and their families in accordance with the provisions of the present Covenant;
(b) Safe and healthy working, conditions;
(c) Equal opportunity for everyone to be promoted in his employment to an appropriate higher level, subject to no considerations other than those of seniority and competence;
(d) Rest, leisure and reasonable limitation of working hours and periodic holidays with pay, as well as remuneration for public holidays.

Article 8

1. The States Parties to the present Covenant undertake to ensure:

(a) The right of everyone to form trade unions and join the trade union of his choice, subject only to the rules of the organization concerned, for the promotion and protection of his economic and social interests. No restrictions may be placed on the exercise of this right other than those prescribed by law and which are necessary in a democratic society in the interests of national security or public order or for the protection of the rights and freedoms of others;
(b) The right of trade unions to establish national federations or confederations and the right of the latter to form or join international trade-union organizations;
(c) The right of trade unions to function freely subject to no limitations other than those prescribed by law and which are necessary in a democratic society

in the interests of national security or public order or for the protection of the rights and freedoms of others;

(d) The right to strike, provided that it is exercised in conformity with the laws of the particular country.

2. This article shall not prevent the imposition of lawful restrictions on the exercise of these rights by members of the armed forces or of the police or of the administration of the State.

3. Nothing in this article shall authorize States Parties to the International Labour Organisation Convention of 1948 concerning Freedom of Association and Protection of the Right to Organize to take legislative measures which would prejudice, or apply the law in such a manner as would prejudice, the guarantees provided for in that Convention.

Article 9
The States Parties to the present Covenant recognize the right of everyone to social security, including social insurance.

Article 10
The States Parties to the present Covenant recognize that:

1. The widest possible protection and assistance should be accorded to the family, which is the natural and fundamental group unit of society, particularly for its establishment and while it is responsible for the care and education of dependent children. Marriage must be entered into with the free consent of the intending spouses.

2. Special protection should be accorded to mothers during a reasonable period before and after childbirth. During such period working mothers should be accorded paid leave or leave with adequate social security benefits.

3. Special measures of protection and assistance should be taken on behalf of all children and young persons without any discrimination for reasons of parentage or other conditions. Children and young persons should be protected from economic and social exploitation. Their employment in work harmful to their morals or health or dangerous to life or likely to hamper their normal development should be punishable by law. States should also set age limits below which the paid employment of child labour should be prohibited and punishable by law.

Article 11
1. The States Parties to the present Covenant recognize the right of everyone to an adequate standard of living for himself and his family, including ade-

quate food, clothing and housing, and to the continuous improvement of living conditions. The States Parties will take appropriate steps to ensure the realization of this right, recognizing to this effect the essential importance of international cooperation based on free consent.

2. The States Parties to the present Covenant, recognizing the fundamental right of everyone to be free from hunger, shall take, individually and through international cooperation, the measures, including specific programmes, which are needed:

(a) To improve methods of production, conservation and distribution of food by making full use of technical and scientific knowledge, by disseminating knowledge of the principles of nutrition and by developing or reforming agrarian systems in such a way as to achieve the most efficient development and utilization of natural resources;
(b) Taking into account the problems of both food-importing and food-exporting countries, to ensure an equitable distribution of world food supplies in relation to need.

Article 12
1. The States Parties to the present Covenant recognize the right of everyone to the enjoyment of the highest attainable standard of physical and mental health.

2. The steps to be taken by the States Parties to the present Covenant to achieve the full realization of this right shall include those necessary for:

(a) The provision for the reduction of the stillbirth-rate and of infant mortality and for the healthy development of the child;
(b) The improvement of all aspects of environmental and industrial hygiene;
(c) The prevention, treatment and control of epidemic, endemic, occupational and other diseases;
(d) The creation of conditions which would assure to all medical service and medical attention in the event of sickness.

Article 13
1. The States Parties to the present Covenant recognize the right of everyone to education. They agree that education shall be directed to the full development of the human personality and the sense of its dignity, and shall strengthen the respect for human rights and fundamental freedoms. They further agree that education shall enable all persons to participate effectively in a free society, promote understanding, tolerance and friendship among all nations and all racial, ethnic or religious groups, and further the activities of the United Nations for the maintenance of peace.

2. The States Parties to the present Covenant recognize that, with a view to achieving the full realization of this right:

(a) Primary education shall be compulsory and available free to all;
(b) Secondary education in its different forms, including technical and vocational secondary education, shall be made generally available and accessible to all by every appropriate means, and in particular by the progressive introduction of free education;
(c) Higher education shall be made equally accessible to all, on the basis of capacity, by every appropriate means, and in particular by the progressive introduction of free education;
(d) Fundamental education shall be encouraged or intensified as far as possible for those persons who have not received or completed the whole period of their primary education;
(e) The development of a system of schools at all levels shall be actively pursued, an adequate fellowship system shall be established, and the material conditions of teaching staff shall be continuously improved.

3. The States Parties to the present Covenant undertake to have respect for the liberty of parents and, when applicable, legal guardians to choose for their children schools, other than those established by the public authorities, which conform to such minimum educational standards as may be laid down or approved by the State and to ensure the religious and moral education of their children in conformity with their own convictions.

4. No part of this article shall be construed so as to interfere with the liberty of individuals and bodies to establish and direct educational institutions, subject always to the observance of the principles set forth in paragraph 1 of this article and to the requirement that the education given in such institutions shall conform to such minimum standards as may be laid down by the State.

Article 14
Each State Party to the present Covenant which, at the time of becoming a Party, has not been able to secure in its metropolitan territory or other territories under its jurisdiction compulsory primary education, free of charge, undertakes within two years, to work out and adopt a detailed plan of action for the progressive implementation, within a reasonable number of years, to be fixed in the plan, of the principle of compulsory education free of charge for all.

Article 15
1. The States Parties to the present Covenant recognize the right of everyone:

(a) To take part in cultural life;
(b) To enjoy the benefits of scientific progress and its applications;
(c) To benefit from the protection of the moral and material interests resulting from any scientific, literary or artistic production of which he is the author.

2. The steps to be taken by the States Parties to the present Covenant to achieve the full realization of this right shall include those necessary for the conservation, the development and the diffusion of science and culture.

3. The States Parties to the present Covenant undertake to respect the freedom indispensable for scientific research and creative activity.

4. The States Parties to the present Covenant recognize the benefits to be derived from the encouragement and development of international contacts and cooperation in the scientific and cultural fields.

**Total Parties to
the International Covenant on Economic, Social and Cultural Rights,
as of 24 November 2004: 151**

APPENDIX D

DECLARATION ON THE RIGHTS OF PERSONS BELONGING TO NATIONAL OR ETHNIC, RELIGIOUS AND LINGUISTIC MINORITIES

ADOPTED BY GENERAL ASSEMBLY RESOLUTION 47/135 OF 18 DECEMBER 1992

The General Assembly,

Reaffirming that one of the basic aims of the United Nations, as proclaimed in the Charter, is to promote and encourage respect for human rights and for fundamental freedoms for all, without distinction as to race, sex, language or religion,

Reaffirming faith in fundamental human rights, in the dignity and worth of the human person, in the equal rights of men and women and of nations large and small,

Desiring to promote the realization of the principles contained in the Charter, the Universal Declaration of Human Rights, the Convention on the Prevention and Punishment of the Crime of Genocide, the International Convention on the Elimination of All Forms of Racial Discrimination, the International Covenant on Civil and Political Rights, the International Covenant on Economic, Social and Cultural Rights, the Declaration on the Elimination of All Forms of Intolerance and of Discrimination Based on Religion or Belief, and the Convention on the Rights of the Child, as well as other relevant international instruments that have been adopted at the universal or regional level and those concluded between individual States Members of the United Nations,

Inspired by the provisions of article 27 of the International Covenant on Civil and Political Rights concerning the rights of persons belonging to ethnic, religious or linguistic minorities,

Considering that the promotion and protection of the rights of persons belonging to national or ethnic, religious and linguistic minorities contribute to the political and social stability of States in which they live,

Emphasizing that the constant promotion and realization of the rights of persons belonging to national or ethnic, religious and linguistic minorities, as an integral part of the development of society as a whole and within a democratic framework based on the rule of law, would contribute to the strengthening of friendship and cooperation among peoples and States,

Considering that the United Nations has an important role to play regarding the protection of minorities,

Bearing in mind the work done so far within the United Nations system, in particular by the Commission on Human Rights, the Sub-Commission on Prevention of Discrimination and Protection of Minorities and the bodies established pursuant to the International Covenants on Human Rights and other relevant international human rights instruments in promoting and protecting the rights of persons belonging to national or ethnic, religious and linguistic minorities,

Taking into account the important work which is done by intergovernmental and non-governmental organizations in protecting minorities and in promoting and protecting the rights of persons belonging to national or ethnic, religious and linguistic minorities,

Recognizing the need to ensure even more effective implementation of international human rights instruments with regard to the rights of persons belonging to national or ethnic, religious and linguistic minorities,

Proclaims this Declaration on the Rights of Persons Belonging to National or Ethnic, Religious and Linguistic Minorities:

Article 1
1. States shall protect the existence and the national or ethnic, cultural, religious and linguistic identity of minorities within their respective territories and shall encourage conditions for the promotion of that identity.

2. States shall adopt appropriate legislative and other measures to achieve those ends.

Article 2

1. Persons belonging to national or ethnic, religious and linguistic minorities (hereinafter referred to as persons belonging to minorities) have the right to enjoy their own culture, to profess and practice their own religion, and to use their own language, in private and in public, freely and without interference or any form of discrimination.

2. Persons belonging to minorities have the right to participate effectively in cultural, religious, social, economic and public life.

3. Persons belonging to minorities have the right to participate effectively in decisions on the national and, where appropriate, regional level concerning the minority to which they belong or the regions in which they live, in a manner not incompatible with national legislation.

4. Persons belonging to minorities have the right to establish and maintain their own associations.

5. Persons belonging to minorities have the right to establish and maintain, without any discrimination, free and peaceful contacts with other members of their group and with persons belonging to other minorities, as well as contacts across frontiers with citizens of other States to whom they are related by national or ethnic, religious or linguistic ties.

Article 3

1. Persons belonging to minorities may exercise their rights, including those set forth in the present Declaration, individually as well as community with other members of their group, without any discrimination.

2. No disadvantage shall result for any person belonging to a minority as the consequence of the exercise or non-exercise of the rights set forth in the present Declaration.

Article 4

1. States shall take measures where required to ensure that persons belonging to minorities may exercise fully and effectively all their human rights and fundamental freedoms without any discrimination and in full equality before the law.

2. States shall take measures to create favourable conditions to enable persons belonging to minorities to express their characteristics and to develop their

culture, language, religion, traditions and customs, except where specific practices are in violation of national law and contrary to international standards.

3. States should take appropriate measures so that, wherever possible, persons belonging to minorities may have adequate opportunities to learn their mother tongue or to have instruction in their mother tongue.

4. States should, where appropriate, take measures in the field of education, in order to encourage knowledge of the history, traditions, language and culture of the minorities existing within their territory. Persons belonging to minorities should have adequate opportunities to gain knowledge of the society as a whole.

5. States should consider appropriate measures so that persons belonging to minorities may participate fully in the economic progress and development in their country.

Article 5
1. National policies and programmes shall be planned and implemented with due regard for the legitimate interests of persons belonging to minorities.

2. Programmes of cooperation and assistance among States should be planned and implemented with due regard for the legitimate interests of persons belonging to minorities.

Article 6
States should cooperate on questions relating to persons belonging to minorities, *inter alia*, exchanging information and experiences, in order to promote mutual understanding and confidence.

Article 7
States should cooperate in order to promote respect for the rights set forth in the present Declaration.

Article 8
1. Nothing in the present Declaration shall prevent the fulfillment of international obligations of States in relation to persons belonging to minorities. In particular, States shall fulfill in good faith the obligations and commitments they have assumed under international treaties and agreements to which they are parties.

2. The exercise of the rights set forth in the present Declaration shall not prejudice the enjoyment by all persons of universally recognized human rights and fundamental freedoms.

3. Measures taken by States to ensure the effective enjoyment of the rights set forth in the present Declaration shall not *prima facie,* be considered contrary to the principle of equality contained in the Universal Declaration of Human Rights.

4. Nothing in the present Declaration may be construed as permitting any activity contrary to the purposes and principles of the United Nations, including sovereign equality, territorial integrity and political independence of States.

Article 9

The specialized agencies and other organizations of the United Nations system shall contribute to the full realization of the rights and principles set forth in the present Declaration, within their respective fields of competence.

Appendix E

Convention on the Rights of the Child

Adopted and Opened for Signature, Ratification and Accession by General Assembly Resolution 44/25 of 20 November 1989 Entry into Force 2 September 1990, in Accordance with Article 49

Preamble
The States Parties to the present Convention,

Considering that, in accordance with the principles proclaimed in the Charter of the United Nations, recognition of the inherent dignity and of the equal and inalienable rights of all members of the human family is the foundation of freedom, justice and peace in the world,

Bearing in mind that the peoples of the United Nations have, in the Charter, reaffirmed their faith in fundamental human rights and in the dignity and worth of the human person, and have determined to promote social progress and better standards of life in larger freedom,

Recognizing that the United Nations has, in the Universal Declaration of Human Rights and in the International Covenants on Human Rights, proclaimed and agreed that everyone is entitled to all the rights and freedoms set forth therein, without distinction of any kind, such as race, colour, sex, language, religion, political or other opinion, national or social origin, property, birth or other status,

Recalling that, in the Universal Declaration of Human Rights, the United Nations has proclaimed that childhood is entitled to special care and assistance,

Convinced that the family, as the fundamental group of society and the natural environment for the growth and well-being of all its members and particularly children, should be afforded the necessary protection and assistance so that it can fully assume its responsibilities within the community,

Recognizing that the child, for the full and harmonious development of his or her personality, should grow up in a family environment, in an atmosphere of happiness, love and understanding,

Considering that the child should be fully prepared to live an individual life in society, and brought up in the spirit of the ideals proclaimed in the Charter of the United Nations, and in particular in the spirit of peace, dignity, tolerance, freedom, equality and solidarity,

Bearing in mind that the need to extend particular care to the child has been stated in the Geneva Declaration of the Rights of the Child of 1924 and in the Declaration of the Rights of the Child adopted by the General Assembly on 20 November 1959 and recognized in the Universal Declaration of Human Rights, in the International Covenant on Civil and Political Rights (in particular in articles 23 and 24), in the International Covenant on Economic, Social and Cultural Rights (in particular in article 10) and in the statutes and relevant instruments of specialized agencies and international organizations concerned with the welfare of children,

Bearing in mind that, as indicated in the Declaration of the Rights of the Child, "the child, by reason of his physical and mental immaturity, needs special safeguards and care, including appropriate legal protection, before as well as after birth",

Recalling the provisions of the Declaration on Social and Legal Principles relating to the Protection and Welfare of Children, with Special Reference to Foster Placement and Adoption Nationally and Internationally; the United Nations Standard Minimum Rules for the Administration of Juvenile Justice (The Beijing Rules); and the Declaration on the Protection of Women and Children in Emergency and Armed Conflict,

Recognizing that, in all countries in the world, there are children living in exceptionally difficult conditions, and that such children need special consideration,

Taking due account of the importance of the traditions and cultural values of each people for the protection and harmonious development of the child,

Recognizing the importance of international co-operation for improving the living conditions of children in every country, in particular in the developing countries,

Have agreed as follows:

PART I

Article 1
For the purposes of the present Convention, a child means every human being below the age of eighteen years unless under the law applicable to the child, majority is attained earlier.

Article 2
1. States Parties shall respect and ensure the rights set forth in the present Convention to each child within their jurisdiction without discrimination of any kind, irrespective of the child's or his or her parent's or legal guardian's race, colour, sex, language, religion, political or other opinion, national, ethnic or social origin, property, disability, birth or other status.

2. States Parties shall take all appropriate measures to ensure that the child is protected against all forms of discrimination or punishment on the basis of the status, activities, expressed opinions, or beliefs of the child's parents, legal guardians, or family members.

Article 3
1. In all actions concerning children, whether undertaken by public or private social welfare institutions, courts of law, administrative authorities or legislative bodies, the best interests of the child shall be a primary consideration.

2. States Parties undertake to ensure the child such protection and care as is necessary for his or her well-being, taking into account the rights and duties of his or her parents, legal guardians, or other individuals legally responsible for him or her, and, to this end, shall take all appropriate legislative and administrative measures.

3. States Parties shall ensure that the institutions, services and facilities responsible for the care or protection of children shall conform with the standards established by competent authorities, particularly in the areas of safety, health, in the number and suitability of their staff, as well as competent supervision.

Article 4

States Parties shall undertake all appropriate legislative, administrative, and other measures for the implementation of the rights recognized in the present Convention. With regard to economic, social and cultural rights, States Parties shall undertake such measures to the maximum extent of their available resources and, where needed, within the framework of international co-operation.

Article 5

States Parties shall respect the responsibilities, rights and duties of parents or, where applicable, the members of the extended family or community as provided for by local custom, legal guardians or other persons legally responsible for the child, to provide, in a manner consistent with the evolving capacities of the child, appropriate direction and guidance in the exercise by the child of the rights recognized in the present Convention.

Article 6

1. States Parties recognize that every child has the inherent right to life.

2. States Parties shall ensure to the maximum extent possible the survival and development of the child.

Article 7

1. The child shall be registered immediately after birth and shall have the right from birth to a name, the right to acquire a nationality and. as far as possible, the right to know and be cared for by his or her parents.

2. States Parties shall ensure the implementation of these rights in accordance with their national law and their obligations under the relevant international instruments in this field, in particular where the child would otherwise be stateless.

Article 8

1. States Parties undertake to respect the right of the child to preserve his or her identity, including nationality, name and family relations as recognized by law without unlawful interference.

2. Where a child is illegally deprived of some or all of the elements of his or her identity, States Parties shall provide appropriate assistance and protection, with a view to re-establishing speedily his or her identity.

Article 9

1. States Parties shall ensure that a child shall not be separated from his or her parents against their will, except when competent authorities subject to judicial review determine, in accordance with applicable law and procedures, that

such separation is necessary for the best interests of the child. Such determination may be necessary in a particular case such as one involving abuse or neglect of the child by the parents, or one where the parents are living separately and a decision must be made as to the child's place of residence.

2. In any proceedings pursuant to paragraph 1 of the present article, all interested parties shall be given an opportunity to participate in the proceedings and make their views known.

3. States Parties shall respect the right of the child who is separated from one or both parents to maintain personal relations and direct contact with both parents on a regular basis, except if it is contrary to the child's best interests.

4. Where such separation results from any action initiated by a State Party, such as the detention, imprisonment, exile, deportation or death (including death arising from any cause while the person is in the custody of the State) of one or both parents or of the child, that State Party shall, upon request, provide the parents, the child or, if appropriate, another member of the family with the essential information concerning the whereabouts of the absent member(s) of the family unless the provision of the information would be detrimental to the well-being of the child. States Parties shall further ensure that the submission of such a request shall of itself entail no adverse consequences for the person(s) concerned.

Article 10
1. In accordance with the obligation of States Parties under article 9, paragraph 1, applications by a child or his or her parents to enter or leave a State Party for the purpose of family reunification shall be dealt with by States Parties in a positive, humane and expeditious manner. States Parties shall further ensure that the submission of such a request shall entail no adverse consequences for the applicants and for the members of their family.

2. A child whose parents reside in different States shall have the right to maintain on a regular basis, save in exceptional circumstances personal relations and direct contacts with both parents. Towards that end and in accordance with the obligation of States Parties under article 9, paragraph 1, States Parties shall respect the right of the child and his or her parents to leave any country, including their own, and to enter their own country. The right to leave any country shall be subject only to such restrictions as are prescribed by law and which are necessary to protect the national security, public order (ordre public), public health or morals or the rights and freedoms of others and are consistent with the other rights recognized in the present Convention.

Article 11

1. States Parties shall take measures to combat the illicit transfer and non-return of children abroad.

2. To this end, States Parties shall promote the conclusion of bilateral or multilateral agreements or accession to existing agreements.

Article 12

1. States Parties shall assure to the child who is capable of forming his or her own views the right to express those views freely in all matters affecting the child, the views of the child being given due weight in accordance with the age and maturity of the child.

2. For this purpose, the child shall in particular be provided the opportunity to be heard in any judicial and administrative proceedings affecting the child, either directly, or through a representative or an appropriate body, in a manner consistent with the procedural rules of national law.

Article 13

1. The child shall have the right to freedom of expression; this right shall include freedom to seek, receive and impart information and ideas of all kinds, regardless of frontiers, either orally, in writing or in print, in the form of art, or through any other media of the child's choice.

2. The exercise of this right may be subject to certain restrictions, but these shall only be such as are provided by law and are necessary:

(a) For respect of the rights or reputations of others; or
(b) For the protection of national security or of public order (ordre public), or of public health or morals.

Article 14

1. States Parties shall respect the right of the child to freedom of thought, conscience and religion.

2. States Parties shall respect the rights and duties of the parents and, when applicable, legal guardians, to provide direction to the child in the exercise of his or her right in a manner consistent with the evolving capacities of the child.

3. Freedom to manifest one's religion or beliefs may be subject only to such limitations as are prescribed by law and are necessary to protect public safety, order, health or morals, or the fundamental rights and freedoms of others.

Article 15

1. States Parties recognize the rights of the child to freedom of association and to freedom of peaceful assembly.

2. No restrictions may be placed on the exercise of these rights other than those imposed in conformity with the law and which are necessary in a democratic society in the interests of national security or public safety, public order (ordre public), the protection of public health or morals or the protection of the rights and freedoms of others.

Article 16

1. No child shall be subjected to arbitrary or unlawful interference with his or her privacy, family, home or correspondence, nor to unlawful attacks on his or her honour and reputation.

2. The child has the right to the protection of the law against such interference or attacks.

Article 17

States Parties recognize the important function performed by the mass media and shall ensure that the child has access to information and material from a diversity of national and international sources, especially those aimed at the promotion of his or her social, spiritual and moral well-being and physical and mental health. To this end, States Parties shall:

(a) Encourage the mass media to disseminate information and material of social and cultural benefit to the child and in accordance with the spirit of article 29;
(b) Encourage international co-operation in the production, exchange and dissemination of such information and material from a diversity of cultural, national and international sources;
(c) Encourage the production and dissemination of children's books;
(d) Encourage the mass media to have particular regard to the linguistic needs of the child who belongs to a minority group or who is indigenous;
(e) Encourage the development of appropriate guidelines for the protection of the child from information and material injurious to his or her well-being, bearing in mind the provisions of articles 13 and 18.

Article 18

1. States Parties shall use their best efforts to ensure recognition of the principle that both parents have common responsibilities for the upbringing and development of the child. Parents or, as the case may be, legal guardians, have the primary responsibility for the upbringing and development of the child. The best interests of the child will be their basic concern.

2. For the purpose of guaranteeing and promoting the rights set forth in the present Convention, States Parties shall render appropriate assistance to parents and legal guardians in the performance of their child-rearing responsibilities and shall ensure the development of institutions, facilities and services for the care of children.

3. States Parties shall take all appropriate measures to ensure that children of working parents have the right to benefit from child-care services and facilities for which they are eligible.

Article 19

1. States Parties shall take all appropriate legislative, administrative, social and educational measures to protect the child from all forms of physical or mental violence, injury or abuse, neglect or negligent treatment, maltreatment or exploitation, including sexual abuse, while in the care of parent(s), legal guardian(s) or any other person who has the care of the child.

2. Such protective measures should, as appropriate, include effective procedures for the establishment of social programmes to provide necessary support for the child and for those who have the care of the child, as well as for other forms of prevention and for identification, reporting, referral, investigation, treatment and follow-up of instances of child maltreatment described heretofore, and, as appropriate, for judicial involvement.

Article 20

1. A child temporarily or permanently deprived of his or her family environment, or in whose own best interests cannot be allowed to remain in that environment, shall be entitled to special protection and assistance provided by the State.

2. States Parties shall in accordance with their national laws ensure alternative care for such a child.

3. Such care could include, inter alia, foster placement, kafalah of Islamic law, adoption or if necessary placement in suitable institutions for the care of children. When considering solutions, due regard shall be paid to the desirability of continuity in a child's upbringing and to the child's ethnic, religious, cultural and linguistic background.

Article 21

States Parties that recognize and/or permit the system of adoption shall ensure that the best interests of the child shall be the paramount consideration and they shall:

(a) Ensure that the adoption of a child is authorized only by competent authorities who determine, in accordance with applicable law and procedures and on the basis of all pertinent and reliable information, that the adoption is permissible in view of the child's status concerning parents, relatives and legal guardians and that, if required, the persons concerned have given their informed consent to the adoption on the basis of such counselling as may be necessary;

(b) Recognize that inter-country adoption may be considered as an alternative means of child's care, if the child cannot be placed in a foster or an adoptive family or cannot in any suitable manner be cared for in the child's country of origin;

(c) Ensure that the child concerned by inter-country adoption enjoys safeguards and standards equivalent to those existing in the case of national adoption;

(d) Take all appropriate measures to ensure that, in inter-country adoption, the placement does not result in improper financial gain for those involved in it;

(e) Promote, where appropriate, the objectives of the present article by concluding bilateral or multilateral arrangements or agreements, and endeavour, within this framework, to ensure that the placement of the child in another country is carried out by competent authorities or organs.

Article 22

1. States Parties shall take appropriate measures to ensure that a child who is seeking refugee status or who is considered a refugee in accordance with applicable international or domestic law and procedures shall, whether unaccompanied or accompanied by his or her parents or by any other person, receive appropriate protection and humanitarian assistance in the enjoyment of applicable rights set forth in the present Convention and in other international human rights or humanitarian instruments to which the said States are Parties.

2. For this purpose, States Parties shall provide, as they consider appropriate, cooperation in any efforts by the United Nations and other competent intergovernmental organizations or non-governmental organizations co-operating with the United Nations to protect and assist such a child and to trace the parents or other members of the family of any refugee child in order to obtain information necessary for reunification with his or her family. In cases where no parents or other members of the family can be found, the child shall be accorded the same protection as any other child permanently or temporarily deprived of his or her family environment for any reason, as set forth in the present Convention.

Article 23

1. States Parties recognize that a mentally or physically disabled child should enjoy a full and decent life, in conditions which ensure dignity, promote self-reliance and facilitate the child's active participation in the community.

2. States Parties recognize the right of the disabled child to special care and shall encourage and ensure the extension, subject to available resources, to the eligible child and those responsible for his or her care, of assistance for which application is made and which is appropriate to the child's condition and to the circumstances of the parents or others caring for the child.

3. Recognizing the special needs of a disabled child, assistance extended in accordance with paragraph 2 of the present article shall be provided free of charge, whenever possible, taking into account the financial resources of the parents or others caring for the child, and shall be designed to ensure that the disabled child has effective access to and receives education, training, health care services, rehabilitation services, preparation for employment and recreation opportunities in a manner conducive to the child's achieving the fullest possible social integration and individual development, including his or her cultural and spiritual development

4. States Parties shall promote, in the spirit of international cooperation, the exchange of appropriate information in the field of preventive health care and of medical, psychological and functional treatment of disabled children, including dissemination of and access to information concerning methods of rehabilitation, education and vocational services, with the aim of enabling States Parties to improve their capabilities and skills and to widen their experience in these areas. In this regard, particular account shall be taken of the needs of developing countries.

Article 24
1. States Parties recognize the right of the child to the enjoyment of the highest attainable standard of health and to facilities for the treatment of illness and rehabilitation of health. States Parties shall strive to ensure that no child is deprived of his or her right of access to such health care services.

2. States Parties shall pursue full implementation of this right and, in particular, shall take appropriate measures:

(a) To diminish infant and child mortality;
(b) To ensure the provision of necessary medical assistance and health care to all children with emphasis on the development of primary health care;
(c) To combat disease and malnutrition, including within the framework of primary health care, through, inter alia, the application of readily available technology and through the provision of adequate nutritious foods and clean drinking-water, taking into consideration the dangers and risks of environmental pollution;

(d) To ensure appropriate pre-natal and post-natal health care for mothers;
(e) To ensure that all segments of society, in particular parents and children, are informed, have access to education and are supported in the use of basic knowledge of child health and nutrition, the advantages of breastfeeding, hygiene and environmental sanitation and the prevention of accidents;
(f) To develop preventive health care, guidance for parents and family planning education and services.

3. States Parties shall take all effective and appropriate measures with a view to abolishing traditional practices prejudicial to the health of children.

4. States Parties undertake to promote and encourage international co-operation with a view to achieving progressively the full realization of the right recognized in the present article. In this regard, particular account shall be taken of the needs of developing countries.

Article 25
States Parties recognize the right of a child who has been placed by the competent authorities for the purposes of care, protection or treatment of his or her physical or mental health, to a periodic review of the treatment provided to the child and all other circumstances relevant to his or her placement.

Article 26
1. States Parties shall recognize for every child the right to benefit from social security, including social insurance, and shall take the necessary measures to achieve the full realization of this right in accordance with their national law.

2. The benefits should, where appropriate, be granted, taking into account the resources and the circumstances of the child and persons having responsibility for the maintenance of the child, as well as any other consideration relevant to an application for benefits made by or on behalf of the child.

Article 27
1. States Parties recognize the right of every child to a standard of living adequate for the child's physical, mental, spiritual, moral and social development.

2. The parent(s) or others responsible for the child have the primary responsibility to secure, within their abilities and financial capacities, the conditions of living necessary for the child's development.

3. States Parties, in accordance with national conditions and within their means, shall take appropriate measures to assist parents and others responsible for the child to implement this right and shall in case of need provide ma-

terial assistance and support programmes, particularly with regard to nutrition, clothing and housing.

4. States Parties shall take all appropriate measures to secure the recovery of maintenance for the child from the parents or other persons having financial responsibility for the child, both within the State Party and from abroad. In particular, where the person having financial responsibility for the child lives in a State different from that of the child, States Parties shall promote the accession to international agreements or the conclusion of such agreements, as well as the making of other appropriate arrangements.

Article 28
1. States Parties recognize the right of the child to education, and with a view to achieving this right progressively and on the basis of equal opportunity, they shall, in particular:

(a) Make primary education compulsory and available free to all;
(b) Encourage the development of different forms of secondary education, including general and vocational education, make them available and accessible to every child, and take appropriate measures such as the introduction of free education and offering financial assistance in case of need;
(c) Make higher education accessible to all on the basis of capacity by every appropriate means;
(d) Make educational and vocational information and guidance available and accessible to all children;
(e) Take measures to encourage regular attendance at schools and the reduction of drop-out rates.

2. States Parties shall take all appropriate measures to ensure that school discipline is administered in a manner consistent with the child's human dignity and in conformity with the present Convention.

3. States Parties shall promote and encourage international cooperation in matters relating to education, in particular with a view to contributing to the elimination of ignorance and illiteracy throughout the world and facilitating access to scientific and technical knowledge and modern teaching methods. In this regard, particular account shall be taken of the needs of developing countries.

Article 29
1. States Parties agree that the education of the child shall be directed to:

(a) The development of the child's personality, talents and mental and physical abilities to their fullest potential;

(b) The development of respect for human rights and fundamental freedoms, and for the principles enshrined in the Charter of the United Nations;

(c) The development of respect for the child's parents, his or her own cultural identity, language and values, for the national values of the country in which the child is living, the country from which he or she may originate, and for civilizations different from his or her own;

(d) The preparation of the child for responsible life in a free society, in the spirit of understanding, peace, tolerance, equality of sexes, and friendship among all peoples, ethnic, national and religious groups and persons of indigenous origin;

(e) The development of respect for the natural environment.

2. No part of the present article or article 28 shall be construed so as to interfere with the liberty of individuals and bodies to establish and direct educational institutions, subject always to the observance of the principle set forth in paragraph 1 of the present article and to the requirements that the education given in such institutions shall conform to such minimum standards as may be laid down by the State.

Article 30

In those States in which ethnic, religious or linguistic minorities or persons of indigenous origin exist, a child belonging to such a minority or who is indigenous shall not be denied the right, in community with other members of his or her group, to enjoy his or her own culture, to profess and practise his or her own religion, or to use his or her own language.

Article 31

1. States Parties recognize the right of the child to rest and leisure, to engage in play and recreational activities appropriate to the age of the child and to participate freely in cultural life and the arts.

2. States Parties shall respect and promote the right of the child to participate fully in cultural and artistic life and shall encourage the provision of appropriate and equal opportunities for cultural, artistic, recreational and leisure activity.

Article 32

1. States Parties recognize the right of the child to be protected from economic exploitation and from performing any work that is likely to be hazardous or to interfere with the child's education, or to be harmful to the child's health or physical, mental, spiritual, moral or social development.

2. States Parties shall take legislative, administrative, social and educational measures to ensure the implementation of the present article. To this end, and

having regard to the relevant provisions of other international instruments, States Parties shall in particular:

(a) Provide for a minimum age or minimum ages for admission to employment;
(b) Provide for appropriate regulation of the hours and conditions of employment;
(c) Provide for appropriate penalties or other sanctions to ensure the effective enforcement of the present article.

Article 33

States Parties shall take all appropriate measures, including legislative, administrative, social and educational measures, to protect children from the illicit use of narcotic drugs and psychotropic substances as defined in the relevant international treaties, and to prevent the use of children in the illicit production and trafficking of such substances.

Article 34

States Parties undertake to protect the child from all forms of sexual exploitation and sexual abuse. For these purposes, States Parties shall in particular take all appropriate national, bilateral and multilateral measures to prevent:

(a) The inducement or coercion of a child to engage in any unlawful sexual activity;
(b) The exploitative use of children in prostitution or other unlawful sexual practices;
(c) The exploitative use of children in pornographic performances and materials.

Article 35

States Parties shall take all appropriate national, bilateral and multilateral measures to prevent the abduction of, the sale of or traffic in children for any purpose or in any form.

Article 36

States Parties shall protect the child against all other forms of exploitation prejudicial to any aspects of the child's welfare.

Article 37

States Parties shall ensure that:

(a) No child shall be subjected to torture or other cruel, inhuman or degrading treatment or punishment. Neither capital punishment nor life imprisonment without possibility of release shall be imposed for offences committed by persons below eighteen years of age;

(b) No child shall be deprived of his or her liberty unlawfully or arbitrarily. The arrest, detention or imprisonment of a child shall be in conformity with the law and shall be used only as a measure of last resort and for the shortest appropriate period of time;

(c) Every child deprived of liberty shall be treated with humanity and respect for the inherent dignity of the human person, and in a manner which takes into account the needs of persons of his or her age. In particular, every child deprived of liberty shall be separated from adults unless it is considered in the child's best interest not to do so and shall have the right to maintain contact with his or her family through correspondence and visits, save in exceptional circumstances;

(d) Every child deprived of his or her liberty shall have the right to prompt access to legal and other appropriate assistance, as well as the right to challenge the legality of the deprivation of his or her liberty before a court or other competent, independent and impartial authority, and to a prompt decision on any such action.

Article 38

1. States Parties undertake to respect and to ensure respect for rules of international humanitarian law applicable to them in armed conflicts which are relevant to the child.

2. States Parties shall take all feasible measures to ensure that persons who have not attained the age of fifteen years do not take a direct part in hostilities.

3. States Parties shall refrain from recruiting any person who has not attained the age of fifteen years into their armed forces. In recruiting among those persons who have attained the age of fifteen years but who have not attained the age of eighteen years, States Parties shall endeavour to give priority to those who are oldest.

4. In accordance with their obligations under international humanitarian law to protect the civilian population in armed conflicts, States Parties shall take all feasible measures to ensure protection and care of children who are affected by an armed conflict.

Article 39

States Parties shall take all appropriate measures to promote physical and psychological recovery and social reintegration of a child victim of: any form of neglect, exploitation, or abuse; torture or any other form of cruel, inhuman or degrading treatment or punishment; or armed conflicts. Such recovery and reintegration shall take place in an environment which fosters the health, self-respect and dignity of the child.

Article 40

1. States Parties recognize the right of every child alleged as, accused of, or recognized as having infringed the penal law to be treated in a manner consistent with the promotion of the child's sense of dignity and worth, which reinforces the child's respect for the human rights and fundamental freedoms of others and which takes into account the child's age and the desirability of promoting the child's reintegration and the child's assuming a constructive role in society.

2. To this end, and having regard to the relevant provisions of international instruments, States Parties shall, in particular, ensure that:

(a) No child shall be alleged as, be accused of, or recognized as having infringed the penal law by reason of acts or omissions that were not prohibited by national or international law at the time they were committed;

(b) Every child alleged as or accused of having infringed the penal law has at least the following guarantees:

(i) To be presumed innocent until proven guilty according to law;

(ii) To be informed promptly and directly of the charges against him or her, and, if appropriate, through his or her parents or legal guardians, and to have legal or other appropriate assistance in the preparation and presentation of his or her defence;

(iii) To have the matter determined without delay by a competent, independent and impartial authority or judicial body in a fair hearing according to law, in the presence of legal or other appropriate assistance and, unless it is considered not to be in the best interest of the child, in particular, taking into account his or her age or situation, his or her parents or legal guardians;

(iv) Not to be compelled to give testimony or to confess guilt; to examine or have examined adverse witnesses and to obtain the participation and examination of witnesses on his or her behalf under conditions of equality;

(v) If considered to have infringed the penal law, to have this decision and any measures imposed in consequence thereof reviewed by a higher competent, independent and impartial authority or judicial body according to law;

(vi) To have the free assistance of an interpreter if the child cannot understand or speak the language used;

(vii) To have his or her privacy fully respected at all stages of the proceedings.

3. States Parties shall seek to promote the establishment of laws, procedures, authorities and institutions specifically applicable to children alleged as, accused of, or recognized as having infringed the penal law and in particular:

(a) The establishment of a minimum age below which children shall be presumed not to have the capacity to infringe the penal law;

(b) Whenever appropriate and desirable, measures for dealing with such children without resorting to judicial proceedings, providing that human rights and legal safeguards are fully respected.

4. A variety of dispositions, such as care, guidance and supervision orders; counselling; probation; foster care; education and vocational training programmes and other alternatives to institutional care shall be available to ensure that children are dealt with in a manner appropriate to their well-being and proportionate both to their circumstances and the offence.

Article 41
Nothing in the present Convention shall affect any provisions which are more conducive to the realization of the rights of the child and which may be contained in:

(a) The law of a State party; or
(b) International law in force for that State.

PART II

Article 42
States Parties undertake to make the principles and provisions of the Convention widely known, by appropriate and active means, to adults and children alike.

Article 43
1. For the purpose of examining the progress made by States Parties in achieving the realization of the obligations undertaken in the present Convention, there shall be established a Committee on the Rights of the Child, which shall carry out the functions hereinafter provided.

2. The Committee shall consist of ten experts of high moral standing and recognized competence in the field covered by this Convention. The members of the Committee shall be elected by States Parties from among their nationals and shall serve in their personal capacity, consideration being given to equitable geographical distribution, as well as to the principal legal systems.

3. The members of the Committee shall be elected by secret ballot from a list of persons nominated by States Parties. Each State Party may nominate one person from among its own nationals.

4. The initial election to the Committee shall be held no later than six months after the date of the entry into force of the present Convention and thereafter every second year. At least four months before the date of each election, the Secretary-General of the United Nations shall address a letter to States Parties inviting them to submit their nominations within two months. The Secretary-

General shall subsequently prepare a list in alphabetical order of all persons thus nominated, indicating States Parties which have nominated them, and shall submit it to the States Parties to the present Convention.

5. The elections shall be held at meetings of States Parties convened by the Secretary-General at United Nations Headquarters. At those meetings, for which two thirds of States Parties shall constitute a quorum, the persons elected to the Committee shall be those who obtain the largest number of votes and an absolute majority of the votes of the representatives of States Parties present and voting.

6. The members of the Committee shall be elected for a term of four years. They shall be eligible for re-election if renominated. The term of five of the members elected at the first election shall expire at the end of two years; immediately after the first election, the names of these five members shall be chosen by lot by the Chairman of the meeting.

7. If a member of the Committee dies or resigns or declares that for any other cause he or she can no longer perform the duties of the Committee, the State Party which nominated the member shall appoint another expert from among its nationals to serve for the remainder of the term, subject to the approval of the Committee.

8. The Committee shall establish its own rules of procedure.

9. The Committee shall elect its officers for a period of two years.

10. The meetings of the Committee shall normally be held at United Nations Headquarters or at any other convenient place as determined by the Committee. The Committee shall normally meet annually. The duration of the meetings of the Committee shall be determined, and reviewed, if necessary, by a meeting of the States Parties to the present Convention, subject to the approval of the General Assembly.

11. The Secretary-General of the United Nations shall provide the necessary staff and facilities for the effective performance of the functions of the Committee under the present Convention.

12. With the approval of the General Assembly, the members of the Committee established under the present Convention shall receive emoluments from United Nations resources on such terms and conditions as the Assembly may decide.

Article 44
1. States Parties undertake to submit to the Committee, through the Secretary-General of the United Nations, reports on the measures they have

adopted which give effect to the rights recognized herein and on the progress made on the enjoyment of those rights:

(a) Within two years of the entry into force of the Convention for the State Party concerned;
(b) Thereafter every five years.

2. Reports made under the present article shall indicate factors and difficulties, if any, affecting the degree of fulfillment of the obligations under the present Convention. Reports shall also contain sufficient information to provide the Committee with a comprehensive understanding of the implementation of the Convention in the country concerned.

3. A State Party which has submitted a comprehensive initial report to the Committee need not, in its subsequent reports submitted in accordance with paragraph 1 (b) of the present article, repeat basic information previously provided.

4. The Committee may request from States Parties further information relevant to the implementation of the Convention.

5. The Committee shall submit to the General Assembly, through the Economic and Social Council, every two years, reports on its activities.

6. States Parties shall make their reports widely available to the public in their own countries.

Article 45
In order to foster the effective implementation of the Convention and to encourage international co-operation in the field covered by the Convention:

(a) The specialized agencies, the United Nations Children's Fund, and other United Nations organs shall be entitled to be represented at the consideration of the implementation of such provisions of the present Convention as fall within the scope of their mandate. The Committee may invite the specialized agencies, the United Nations Children's Fund and other competent bodies as it may consider appropriate to provide expert advice on the implementation of the Convention in areas falling within the scope of their respective mandates. The Committee may invite the specialized agencies, the United Nations Children's Fund, and other United Nations organs to submit reports on the implementation of the Convention in areas falling within the scope of their activities;
(b) The Committee shall transmit, as it may consider appropriate, to the specialized agencies, the United Nations Children's Fund and other competent bodies, any reports from States Parties that contain a request, or indicate a

need, for technical advice or assistance, along with the Committee's observations and suggestions, if any, on these requests or indications;

(c) The Committee may recommend to the General Assembly to request the Secretary-General to undertake on its behalf studies on specific issues relating to the rights of the child;

(d) The Committee may make suggestions and general recommendations based on information received pursuant to articles 44 and 45 of the present Convention. Such suggestions and general recommendations shall be transmitted to any State Party concerned and reported to the General Assembly, together with comments, if any, from States Parties.

PART III

Article 46
The present Convention shall be open for signature by all States.

Article 47
The present Convention is subject to ratification. Instruments of ratification shall be deposited with the Secretary-General of the United Nations.

Article 48
The present Convention shall remain open for accession by any State. The instruments of accession shall be deposited with the Secretary-General of the United Nations.

Article 49
1. The present Convention shall enter into force on the thirtieth day following the date of deposit with the Secretary-General of the United Nations of the twentieth instrument of ratification or accession.

2. For each State ratifying or acceding to the Convention after the deposit of the twentieth instrument of ratification or accession, the Convention shall enter into force on the thirtieth day after the deposit by such State of its instrument of ratification or accession.

Article 50
1. Any State Party may propose an amendment and file it with the Secretary-General of the United Nations. The Secretary-General shall thereupon communicate the proposed amendment to States Parties, with a request that they indicate whether they favour a conference of States Parties for the purpose of considering and voting upon the proposals. In the event that, within four months from the date of such communication, at least one third of the States Parties favour such a conference, the Secretary-General shall convene the con-

ference under the auspices of the United Nations. Any amendment adopted by a majority of States Parties present and voting at the conference shall be submitted to the General Assembly for approval.

2. An amendment adopted in accordance with paragraph 1 of the present article shall enter into force when it has been approved by the General Assembly of the United Nations and accepted by a two-thirds majority of States Parties.

3. When an amendment enters into force, it shall be binding on those States Parties which have accepted it, other States Parties still being bound by the provisions of the present Convention and any earlier amendments which they have accepted.

Article 51
1. The Secretary-General of the United Nations shall receive and circulate to all States the text of reservations made by States at the time of ratification or accession.

2. A reservation incompatible with the object and purpose of the present Convention shall not be permitted.

3. Reservations may be withdrawn at any time by notification to that effect addressed to the Secretary-General of the United Nations, who shall then inform all States. Such notification shall take effect on the date on which it is received by the Secretary-General

Article 52
A State Party may denounce the present Convention by written notification to the Secretary-General of the United Nations. Denunciation becomes effective one year after the date of receipt of the notification by the Secretary-General.

Article 53
The Secretary-General of the United Nations is designated as the depositary of the present Convention.

Article 54
The original of the present Convention, of which the Arabic, Chinese, English, French, Russian and Spanish texts are equally authentic, shall be deposited with the Secretary-General of the United Nations.

IN WITNESS THEREOF the undersigned plenipotentiaries,
being duly authorized thereto by their respective governments,
have signed the present Convention.

As of 24 November 2004, Somalia and the United States of America were the only U.N. member states not having ratified this convention.

Appendix F

Convention on the Elimination of All Forms of Discrimination against Women

Adopted and Opened for Signature, Ratification and Accession by General Assembly Resolution 34/180 of 18 December 1979 Entry into Force 3 September 1981, in Accordance with Article 27(1)

(Excerpt of substantive provisions)

Article 1

For the purposes of the present Convention, the term "discrimination against women" shall mean any distinction, exclusion or restriction made on the basis of sex which has the effect or purpose of impairing or nullifying the recognition, enjoyment or exercise by women, irrespective of their marital status, on a basis of equality of men and women, of human rights and fundamental freedoms in the political, economic, social, cultural, civil or any other field.

Article 2

States Parties condemn discrimination against women in all its forms, agree to pursue by all appropriate means and without delay a policy of eliminating discrimination against women and, to this end, undertake:

(a) To embody the principle of the equality of men and women in their national constitutions or other appropriate legislation if not yet incorporated therein and to ensure, through law and other appropriate means, the practical realization of this principle;

(b) To adopt appropriate legislative and other measures, including sanctions where appropriate, prohibiting all discrimination against women;

(c) To establish legal protection of the rights of women on an equal basis with men and to ensure through competent national tribunals and other public institutions the effective protection of women against any act of discrimination;

(d) To refrain from engaging in any act or practice of discrimination against women and to ensure that public authorities and institutions shall act in conformity with this obligation;

(e) To take all appropriate measures to eliminate discrimination against women by any person, organization or enterprise;

(f) To take all appropriate measures, including legislation, to modify or abolish existing laws, regulations, customs and practices which constitute discrimination against women;

(g) To repeal all national penal provisions which constitute discrimination against women.

Article 3

States Parties shall take in all fields, in particular in the political, social, economic and cultural fields, all appropriate measures, including legislation, to ensure the full development and advancement of women, for the purpose of guaranteeing them the exercise and enjoyment of human rights and fundamental freedoms on a basis of equality with men.

Article 4

1. Adoption by States Parties of temporary special measures aimed at accelerating de facto equality between men and women shall not be considered discrimination as defined in the present Convention, but shall in no way entail as a consequence the maintenance of unequal or separate standards; these measures shall be discontinued when the objectives of equality of opportunity and treatment have been achieved.

2. Adoption by States Parties of special measures, including those measures contained in the present Convention, aimed at protecting maternity shall not be considered discriminatory.

Article 5

States Parties shall take all appropriate measures:

(a) To modify the social and cultural patterns of conduct of men and women, with a view to achieving the elimination of prejudices and customary and all other practices which are based on the idea of the inferiority or the superiority of either of the sexes or on stereotyped roles for men and women;

(b) To ensure that family education includes a proper understanding of maternity as a social function and the recognition of the common responsibility of men and women in the upbringing and development of their children, it being understood that the interest of the children is the primordial consideration in all cases.

Article 6

States Parties shall take all appropriate measures, including legislation, to suppress all forms of traffic in women and exploitation of prostitution of women.

Article 7

States Parties shall take all appropriate measures to eliminate discrimination against women in the political and public life of the country and, in particular, shall ensure to women, on equal terms with men, the right:

(a) To vote in all elections and public referenda and to be eligible for election to all publicly elected bodies;

(b) To participate in the formulation of government policy and the implementation thereof and to hold public office and perform all public functions at all levels of government;

(c) To participate in non-governmental organizations and associations concerned with the public and political life of the country.

Article 8

States Parties shall take all appropriate measures to ensure to women, on equal terms with men and without any discrimination, the opportunity to represent their Governments at the international level and to participate in the work of international organizations.

Article 9

1. States Parties shall grant women equal rights with men to acquire, change or retain their nationality. They shall ensure in particular that neither marriage to an alien nor change of nationality by the husband during marriage shall automatically change the nationality of the wife, render her stateless or force upon her the nationality of the husband.

2. States Parties shall grant women equal rights with men with respect to the nationality of their children.

Article 10

States Parties shall take all appropriate measures to eliminate discrimination against women in order to ensure to them equal rights with men in the field of education and in particular to ensure, on a basis of equality of men and women:

(a) The same conditions for career and vocational guidance, for access to studies and for the achievement of diplomas in educational establishments of all categories in rural as well as in urban areas; this equality shall be ensured in preschool, general, technical, professional and higher technical education, as well as in all types of vocational training;
(b) Access to the same curricula, the same examinations, teaching staff with qualifications of the same standard and school premises and equipment of the same quality;
(c) The elimination of any stereotyped concept of the roles of men and women at all levels and in all forms of education by encouraging coeducation and other types of education which will help to achieve this aim and, in particular, by the revision of textbooks and school programmes and the adaptation of teaching methods;
(d) The same opportunities to benefit from scholarships and other study grants;
(e) The same opportunities for access to programmes of continuing education, including adult and functional literacy programmes, particularly those aimed at reducing, at the earliest possible time, any gap in education existing between men and women;
(f) The reduction of female student drop-out rates and the organization of programmes for girls and women who have left school prematurely;
(g) The same opportunities to participate actively in sports and physical education;
(h) Access to specific educational information to help to ensure the health and well-being of families, including information and advice on family planning.

Article 11

1. States Parties shall take all appropriate measures to eliminate discrimination against women in the field of employment in order to ensure, on a basis of equality of men and women, the same rights, in particular:

(a) The right to work as an inalienable right of all human beings;
(b) The right to the same employment opportunities, including the application of the same criteria for selection in matters of employment;
(c) The right to free choice of profession and employment, the right to promotion, job security and all benefits and conditions of service and the right

to receive vocational training and retraining, including apprenticeships, advanced vocational training and recurrent training;

(d) The right to equal remuneration, including benefits, and to equal treatment in respect of work of equal value, as well as equality of treatment in the evaluation of the quality of work;

(e) The right to social security, particularly in cases of retirement, unemployment, sickness, invalidity and old age and other incapacity to work, as well as the right to paid leave;

(f) The right to protection of health and to safety in working conditions, including the safeguarding of the function of reproduction.

2. In order to prevent discrimination against women on the grounds of marriage or maternity and to ensure their effective right to work, States Parties shall take appropriate measures:

(a) To prohibit, subject to the imposition of sanctions, dismissal on the grounds of pregnancy or of maternity leave and discrimination in dismissals on the basis of marital status;

(b) To introduce maternity leave with pay or with comparable social benefits without loss of former employment, seniority or social allowances;

(c) To encourage the provision of the necessary supporting social services to enable parents to combine family obligations with work responsibilities and participation in public life, in particular through promoting the establishment and development of a network of child-care facilities;

(d) To provide special protection to women during pregnancy in types of work proved to be harmful to them.

3. Protective legislation relating to matters covered in this article shall be reviewed periodically in the light of scientific and technological knowledge and shall be revised, repealed or extended as necessary.

Article 12

1. States Parties shall take all appropriate measures to eliminate discrimination against women in the field of health care in order to ensure, on a basis of equality of men and women, access to health care services, including those related to family planning.

2. Notwithstanding the provisions of paragraph 1 of this article, States Parties shall ensure to women appropriate services in connection with pregnancy, confinement and the post-natal period, granting free services where necessary, as well as adequate nutrition during pregnancy and lactation.

Article 13
States Parties shall take all appropriate measures to eliminate discrimination against women in other areas of economic and social life in order to ensure, on a basis of equality of men and women, the same rights, in particular:

(a) The right to family benefits;
(b) The right to bank loans, mortgages and other forms of financial credit;
(c) The right to participate in recreational activities, sports and all aspects of cultural life.

Article 14
1. States Parties shall take into account the particular problems faced by rural women and the significant roles which rural women play in the economic survival of their families, including their work in the non-monetized sectors of the economy, and shall take all appropriate measures to ensure the application of the provisions of the present Convention to women in rural areas.

2. States Parties shall take all appropriate measures to eliminate discrimination against women in rural areas in order to ensure, on a basis of equality of men and women, that they participate in and benefit from rural development and, in particular, shall ensure to such women the right:

(a) To participate in the elaboration and implementation of development planning at all levels;
(b) To have access to adequate health care facilities, including information, counselling and services in family planning;
(c) To benefit directly from social security programmes;
(d) To obtain all types of training and education, formal and non-formal, including that relating to functional literacy, as well as, inter alia, the benefit of all community and extension services in order to increase their technical proficiency;
(e) To organize self-help groups and cooperatives in order to obtain equal access to economic opportunities through employment or self-employment;
(f) To participate in all community activities;
(g) To have access to agricultural credit and loans, marketing facilities, appropriate technology and equal treatment in land and agrarian reform as well as in land resettlement schemes;
(h) To enjoy adequate living conditions, particularly in relation to housing, sanitation, electricity and water supply, transport and communications.

Article 15
1. States Parties shall accord to women equality with men before the law.

2. States Parties shall accord to women, in civil matters, a legal capacity identical to that of men and the same opportunities to exercise that capacity. In particular, they shall give women equal rights to conclude contracts and to administer property and shall treat them equally in all stages of procedure in courts and tribunals.

3. States Parties agree that all contracts and all other private instruments of any kind with a legal effect which is directed at restricting the legal capacity of women shall be deemed null and void.

4. States Parties shall accord to men and women the same rights with regard to the law relating to the movement of persons and the freedom to choose their residence and domicile.

Article 16
1. States Parties shall take all appropriate measures to eliminate discrimination against women in all matters relating to marriage and family relations and in particular shall ensure, on a basis of equality of men and women:

(a) The same right to enter into marriage;
(b) The same right freely to choose a spouse and to enter into marriage only with their free and full consent;
(c) The same rights and responsibilities during marriage and at its dissolution;
(d) The same rights and responsibilities as parents, irrespective of their marital status, in matters relating to their children; in all cases the interests of the children shall be paramount;
(e) The same rights to decide freely and responsibly on the number and spacing of their children and to have access to the information, education and means to enable them to exercise these rights;
(f) The same rights and responsibilities with regard to guardianship, wardship, trusteeship and adoption of children, or similar institutions where these concepts exist in national legislation; in all cases the interests of the children shall be paramount;
(g) The same personal rights as husband and wife, including the right to choose a family name, a profession and an occupation;
(h) The same rights for both spouses in respect of the ownership, acquisition, management, administration, enjoyment and disposition of property, whether free of charge or for a valuable consideration.

2. The betrothal and the marriage of a child shall have no legal effect, and all necessary action, including legislation, shall be taken to specify a minimum

age for marriage and to make the registration of marriages in an official registry compulsory.

* * *

Article 28 (para. 2):
A reservation incompatible with the object and purpose of the present Convention shall not be permitted.

* * *

**Total State Parties to the Convention on the Elimination
of All Forms of Discrimination against Women,
as of 20 October 2004: 179**

Appendix G

International Convention on the Protection of the Rights of All Migrant Workers and Members of Their Families

Adopted by General Assembly Resolution 45/158 of 18 December 1990 Entry into Force on 1 July 2003

Preamble

The States Parties to the present Convention,

Taking into account the principles embodied in the basic instruments of the United Nations concerning human rights, in particular the Universal Declaration of Human Rights, the International Covenant on Economic, Social and Cultural Rights, the International Covenant on Civil and Political Rights, the International Convention on the Elimination of All Forms of Racial Discrimination, the Convention on the Elimination of All Forms of Discrimination against Women and the Convention on the Rights of the Child,

Taking into account also the principles and standards set forth in the relevant instruments elaborated within the framework of the International Labour Organisation, especially the Convention concerning Migration for Employment (No. 97), the Convention concerning Migrations in Abusive Conditions and the Promotion of Equality of Opportunity and Treatment of Migrant Workers (No.143), the Recommendation concerning Migration for Employment

(No. 86), the Recommendation concerning Migrant Workers (No.151), the Convention concerning Forced or Compulsory Labour (No. 29) and the Convention concerning Abolition of Forced Labour (No. 105),

Reaffirming the importance of the principles contained in the Convention against Discrimination in Education of the United Nations Educational, Scientific and Cultural Organization,

Recalling the Convention against Torture and Other Cruel, Inhuman or Degrading Treatment or Punishment, the Declaration of the Fourth United Nations Congress on the Prevention of Crime and the Treatment of Offenders, the Code of Conduct for Law Enforcement Officials, and the Slavery Conventions,

Recalling that one of the objectives of the International Labour Organisation, as stated in its Constitution, is the protection of the interests of workers when employed in countries other than their own, and bearing in mind the expertise and experience of that organization in matters related to migrant workers and members of their families,

Recognizing the importance of the work done in connection with migrant workers and members of their families in various organs of the United Nations, in particular in the Commission on Human Rights and the Commission for Social Development, and in the Food and Agriculture Organization of the United Nations, the United Nations Educational, Scientific and Cultural Organization and the World Health Organization, as well as in other international organizations,

Recognizing also the progress made by certain States on a regional or bilateral basis towards the protection of the rights of migrant workers and members of their families, as well as the importance and usefulness of bilateral and multilateral agreements in this field,

Realizing the importance and extent of the migration phenomenon, which involves millions of people and affects a large number of States in the international community,

Aware of the impact of the flows of migrant workers on States and people concerned, and desiring to establish norms which may contribute to the harmonization of the attitudes of States through the acceptance of basic principles concerning the treatment of migrant workers and members of their families,

Considering the situation of vulnerability in which migrant workers and members of their families frequently-find themselves owing, among other things, to their absence from their State of origin and to the difficulties they may encounter arising from their presence in the State of employment,

Convinced that the rights of migrant workers and members of their families have not been sufficiently recognized everywhere and therefore require appropriate international protection,

Taking into account the fact that migration is often the cause of serious problems for the members of the families of migrant workers as well as for the workers themselves, in particular because of the scattering of the family,

Bearing in mind that the human problems involved in migration are even more serious in the case of irregular migration and convinced therefore that appropriate action should be encouraged in order to prevent and eliminate clandestine movements and trafficking in migrant workers, while at the same time assuring the protection of their fundamental human rights,

Considering that workers who are non-documented or in an irregular situation are frequently employed under less favourable conditions of work than other workers and that certain employers find this an inducement to seek such labour in order to reap the benefits of unfair competition,

Considering also that recourse to the employment of migrant workers who are in an irregular situation will be discouraged if the fundamental human rights of all migrant workers are more widely recognized and, moreover, that granting certain additional rights to migrant workers and members of their families in a regular situation will encourage all migrants and employers to respect and comply with the laws and procedures established by the States concerned,

Convinced, therefore, of the need to bring about the international protection of the rights of all migrant workers and members of their families, reaffirming and establishing basic norms in a comprehensive convention which could be applied universally,

Have agreed as follows:

PART I: SCOPE AND DEFINITIONS

Article 1

1. The present Convention is applicable, except as otherwise provided hereafter, to all migrant workers and members of their families without distinction of any kind such as sex, race, colour, language, religion or conviction, political or other opinion, national, ethnic or social origin, nationality, age, economic position, property, marital status, birth or other status.

2. The present Convention shall apply during the entire migration process of migrant workers and members of their families, which comprises preparation

for migration, departure, transit and the entire period of stay and remunerated activity in the State of employment as well as return to the State of origin or the State of habitual residence.

Article 2
For the purposes of the present Convention:

1. The term "migrant worker" refers to a person who is to be engaged, is engaged or has been engaged in a remunerated activity in a State of which he or she is not a national.

2. (a) The term "frontier worker" refers to a migrant worker who retains his or her habitual residence in a neighbouring State to which he or she normally returns every day or at least once a week;
(b) The term "seasonal worker" refers to a migrant worker whose work by its character is dependent on seasonal conditions and is performed only during part of the year;
(c) The term "seafarer", which includes a fisherman, refers to a migrant worker employed on board a vessel registered in a State of which he or she is not a national;
(d) The term "worker on an offshore installation" refers to a migrant worker employed on an offshore installation that is under the jurisdiction of a State of which he or she is not a national;
(e) The term "itinerant worker" refers to a migrant worker who, having his or her habitual residence in one State, has to travel to another State or States for short periods, owing to the nature of his or her occupation;
(f) The term "project-tied worker" refers to a migrant worker admitted to a State of employment for a defined period to work solely on a specific project being carried out in that State by his or her employer;
(g) The term "specified-employment worker" refers to a migrant worker:
(i) Who has been sent by his or her employer for a restricted and defined period of time to a State of employment to undertake a specific assignment or duty; or
(ii) Who engages for a restricted and defined period of time in work that requires professional, commercial, technical or other highly specialized skill; or
(iii) Who, upon the request of his or her employer in the State of employment, engages for a restricted and defined period of time in work whose nature is transitory or brief; and who is required to depart from the State of employment either at the expiration of his or her authorized period of stay, or earlier if he or she no longer undertakes that specific assignment or duty or engages in that work;
(h) The term "self-employed worker" refers to a migrant worker who is engaged in a remunerated activity otherwise than under a contract of employ-

ment and who earns his or her living through this activity normally working alone or together with members of his or her family, and to any other migrant worker recognized as self-employed by applicable legislation of the State of employment or bilateral or multilateral agreements.

Article 3

The present Convention shall not apply to:

(a) Persons sent or employed by international organizations and agencies or persons sent or employed by a State outside its territory to perform official functions, whose admission and status are regulated by general international law or by specific international agreements or conventions;

(b) Persons sent or employed by a State or on its behalf outside its territory who participate in development programmes and other co-operation programmes, whose admission and status are regulated by agreement with the State of employment and who, in accordance with that agreement, are not considered migrant workers;

(c) Persons taking up residence in a State different from their State of origin as investors;

(d) Refugees and stateless persons, unless such application is provided for in the relevant national legislation of, or international instruments in force for, the State Party concerned;

(e) Students and trainees;

(f) Seafarers and workers on an offshore installation who have not been admitted to take up residence and engage in a remunerated activity in the State of employment.

Article 4

For the purposes of the present Convention the term "members of the family" refers to persons married to migrant workers or having with them a relationship that, according to applicable law, produces effects equivalent to marriage, as well as their dependent children and other dependent persons who are recognized as members of the family by applicable legislation or applicable bilateral or multilateral agreements between the States concerned.

Article 5

For the purposes of the present Convention, migrant workers and members of their families:

(a) Are considered as documented or in a regular situation if they are authorized to enter, to stay and to engage in a remunerated activity in the State of employment pursuant to the law of that State and to international agreements to which that State is a party;

(b) Are considered as non-documented or in an irregular situation if they do not comply with the conditions provided for in subparagraph (a) of the present article.

Article 6

For the purposes of the present Convention:

(a) The term "State of origin" means the State of which the person concerned is a national;

(b) The term "State of employment" means a State where the migrant worker is to be engaged, is engaged or has been engaged in a remunerated activity, as the case may be;

(c) The term "State of transit," means any State through which the person concerned passes on any journey to the State of employment or from the State of employment to the State of origin or the State of habitual residence.

PART II: NON-DISCRIMINATION WITH RESPECT TO RIGHTS

Article 7

States Parties undertake, in accordance with the international instruments concerning human rights, to respect and to ensure to all migrant workers and members of their families within their territory or subject to their jurisdiction the rights provided for in the present Convention without distinction of any kind such as to sex, race, colour, language, religion or conviction, political or other opinion, national, ethnic or social origin, nationality, age, economic position, property, marital status, birth or other status.

PART III: HUMAN RIGHTS OF ALL MIGRANT WORKERS AND MEMBERS OF THEIR FAMILIES

Article 8

1. Migrant workers and members of their families shall be free to leave any State, including their State of origin. This right shall not be subject to any restrictions except those that are provided by law, are necessary to protect national security, public order (ordre public), public health or morals or the rights and freedoms of others and are consistent with the other rights recognized in the present part of the Convention.

2. Migrant workers and members of their families shall have the right at any time to enter and remain in their State of origin.

Article 9

The right to life of migrant workers and members of their families shall be protected by law.

Article 10

No migrant worker or member of his or her family shall be subjected to torture or to cruel, inhuman or degrading treatment or punishment.

Article 11

1. No migrant worker or member of his or her family shall be held in slavery or servitude.

2. No migrant worker or member of his or her family shall be required to perform forced or compulsory labour.

3. Paragraph 2 of the present article shall not be held to preclude, in States where imprisonment with hard labour may be imposed as a punishment for a crime, the performance of hard labour in pursuance of a sentence to such punishment by a competent court.

4. For the purpose of the present article the term "forced or compulsory labour" shall not include:

(a) Any work or service not referred to in paragraph 3 of the present article normally required of a person who is under detention in consequence of a lawful order of a court or of a person during conditional release from such detention;
(b) Any service exacted in cases of emergency or clamity threatening the life or well-being of the community;
(c) Any work or service that forms part of normal civil obligations so far as it is imposed also on citizens of the State concerned.

Article 12

1. Migrant workers and members of their families shall have the right to freedom of thought, conscience and religion. This right shall include freedom to have or to adopt a religion or belief of their choice and freedom either individually or in community with others and in public or private to manifest their religion or belief in worship, observance, practice and teaching.

2. Migrant workers and members of their families shall not be subject to coercion that would impair their freedom to have or to adopt a religion or belief of their choice.

3. Freedom to manifest one's religion or belief may be subject only to such limitations as are prescribed by law and are necessary to protect public safety, order, health or morals or the fundamental rights and freedoms of others.

4. States Parties to the present Convention undertake to have respect for the liberty of parents, at least one of whom is a migrant worker, and, when applicable, legal guardians to ensure the religious and moral education of their children in conformity with their own convictions.

Article 13
1. Migrant workers and members of their families shall have the right to hold opinions without interference.

2. Migrant workers and members of their families shall have the right to freedom of expression; this right shall include freedom to seek, receive and impart information and ideas of all kinds, regardless of frontiers, either orally, in writing or in print, in the form of art or through any other media of their choice.

3. The exercise of the right provided for in paragraph 2 of the present article carries with it special duties and responsibilities. It may therefore be subject to certain restrictions, but these shall only be such as are provided by law and are necessary:

(a) For respect of the rights or reputation of others;
(b) For the protection of the national security of the States concerned or of public order (ordre public) or of public health or morals;
(c) For the purpose of preventing any propaganda for war;
(d) For the purpose of preventing any advocacy of national, racial or religious hatred that constitutes incitement to discrimination, hostility or violence.

Article 14
No migrant worker or member of his or her family shall be subjected to arbitrary or unlawful interference with his or her privacy, family, home, correspondence or other communications, or to unlawful attacks on his or her honour and reputation. Each migrant worker and member of his or her family shall have the right to the protection of the law against such interference or attacks.

Article 15
No migrant worker or member of his or her family shall be arbitrarily deprived of property, whether owned individually or in association with others. Where, under the legislation in force in the State of employment, the assets of a migrant worker or a member of his or her family are expropriated in whole or

in part, the person concerned shall have the right to fair and adequate compensation.

Article 16

1. Migrant workers and members of their families shall have the right to liberty and security of person.

2. Migrant workers and members of their families shall be entitled to effective protection by the State against violence, physical injury, threats and intimidation, whether by public officials or by private individuals, groups or institutions.

3. Any verification by law enforcement officials of the identity of migrant workers or members of their families shall be carried out in accordance with procedure established by law.

4. Migrant workers and members of their families shall not be subjected individually or collectively to arbitrary arrest or detention; they shall not be deprived o their liberty except on such grounds and in accordance with such procedures as are established by law.

5. Migrant workers and members of their families who are arrested shall be informed at the time of arrest as far as possible in a language they understand of the reasons for their arrest and they shall be promptly informed in a language they understand of any charges against them.

6. Migrant workers and members of their families who are arrested or detained on a criminal charge shall be brought promptly before a judge or other officer authorized by law to exercise judicial power and shall be entitled to trial within a reasonable time or to release. It shall not be the general rule that while awaiting trial they shall be detained in custody, but release may be subject to guarantees to appear for trial, at any other stage of the judicial proceedings and, should the occasion arise, for the execution of the judgment.

7. When a migrant worker or a member of his or her family is arrested or committed to prison or custody pending trial or is detained in any other manner:

(a) The consular or diplomatic authorities of his or her State of origin or of a State representing the interests of that State shall, if he or she so requests, be informed without delay of his or her arrest or detention and of the reasons therefore;
(b) The person concerned shall have the right to communicate with the said authorities. Any communication by the person concerned to the said authorities shall be forwarded without delay, and he or she shall also have the right to receive communications sent by the said authorities without delay;

(c) The person concerned shall be informed without delay of this right and of rights deriving from relevant treaties, if any, applicable between the States concerned, to correspond and to meet with representatives of the said authorities and to make arrangements with them for his or her legal representation.

8. Migrant workers and members of their families who are deprived of their liberty by arrest or detention shall be entitled to take proceedings before a court, in order that that court may decide without delay on the lawfulness of their detention and order their release if the detention is not lawful. When they attend such proceedings, they shall have the assistance, if necessary without cost to them, of an interpreter, if they cannot understand or speak the language used.

9. Migrant workers and members of their families who have been victims of unlawful arrest or detention shall have an enforceable right to compensation.

Article 17
1. Migrant workers and members of their families who are deprived of their liberty shall be treated with humanity and with respect for the inherent dignity of the human person and for their cultural identity.

2. Accused migrant workers and members of their families shall, save in exceptional circumstances, be separated from convicted persons and shall be subject to separate treatment appropriate to their status as unconvicted persons. Accused juvenile persons shall be separated from adults and brought as speedily as possible for adjudication.

3. Any migrant worker or member of his or her family who is detained in a State of transit or in a State of employment for violation of provisions relating to migration shall be held, in so far as practicable, separately from convicted persons or persons detained pending trial.

4. During any period of imprisonment in pursuance of a sentence imposed by a court of law, the essential aim of the treatment of a migrant worker or a member of his or her family shall be his or her reformation and social rehabilitation. Juvenile offenders shall be separated from adults and be accorded treatment appropriate to their age and legal status.

5. During detention or imprisonment, migrant workers and members of their families shall enjoy the same rights as nationals to visits by members of their families.

6. Whenever a migrant worker is deprived of his or her liberty, the competent authorities of the State concerned shall pay attention to the problems that may

be posed for members of his or her family, in particular for spouses and minor children.

7. Migrant workers and members of their families who are subjected to any form of detention or imprisonment in accordance with the law in force in the State of employment or in the State of transit shall enjoy the same rights as nationals of those States who are in the same situation.

8. If a migrant worker or a member of his or her family is detained for the purpose of verifying any infraction of provisions related to migration, he or she shall not bear any costs arising therefrom.

Article 18

1. Migrant workers and members of their families shall have the right to equality with nationals of the State concerned before the courts and tribunals. In the determination of any criminal charge against them or of their rights and obligations in a suit of law, they shall be entitled to a fair and public hearing by a competent, independent and impartial tribunal established by law.

2. Migrant workers and members of their families who are charged with a criminal offence shall have the right to be presumed innocent until proven guilty according to law.

3. In the determination of any criminal charge against them, migrant workers and members of their families shall be entitled to the following minimum guarantees:

(a) To be informed promptly and in detail in a language they understand of the nature and cause of the charge against them;
(b) To have adequate time and facilities for the preparation of their defence and to communicate with counsel of their own choosing;
(c) To be tried without undue delay;
(d) To be tried in their presence and to defend themselves in person or through legal assistance of their own choosing; to be informed, if they do not have legal assistance, of this right; and to have legal assistance assigned to them, in any case where the interests of justice so require and without payment by them in any such case if they do not have sufficient means to pay;
(e) To examine or have examined the witnesses against them and to obtain the attendance and examination of witnesses on their behalf under the same conditions as witnesses against them;
(f) To have the free assistance of an interpreter if they cannot understand or speak the language used in court;
(g) Not to be compelled to testify against themselves or to confess guilt.

4. In the case of juvenile persons, the procedure shall be such as will take account of their age and the desirability of promoting their rehabilitation.

5. Migrant workers and members of their families convicted of a crime shall have the right to their conviction and sentence being reviewed by a higher tribunal according to law.

6. When a migrant worker or a member of his or her family has, by a final decision, been convicted of a criminal offence and when subsequently his or her conviction has been reversed or he or she has been pardoned on the ground that a new or newly discovered fact shows conclusively that there has been a miscarriage of justice, the person who has suffered punishment as a result of such conviction shall be compensated according to law, unless it is proved that the non-disclosure of the unknown fact in time is wholly or partly attributable to that person.

7. No migrant worker or member of his or her family shall be liable to be tried or punished again for an offence for which he or she has already been finally convicted or acquitted in accordance with the law and penal procedure of the State concerned.

Article 19
1. No migrant worker or member of his or her family shall be held guilty of any criminal offence on account of any act or omission that did not constitute a criminal offence under national or international law at the time when the criminal offence was committed, nor shall a heavier penalty be imposed than the one that was applicable at the time when it was committed. If, subsequent to the commission of the offence, provision is made by law for the imposition of a lighter penalty, he or she shall benefit thereby.

2. Humanitarian considerations related to the status of a migrant worker, in particular with respect to his or her right of residence or work, should be taken into account in imposing a sentence for a criminal offence committed by a migrant worker or a member of his or her family.

Article 20
1. No migrant worker or member of his or her family shall be imprisoned merely on the ground of failure to fulfill a contractual obligation.

2. No migrant worker or member of his or her family shall be deprived of his or her authorization of residence or work permit or expelled merely on the ground of failure to fulfill an obligation arising out of a work contract unless fulfillment of that obligation constitutes a condition for such authorization or permit.

Article 21

It shall be unlawful for anyone, other than a public official duly authorized by law, to confiscate, destroy or attempt to destroy identity documents, documents authorizing entry to or stay, residence or establishment in the national territory or work permits. No authorized confiscation of such documents shall take place without delivery of a detailed receipt. In no case shall it be permitted to destroy the passport or equivalent document of a migrant worker or a member of his or her family.

Article 22

1. Migrant workers and members of their families shall not be subject to measures of collective expulsion. Each case of expulsion shall be examined and decided individually.

2. Migrant workers and members of their families may be expelled from the territory of a State Party only in pursuance of a decision taken by the competent authority in accordance with law.

3. The decision shall be communicated to them in a language they understand. Upon their request where not otherwise mandatory, the decision shall be communicated to them in writing and, save in exceptional circumstances on account of national security, the reasons for the decision likewise stated. The persons concerned shall be informed of these rights before or at the latest at the time the decision is rendered.

4. Except where a final decision is pronounced by a judicial authority, the person concerned shall have the right to submit the reason he or she should not be expelled and to have his or her case reviewed by the competent authority, unless compelling reasons of national security require otherwise. Pending such review, the person concerned shall have the right to seek a stay of the decision of expulsion.

5. If a decision of expulsion that has already been executed is subsequently annulled, the person concerned shall have the right to seek compensation according to law and the earlier decision shall not be used to prevent him or her from re-entering the State concerned.

6. In case of expulsion, the person concerned shall have a reasonable opportunity before or after departure to settle any claims for wages and other entitlements due to him or her and any pending liabilities.

7. Without prejudice to the execution of a decision of expulsion, a migrant worker or a member of his or her family who is subject to such a decision may seek entry into a State other than his or her State of origin.

8. In case of expulsion of a migrant worker or a member of his or her family the costs of expulsion shall not be borne by him or her. The person concerned may be required to pay his or her own travel costs.

9. Expulsion from the State of employment shall not in itself prejudice any rights of a migrant worker or a member of his or her family acquired in accordance with the law of that State, including the right to receive wages and other entitlements due to him or her.

Article 23
Migrant workers and members of their families shall have the right to have recourse to the protection and assistance of the consular or diplomatic authorities of their State of origin or of a State representing the interests of that State whenever the rights recognized in the present Convention are impaired. In particular, in case of expulsion, the person concerned shall be informed of this right without delay and the authorities of the expelling State shall facilitate the exercise of such right.

Article 24
Every migrant worker and every member of his or her family shall have the right to recognition everywhere as a person before the law.

Article 25
1. Migrant workers shall enjoy treatment not less favourable than that which applies to nationals of the State of employment in respect of remuneration and:

(a) Other conditions of work, that is to say, overtime, hours of work, weekly rest, holidays with pay, safety, health, termination of the employment relationship and any other conditions of work which, according to national law and practice, are covered by these terms;
(b) Other terms of employment, that is to say, minimum age of employment, restriction on home work and any other matters which, according to national law and practice, are considered a term of employment.

2. It shall not be lawful to derogate in private contracts of employment from the principle of equality of treatment referred to in paragraph 1 of the present article.

3. States Parties shall take all appropriate measures to ensure that migrant workers are not deprived of any rights derived from this principle by reason of any irregularity in their stay or employment. In particular, employers shall

not be relieved of any legal or contractual obligations, nor shall their obligations be limited in any manner by reason of such irregularity.

Article 26
1. States Parties recognize the right of migrant workers and members of their families:

(a) To take part in meetings and activities of trade unions and of any other associations established in accordance with law, with a view to protecting their economic, social, cultural and other interests, subject only to the rules of the organization concerned;
(b) To join freely any trade union and any such association as aforesaid, subject only to the rules of the organization concerned;
(c) To seek the aid and assistance of any trade union and of any such association as aforesaid.

2. No restrictions may be placed on the exercise of these rights other than those that are prescribed by law and which are necessary in a democratic society in the interests of national security, public order (ordre public) or the protection of the rights and freedoms of others.

Article 27
1. With respect to social security, migrant workers and members of their families shall enjoy in the State of employment the same treatment granted to nationals in so far as they fulfill the requirements provided for by the applicable legislation of that State and the applicable bilateral and multilateral treaties. The competent authorities of the State of origin and the State of employment can at any time establish the necessary arrangements to determine the modalities of application of this norm.

2. Where the applicable legislation does not allow migrant workers and members of their families a benefit, the States concerned shall examine the possibility of reimbursing interested persons the amount of contributions made by them with respect to that benefit on the basis of the treatment granted to nationals who are in similar circumstances.

Article 28
Migrant workers and members of their families shall have the right to receive any medical care that is urgently required for the preservation of their life or the avoidance of irreparable harm to their health on the basis of equality of treatment with nationals of the State concerned. Such emergency medical care shall not be refused them by reason of any irregularity with regard to stay or employment.

Article 29
Each child of a migrant worker shall have the right to a name, to registration of birth and to a nationality.

Article 30
Each child of a migrant worker shall have the basic right of access to education on the basis of equality of treatment with nationals of the State concerned. Access to public pre-school educational institutions or schools shall not be refused or limited by reason of the irregular situation with respect to stay or employment of either parent or by reason of the irregularity of the child's stay in the State of employment.

Article 31
1. States Parties shall ensure respect for the cultural identity of migrant workers and members of their families and shall not prevent them from maintaining their cultural links with their State of origin.
2. States Parties may take appropriate measures to assist and encourage efforts in this respect.

Article 32
Upon the termination of their stay in the State of employment, migrant workers and members of their families shall have the right to transfer their earnings and savings and, in accordance with the applicable legislation of the States concerned, their personal effects and belongings.

Article 33
1. Migrant workers and members of their families shall have the right to be informed by the State of origin, the State of employment or the State of transit as the case may be concerning:

(a) Their rights arising out of the present Convention;
(b) The conditions of their admission, their rights and obligations under the law and practice of the State concerned and such other matters as will enable them to comply with administrative or other formalities in that State.

2. States Parties shall take all measures they deem appropriate to disseminate the said information or to ensure that it is provided by employers, trade unions or other appropriate bodies or institutions. As appropriate, they shall co-operate with other States concerned.

3. Such adequate information shall be provided upon request to migrant workers and members of their families, free of charge, and, as far as possible, in a language they are able to understand.

Article 34
Nothing in the present part of the Convention shall have the effect of relieving migrant workers and the members of their families from either the obligation to comply with the laws and regulations of any State of transit and the State of employment or the obligation to respect the cultural identity of the inhabitants of such States.

Article 35
Nothing in the present part of the Convention shall be interpreted as implying the regularization of the situation of migrant workers or members of their families who are non-documented or in an irregular situation or any right to such regularization of their situation, nor shall it prejudice the measures intended to ensure sound and equitable-conditions for international migration as provided in part VI of the present Convention.

PART IV: OTHER RIGHTS OF MIGRANT WORKERS AND MEMBERS OF THEIR FAMILIES WHO ARE DOCUMENTED OR IN A REGULAR SITUATION

Article 36
Migrant workers and members of their families who are documented or in a regular situation in the State of employment shall enjoy the rights set forth in the present part of the Convention in addition to those set forth in part III.

Article 37
Before their departure, or at the latest at the time of their admission to the State of employment, migrant workers and members of their families shall have the right to be fully informed by the State of origin or the State of employment, as appropriate, of all conditions applicable to their admission and particularly those concerning their stay and the remunerated activities in which they may engage as well as of the requirements they must satisfy in the State of employment and the authority to which they must address themselves for any modification of those conditions.

Article 38
1. States of employment shall make every effort to authorize migrant workers and members of the families to be temporarily absent without effect upon their authorization to stay or to work, as the case may be. In doing so, States of employment shall take into account the special needs and obligations of

migrant workers and members of their families, in particular in their States of origin.

2. Migrant workers and members of their families shall have the right to be fully informed of the terms on which such temporary absences are authorized.

Article 39

1. Migrant workers and members of their families shall have the right to liberty of movement in the territory of the State of employment and freedom to choose their residence there.

2. The rights mentioned in paragraph 1 of the present article shall not be subject to any restrictions except those that are provided by law, are necessary to protect national security, public order (ordre public), public health or morals, or the rights and freedoms of others and are consistent with the other rights recognized in the present Convention.

Article 40

1. Migrant workers and members of their families shall have the right to form associations and trade unions in the State of employment for the promotion and protection of their economic, social, cultural and other interests.

2. No restrictions may be placed on the exercise of this right other than those that are prescribed by law and are necessary in a democratic society in the interests of national security, public order (ordre public) or the protection of the rights and freedoms of others.

Article 41

1. Migrant workers and members of their families shall have the right to participate in public affairs of their State of origin and to vote and to be elected at elections of that State, in accordance with its legislation.

2. The States concerned shall, as appropriate and in accordance with their legislation, facilitate the exercise of these rights.

Article 42

1. States Parties shall consider the establishment of procedures or institutions through which account may be taken, both in States of origin and in States of employment, of special needs, aspirations and obligations of migrant workers and members of their families and shall envisage, as appropriate, the possibility for migrant workers and members of their families to have their freely chosen representatives in those institutions.

2. States of employment shall facilitate, in accordance with their national legislation, the consultation or participation of migrant workers and members of their families in decisions concerning the life and administration of local communities.

3. Migrant workers may enjoy political rights in the State of employment if that State, in the exercise of its sovereignty, grants them such rights.

Article 43

1. Migrant workers shall enjoy equality of treatment with nationals of the State of employment in relation to:

(a) Access to educational institutions and services subject to the admission requirements and other regulations of the institutions and services concerned;
(b) Access to vocational guidance and placement services;
(c) Access to vocational training and retraining facilities and institutions;
(d) Access to housing, including social housing schemes, and protection against exploitation in respect of rents;
(e) Access to social and health services, provided that the requirements for participation in the respective schemes are met;
(f) Access to co-operatives and self-managed enterprises, which shall not imply a change of their migration status and shall be subject to the rules and regulations of the bodies concerned;
(g) Access to and participation in cultural life.

2. States Parties shall promote conditions to ensure effective equality of treatment to enable migrant workers to enjoy the rights mentioned in paragraph 1 of the present article whenever the terms of their stay, as authorized by the State of employment, meet the appropriate requirements.

3. States of employment shall not prevent an employer of migrant workers from establishing housing or social or cultural facilities for them. Subject to article 70 of the present Convention, a State of employment may make the establishment of such facilities subject to the requirements generally applied in that State concerning their installation.

Article 44

1. States Parties, recognizing that the family is the natural and fundamental group unit of society and is entitled to protection by society and the State, shall take appropriate measures to ensure the protection of the unity of the families of migrant workers.

2. States Parties shall take measures that they deem appropriate and that fall within their competence to facilitate the reunification of migrant workers with their spouses or persons who have with the migrant worker a relationship that, according to applicable law, produces effects equivalent to marriage, as well as with their minor dependent unmarried children.

3. States of employment, on humanitarian grounds, shall favourably consider granting equal treatment, as set forth in paragraph 2 of the present article, to other family members of migrant workers.

Article 45
1. Members of the families of migrant workers shall, in the State of employment, enjoy equality of treatment with nationals of that State in relation to:

(a) Access to educational institutions and services, subject to the admission requirements and other regulations of the institutions and services concerned;
(b) Access to vocational guidance and training institutions and services, provided that requirements for participation are met;
(c) Access to social and health services, provided that requirements for participation in the respective schemes are met;
(d) Access to and participation in cultural life.

2. States of employment shall pursue a policy, where appropriate in collaboration with the States of origin, aimed at facilitating the integration of children of migrant workers in the local school system, particularly in respect of teaching them the local language.

3. States of employment shall endeavour to facilitate for the children of migrant workers the teaching of their mother tongue and culture and, in this regard, States of origin shall collaborate whenever appropriate.

4. States of employment may provide special schemes of education in the mother tongue of children of migrant workers, if necessary in collaboration with the States of origin.

Article 46
Migrant workers and members of their families shall, subject to the applicable legislation of the States concerned, as well as relevant international agreements and the obligations of the States concerned arising out of their participation in customs unions, enjoy exemption from import and export duties and taxes in respect of their personal and household effects as well as the equipment necessary to engage in the remunerated activity for which they were admitted to the State of employment:

(a) Upon departure from the State of origin or State of habitual residence;
(b) Upon initial admission to the State of employment;
(c) Upon final departure from the State of employment;
(d) Upon final return to the State of origin or State of habitual residence.

Article 47

1. Migrant workers shall have the right to transfer their earnings and savings, in particular those funds necessary for the support of their families, from the State of employment to their State of origin or any other State. Such transfers shall be made in conformity with procedures established by applicable legislation of the State concerned and in conformity with applicable international agreements.

2. States concerned shall take appropriate measures to facilitate such transfers.

Article 48

1. Without prejudice to applicable double taxation agreements, migrant workers and members of their families shall, in the matter of earnings in the State of employment:

(a) Not be liable to taxes, duties or charges of any description higher or more onerous than those imposed on nationals in similar circumstances;
(b) Be entitled to deductions or exemptions from taxes of any description and to any tax allowances applicable to nationals in similar circumstances, including tax allowances for dependent members of their families.

2. States Parties shall endeavour to adopt appropriate measures to avoid double taxation of the earnings and savings of migrant workers and members of their families.

Article 49

1. Where separate authorizations to reside and to engage in employment are required by national legislation, the States of employment shall issue to migrant workers authorization of residence for at least the same period of time as their authorization to engage in remunerated activity.

2. Migrant workers who in the State of employment are allowed freely to choose their remunerated activity shall neither be regarded as in an irregular situation nor shall they lose their authorization of residence by the mere fact of the termination of their remunerated activity prior to the expiration of their work permits or similar authorizations.

3. In order to allow migrant workers referred to in paragraph 2 of the present article sufficient time to find alternative remunerated activities, the authori-

zation of residence shall not be withdrawn at least for a period corresponding to that during which they may be entitled to unemployment benefits.

Article 50
1. In the case of death of a migrant worker or dissolution of marriage, the State of employment shall favourably consider granting family members of that migrant worker residing in that State on the basis of family reunion an authorization to stay; the State of employment shall take into account the length of time they have already resided in that State.

2. Members of the family to whom such authorization is not granted shall be allowed before departure a reasonable period of time in order to enable them to settle their affairs in the State of employment.

3. The provisions of paragraphs 1 and 2 of the present article may not be interpreted as adversely affecting any right to stay and work otherwise granted to such family members by the legislation of the State of employment or by bilateral and multilateral treaties applicable to that State.

Article 51
Migrant workers who in the State of employment are not permitted freely to choose their remunerated activity shall neither be regarded as in an irregular situation nor shall they lose their authorization of residence by the mere fact of the termination of their remunerated activity prior to the expiration of their work permit, except where the authorization of residence is expressly dependent upon the specific remunerated activity for which they were admitted. Such migrant workers shall have the right to seek alternative employment, participation in public work schemes and retraining during the remaining period of their authorization to work, subject to such conditions and limitations as are specified in the authorization to work.

Article 52
1. Migrant workers in the State of employment shall have the right freely to choose their remunerated activity, subject to the following restrictions or conditions.

2. For any migrant worker a State of employment may:

(a) Restrict access to limited categories of employment, functions, services or activities where this is necessary in the interests of this State and provided for by national legislation;
(b) Restrict free choice of remunerated activity in accordance with its legislation concerning recognition of occupational qualifications acquired outside

its territory. However, States Parties concerned shall endeavour to provide for recognition of such qualifications.

3. For migrant workers whose permission to work is limited in time, a State of employment may also:

(a) Make the right freely to choose their remunerated activities subject to the condition that the migrant worker has resided lawfully in its territory for the purpose of remunerated activity for a period of time prescribed in its national legislation that should not exceed two years;   •
(b) Limit access by a migrant worker to remunerated activities in pursuance of a policy of granting priority to its nationals or to persons who are assimilated to them for these purposes by virtue of legislation or bilateral or multilateral agreements. Any such limitation shall cease to apply to a migrant worker who has resided lawfully in its territory for the purpose of remunerated activity for a period of time prescribed in its national legislation that should not exceed five years.

4. States of employment shall prescribe the conditions under which a migrant worker who has been admitted to take up employment may be authorized to engage in work on his or her own account. Account shall be taken of the period during which the worker has already been lawfully in the State of employment.

Article 53
1. Members of a migrant worker's family who have themselves an authorization of residence or admission that is without limit of time or is automatically renewable shall be permitted freely to choose their remunerated activity under the same conditions as are applicable to the said migrant worker in accordance with article 52 of the present Convention.

2. With respect to members of a migrant worker's family who are not permitted freely to choose their remunerated activity, States Parties shall consider favourably granting them priority in obtaining permission to engage in a remunerated activity over other workers who seek admission to the State of employment, subject to applicable bilateral and multilateral agreements.

Article 54
1. Without prejudice to the terms of their authorization of residence or their permission to work and the rights provided for in articles 25 and 27 of the present Convention, migrant workers shall enjoy equality of treatment with nationals of the State of employment in respect of:

(a) Protection against dismissal;
(b) Unemployment benefits;

(c) Access to public work schemes intended to combat unemployment;

(d) Access to alternative employment in the event of loss of work or termination of other remunerated activity, subject to article 52 of the present Convention.

2. If a migrant worker claims that the terms of his or her work contract have been violated by his or her employer, he or she shall have the right to address his or her case to the competent authorities of the State of employment, on terms provided for in article 18, paragraph 1, of the present Convention.

Article 55

Migrant workers who have been granted permission to engage in a remunerated activity, subject to the conditions attached to such permission, shall be entitled to equality of treatment with nationals of the State of employment in the exercise of that remunerated activity.

Article 56

1. Migrant workers and members of their families referred to in the present part of the Convention may not be expelled from a State of employment, except for reasons defined in the national legislation of that State, and subject to the safeguards established in part III.

2. Expulsion shall not be resorted to for the purpose of depriving a migrant worker or a member of his or her family of the rights arising out of the authorization of residence and the work permit.

3. In considering whether to expel a migrant worker or a member of his or her family, account should be taken of humanitarian considerations and of the length of time that the person concerned has already resided in the State of employment.

PART V: PROVISIONS APPLICABLE TO PARTICULAR CATEGORIES OF MIGRANT WORKERS AND OF THEIR FAMILIES

Article 57

The particular categories of migrant workers and members of their families specified in the present part of the Convention who are documented or in a regular situation shall enjoy the rights set forth in part m and, except as modified below, the rights set forth in part IV.

Article 58

1. Frontier workers, as defined in article 2, paragraph 2 (a), of the present Convention, shall be entitled to the rights provided for in part IV that can be applied to them by reason of their presence and work in the territory of the

State of employment, taking into account that they do not have their habitual residence in that State.

2. States of employment shall consider favourably granting frontier workers the right freely to choose their remunerated activity after a specified period of time. The granting of that right shall not affect their status as frontier workers.

Article 59

1. Seasonal workers, as defined in article 2, paragraph 2 (b), of the present Convention, shall be entitled to the rights provided for in part IV that can be applied to them by reason of their presence and work in the territory of the State of employment and that are compatible with their status in that State as seasonal workers, taking into account the fact that they are present in that State for only part of the year.

2. The State of employment shall, subject to paragraph 1 of the present article, consider granting seasonal workers who have been employed in its territory for a significant period of time the possibility of taking up other remunerated activities and giving them priority over other workers who seek admission to that State, subject to applicable bilateral and multilateral agreements.

Article 60

Itinerant workers, as defined in article 2, paragraph 2 (e), of the present Convention, shall be entitled to the rights provided for in part IV that can be granted to them by reason of their presence and work in the territory of the State of employment and that are compatible with their status as itinerant workers in that State.

Article 61

1. Project-tied workers, as defined in article 2, paragraph 2 (f), of the present Convention, and members of their families shall be entitled to the rights provided for in part IV except the provisions of article 43, paragraphs 1 (b) and (c), article 43, paragraph 1 (d), as it pertains to social housing schemes, article 45, paragraph 1 (b), and articles 52 to 55.

2. If a project-tied worker claims that the terms of his or her work contract have been violated by his or her employer, he or she shall have the right to address his or her case to the competent authorities of the State which has jurisdiction over that employer, on terms provided for in article 18, paragraph 1, of the present Convention.

3. Subject to bilateral or multilateral agreements in force for them, the States Parties concerned shall endeavour to enable project-tied workers to remain

adequately protected by the social security systems of their States of origin or habitual residence during their engagement in the project. States Parties concerned shall take appropriate measures with the aim of avoiding any denial of rights or duplication of payments in this respect.

4. Without prejudice to the provisions of article 47 of the present Convention and to relevant bilateral or multilateral agreements, States Parties concerned shall permit payment of the earnings of project-tied workers in their State of origin or habitual residence.

Article 62
1. Specified-employment workers as defined in article 2, paragraph 2 (g), of the present Convention, shall be entitled to the rights provided for in part IV, except the provisions of article 43, paragraphs 1 (b) and (c), article 43, paragraph 1 (d), as it pertains to social housing schemes, article 52, and article 54, paragraph 1 (d).

2. Members of the families of specified-employment workers shall be entitled to the rights relating to family members of migrant workers provided for in part IV of the present Convention, except the provisions of article 53.

Article 63
1. Self-employed workers, as defined in article 2, paragraph 2 (h), of the present Convention, shall be entitled to the rights provided for in part IV with the exception of those rights which are exclusively applicable to workers having a contract of employment.

2. Without prejudice to articles 52 and 79 of the present Convention, the termination of the economic activity of the self-employed workers shall not in itself imply the withdrawal of the authorization for them or for the members of their families to stay or to engage in a remunerated activity in the State of employment except where the authorization of residence is expressly dependent upon the specific remunerated activity for which they were admitted.

PART VI: PROMOTION OF SOUND, EQUITABLE, HUMANE AND LAWFUL CONDITIONS CONNECTION WITH INTERNATIONAL MIGRATION OF WORKERS AND MEMBERS OF THEIR FAMILIES

Article 64
1. Without prejudice to article 79 of the present Convention, the States Parties concerned shall as appropriate consult and co-operate with a view to promoting sound, equitable and humane conditions in connection with international migration of workers and members of their families.

2. In this respect, due regard shall be paid not only to labour needs and resources, but also to the social, economic, cultural and other needs of migrant workers and members of their families involved, as well as to the consequences of such migration for the communities concerned.

Article 65

1. States Parties shall maintain appropriate services to deal with questions concerning international migration of workers and members of their families. Their functions shall include, *inter alia*:

(a) The formulation and implementation of policies regarding such migration;
(b) An exchange of information. consultation and co-operation with the competent authorities of other States Parties involved in such migration;
(c) The provision of appropriate information, particularly to employers, workers and their organizations on policies, laws and regulations relating to migration and employment, on agreements concluded with other States concerning migration and on other relevant matters;
(d) The provision of information and appropriate assistance to migrant workers and members of their families regarding requisite authorizations and formalities and arrangements for departure, travel, arrival, stay, remunerated activities, exit and return, as well as on conditions of work and life in the State of employment and on customs, currency, tax and other relevant laws and regulations.

2. States Parties shall facilitate as appropriate the provision of adequate consular and other services that are necessary to meet the social, cultural and other needs of migrant workers and members of their families.

Article 66

1. Subject to paragraph 2 of the present article, the right to undertake operations with a view to the recruitment of workers for employment in another State shall be restricted to:

(a) Public services or bodies of the State in which such operations take place;
(b) Public services or bodies of the State of employment on the basis of agreement between the States concerned;
(c) A body established by virtue of a bilateral or multilateral agreement.

2. Subject to any authorization, approval and supervision by the public authorities of the States Parties concerned as may be established pursuant to the legislation and practice of those States, agencies, prospective employers or persons acting on their behalf may also be permitted to undertake the said operations.

Article 67

1. States Parties concerned shall co-operate as appropriate in the adoption of measures regarding the orderly return of migrant workers and members of their families to the State of origin when they decide to return or their authorization of residence or employment expires or when they are in the State of employment in an irregular situation.

2. Concerning migrant workers and members of their families in a regular situation, States Parties concerned shall co-operate as appropriate, on terms agreed upon by those States, with a view to promoting adequate economic conditions for their resettlement and to facilitating their durable social and cultural reintegration in the State of origin.

Article 68

1. States Parties, including States of transit, shall collaborate with a view to preventing and eliminating illegal or clandestine movements and employment of migrant workers in an irregular situation. The measures to be taken to this end within the jurisdiction of each State concerned shall include:

(a) Appropriate measures against the dissemination of misleading information relating to emigration and immigration;

(b) Measures to detect and eradicate illegal or clandestine movements of migrant workers and members of their families and to impose effective sanctions on persons, groups or entities which organize, operate or assist in organizing or operating such movements;

(c) Measures to impose effective sanctions on persons, groups or entities which use violence, threats or intimidation against migrant workers or members of their families in an irregular situation.

2. States of employment shall take all adequate and effective measures to eliminate employment in their territory of migrant workers in an irregular situation, including, whenever appropriate, sanctions on employers of such workers. The rights of migrant workers vis-à-vis their employer arising from employment shall not be impaired by these measures.

Article 69

1. States Parties shall, when there are migrant workers and members of their families within their territory in an irregular situation, take appropriate measures to ensure that such a situation does not persist.

2. Whenever States Parties concerned consider the possibility of regularizing the situation of such persons in accordance with applicable national legislation and bilateral or multilateral agreements, appropriate account shall be

taken of the circumstances of their entry, the duration of their stay in the States of employment and other relevant considerations, in particular those relating to their family situation.

Article 70

States Parties shall take measures not less favourable than those applied to nationals to ensure that working and living conditions of migrant workers and members of their families in a regular situation are in keeping with the standards of fitness, safety, health and principles of human dignity.

Article 71

1. States Parties shall facilitate, whenever necessary, the repatriation to the State of origin of the bodies of deceased migrant workers or members of their families.

2. As regards compensation matters relating to the death of a migrant worker or a member of his or her family, States Parties shall, as appropriate, provide assistance to the persons concerned with a view to the prompt settlement of such matters. Settlement of these matters shall be carried out on the basis of applicable national law in accordance with the provisions of the present Convention and any relevant bilateral or multilateral agreements.

PART VII: APPLICATION OF THE CONVENTION

Article 72

1. (a) For the purpose of reviewing the application of the present Convention, there shall be established a Committee on the Protection of the Rights of All Migrant Workers and Members of Their Families (hereinafter referred to as "the Committee");
(b) The Committee shall consist, at the time of entry into force of the present Convention, of ten and, after the entry into force of the Convention for the forty-first State Party, of fourteen experts of high moral standing, impartiality and recognized competence in the field covered by the Convention.

2. (a) Members of the Committee shall be elected by secret ballot by the States Parties from a list of persons nominated by the States Parties, due consideration being given to equitable geographical distribution, including both States of origin and States of employment, and to the representation of the principal legal system. Each State Party may nominate one person from among its own nationals;
(b) Members shall be elected and shall serve in their personal capacity.

3. The initial election shall be held no later than six months after the date of the entry into force of the present Convention and subsequent elections every second year. At least four months before the date of each election, the Secretary-General of the United Nations shall address a letter to all States Parties inviting them to submit their nominations within two months. The Secretary-General shall prepare a list in alphabetical order of all persons thus nominated, indicating the States Parties that have nominated them, and shall submit it to the States Parties not later than one month before the date of the corresponding election, together with the curricula vitae of the persons thus nominated.

4. Elections of members of the Committee shall be held at a meeting of States Parties convened by the Secretary-General at United Nations Headquarters. At that meeting, for which two thirds of the States Parties shall constitute a quorum, the persons elected to the Committee shall be those nominees who obtain the largest number of votes and an absolute majority of the votes of the States Parties present and voting.

5. (a) The members of the Committee shall serve for a term of four years. However, the terms of five of the members elected in the first election shall expire at the end of two years; immediately after the first election, the names of these five members shall be chosen by lot by the Chairman of the meeting of States Parties;
(b) The election of the four additional members of the Committee shall be held in accordance with the provisions of paragraphs 2, 3 and 4 of the present article, following the entry into force of the Convention for the forty-first State Party. The term of two of the additional members elected on this occasion shall expire at the end of two years; the names of these members shall be chosen by lot by the Chairman of the meeting of States Parties;
(c) The members of the Committee shall be eligible for re-election if renominated.

6. If a member of the Committee dies or resigns or declares that for any other cause he or she can no longer perform the duties of the Committee, the State Party that nominated the expert shall appoint another expert from among its own nationals for the remaining part of the term. The new appointment is subject to the approval of the Committee.

7. The Secretary-General of the United Nations shall provide the necessary staff and facilities for the effective performance of the functions of the Committee.

8. The members of the Committee shall receive emoluments from United Nations resources on such terms and conditions as the General Assembly may decide.

9. The members of the Committee shall be entitled to the facilities, privileges and immunities of experts on mission for the United Nations as laid down in the relevant sections of the Convention on the Privileges and Immunities of the United Nations.

Article 73
1. States Parties undertake to submit to the Secretary-General of the United Nations for consideration by the Committee a report on the legislative, judicial, administrative and other measures they have taken to give effect to the provisions of the present Convention:

(a) Within one year after the entry into force of the Convention for the State Party concerned;
(b) Thereafter every five years and whenever the Committee so requests.

2. Reports prepared under the present article shall also indicate factors and difficulties, if any, affecting the implementation of the Convention and shall include information on the characteristics of migration flows in which the State Party concerned is involved.

3. The Committee shall decide any further guidelines applicable to the content of the reports.

4. States Parties shall make their reports widely available to the public in their own countries.

Article 74
1. The Committee shall examine the reports submitted by each State Party and shall transmit such comments as it may consider appropriate to the State Party concerned. This State Party may submit to the Committee observations on any comment made by the Committee in accordance with the present article. The Committee may request supplementary information from States Parties when considering these reports.

2. The Secretary-General of the United Nations shall, in due time before the opening of each regular session of the Committee, transmit to the Director-General of the International Labour Office copies of the reports submitted by States Parties concerned and information relevant to the consideration of these reports, in order to enable the Office to assist the Committee with the expertise the Office may provide regarding those matters dealt with by the pres-

ent Convention that fall within the sphere of competence of the International Labour Organisation. The Committee shall consider in its deliberations such comments and materials as the Office may provide.

3. The Secretary-General of the United Nations may also, after consultation with the Committee, transmit to other specialized agencies as well as to intergovernmental organizations, copies of such parts of these reports as may fall within their competence.

4. The Committee may invite the specialized agencies and organs of the United Nations, as well as intergovernmental organizations and other concerned bodies to submit, for consideration by the Committee, written information on such matters dealt with in the present Convention as fall within the scope of their activities.

5. The International Labour Office shall be invited by the Committee to appoint representatives to participate, in a consultative capacity, in the meetings of the Committee.

6. The Committee may invite representatives of other specialized agencies and organs of the United Nations, as well as of intergovernmental organizations, to be present and to be heard in its meetings whenever matters falling within their field of competence are considered.

7. The Committee shall present an annual report to the General Assembly of the United Nations on the implementation of the present Convention, containing its own considerations and recommendations, based, in particular, on the examination of the reports and any observations presented by States Parties.

8. The Secretary-General of the United Nations shall transmit the annual reports of the Committee to the States Parties to the present Convention, the Economic and Social Council, the Commission on Human Rights of the United Nations, the Director-General of the International Labour Office and other relevant organizations.

Article 75

1. The Committee shall adopt its own rules of procedure.

2. The Committee shall elect its officers for a term of two years.

3. The Committee shall normally meet annually.

4. The meetings of the Committee shall normally be held at United Nations Headquarters.

Article 76

1. A State Party to the present Convention may at any time declare under this article that it recognizes the competence of the Committee to receive and consider communications to the effect that a State Party claims that another State Party is not fulfilling its obligations under the present Convention. Communications under this article may be received and considered only if submitted by a State Party that has made a declaration recognizing in regard to itself the competence of the Committee. No communication shall be received by the Committee if it concerns a State Party which has not made such a declaration. Communications received under this article shall be dealt with in accordance with the following procedure:

(a) If a State Party to the present Convention considers that another State Party is not fulfilling its obligations under the present Convention, it may, by written communication, bring the matter to the attention of that State Party. The State Party may also inform the Committee of the matter. Within three months after the receipt of the communication the receiving State shall afford the State that sent the communication an explanation, or any other statement in writing clarifying the matter which should include, to the extent possible and pertinent, reference to domestic procedures and remedies taken, pending or available in the matter;

(b) If the matter is not adjusted to the satisfaction of both States Parties concerned within six months after the receipt by the receiving State of the initial communication, either State shall have the right to refer the matter to the Committee, by notice given to the Committee and to the other State;

(c) The Committee shall deal with a matter referred to it only after it has ascertained that all available domestic remedies have been invoked and exhausted in the matter, in conformity with the generally recognized principles of international law. This shall not be the rule where, in the view of the Committee, the application of the remedies is unreasonably prolonged;

(d) Subject to the provisions of subparagraph (c) of the present paragraph, the Committee shall make available its good offices to the States Parties concerned with a view to a friendly solution of the matter on the basis of the respect for the obligations set forth in the present Convention;

(e) The Committee shall hold closed meetings when examining communications under the present article;

(f) In any matter referred to it in accordance with subparagraph (b) of the present paragraph, the Committee may call upon the States Parties concerned, referred to in subparagraph (b), to supply any relevant information;

(g) The States Parties concerned, referred to in subparagraph (b) of the present paragraph, shall have the right to be represented when the matter is being considered by the Committee and to make submissions orally and/or in writing;

(h) The Committee shall, within twelve months after the date of receipt of notice under subparagraph (b) of the present paragraph, submit a report, as follows:

(i) If a solution within the terms of subparagraph (d) of the present paragraph is reached, the Committee shall confine its report to a brief statement of the facts and of the solution reached;

(ii) If a solution within the terms of subparagraph (d) is not reached, the Committee shall, in its report, set forth the relevant facts concerning the issue between the States Parties concerned. The written submissions and record of the oral submissions made by the States Parties concerned shall be attached to the report. The Committee may also communicate only to the States Parties concerned any views that it may consider relevant to the issue between them.

In every matter, the report shall be communicated to the States Parties concerned.

2. The provisions of the present article shall come into force when ten States Parties to the present Convention have made a declaration under paragraph 1 of the present article. Such declarations shall be deposited by the States Parties with the Secretary-General of the United Nations, who shall transmit copies thereof to the other States Parties. A declaration may be withdrawn at any time by notification to the Secretary-General. Such a withdrawal shall not prejudice the consideration of any matter that is the subject of a communication already transmitted under the present article; no further communication by any State Party shall be received under the present article after the notification of withdrawal of the declaration has been received by the Secretary-General, unless the State Party concerned has made a new declaration.

Article 77

1. A State Party to the present Convention may at any time declare under the present article that it recognizes the competence of the Committee to receive and consider communications from or on behalf of individuals subject to its jurisdiction who claim that their individual rights as established by the present Convention have been violated by that State Party. No communication shall be received by the Committee if it concerns a State Party that has not made such a declaration.

2. The Committee shall consider inadmissible any communication under the present article which is anonymous or which it considers to be an abuse of the

right of submission of such communications or to be incompatible with the provisions of the present Convention.

3. The Committee shall not consider any communication from an individual under the present article unless it has ascertained that:

(a) The same matter has not been, and is not being, examined under another procedure of international investigation or settlement;
(b) The individual has exhausted all available domestic remedies; this shall not be the rule where, in the view of the Committee, the application of the remedies is unreasonably prolonged or is unlikely to bring effective relief to that individual.

4. Subject to the provisions of paragraph 2 of the present article, the Committee shall bring any communications submitted to it under this article to the attention of the State Party to the present Convention that has made a declaration under paragraph 1 and is alleged to be violating any provisions of the Convention. Within six months, the receiving State shall submit to the Committee written explanations or statements clarifying the matter and the remedy, if any, that may have been taken by that State.

5. The Committee shall consider communications received under the present article in the light of all information made available to it by or on behalf of the individual and by the State Party concerned.

6. The Committee shall hold closed meetings when examining communications under the present article.

7. The Committee shall forward its views to the State Party concerned and to the individual.

8. The provisions of the present article shall come into force when ten States Parties to the present Convention have made declarations under paragraph 1 of the present article. Such declarations shall be deposited by the States Parties with the Secretary-General of the United Nations, who shall transmit copies thereof to the other States Parties. A declaration may be withdrawn at any time by notification to the Secretary-General. Such a withdrawal shall not prejudice the consideration of any matter that is the subject of a communication already transmitted under the present article; no further communication by or on behalf of an individual shall be received under the present article after the notification of withdrawal of the declaration has been received by the Secretary-General, unless the State Party has made a new declaration.

Article 78

The provisions of article 76 of the present Convention shall be applied without prejudice to any procedures for settling disputes or complaints in the field covered by the present Convention laid down in the constituent instruments of, or in conventions adopted by, the United Nations and the specialized agencies and shall not prevent the States Parties from having recourse to any procedures for settling a dispute in accordance with international agreements in force between them.

PART VIII: GENERAL PROVISIONS

Article 79

Nothing in the present Convention shall affect the right of each State Party to establish the criteria governing admission of migrant workers and members of their families. Concerning other matters related to their legal situation and treatment as migrant workers and members of their families, States Parties shall be subject to the limitations set forth in the present Convention.

Article 80

Nothing in the present Convention shall be interpreted as impairing the provisions of the Charter of the United Nations and of the constitutions of the specialized agencies which define the respective responsibilities of the various organs of the United Nations and of the specialized agencies in regard to the matters dealt with in the present Convention.

Article 81

1. Nothing in the present Convention shall affect more favourable rights or freedoms granted to migrant workers and members of their families by virtue of:

(a) The law or practice of a State Party; or
(b) Any bilateral or multilateral treaty in force for the State Party concerned.

2. Nothing in the present Convention may be interpreted as implying for any State, group or person any right to engage in any activity or perform any act that would impair any of the rights and freedoms as set forth in the present Convention.

Article 82

The rights of migrant workers and members of their families provided for in the present Convention may not be renounced. It shall not be permissible to exert any form of pressure upon migrant workers and members of their families with a view to their relinquishing or foregoing any of the said rights. It shall not be possible to derogate by contract from rights recognized in the present Convention. States Parties shall take appropriate measures to ensure that these principles are respected.

Article 83
Each State Party to the present Convention undertakes:

(a) To ensure that any person whose rights or freedoms as herein recognized are violated shall have an effective remedy, notwithstanding that the violation has been committed by persons acting in an official capacity;

(b) To ensure that any persons seeking such a remedy shall have his or her claim reviewed and decided by competent judicial, administrative or legislative authorities, or by any other competent authority provided for by the legal system of the State, and to develop the possibilities of judicial remedy;

(c) To ensure that the competent authorities shall enforce such remedies when granted.

Article 84
Each State Party undertakes to adopt the legislative and other measures that are necessary to implement the provisions of the present Convention.

PART IX: FINAL PROVISIONS

Article 85
The Secretary-General of the United Nations is designated as the depositary of the present Convention.

Article 86
1. The present Convention shall be open for signature by all States. It is subject to ratification.

2. The present Convention shall be open to accession by any State.

3. Instruments of ratification or accession shall be deposited with the Secretary-General of the United Nations.

Article 87
1. The present Convention shall enter into force on the first day of the month following a period of three months after the date of the deposit of the twentieth instrument of ratification or accession.

2. For each State ratifying or acceding to the present Convention after its entry into force, the Convention shall enter into force on the first day of the month following a period of three months after the date of the deposit of its own instrument of ratification or accession.

Article 88

A State ratifying or acceding to the present Convention may not exclude the application of any Part of it, or, without prejudice to article 3, exclude any particular category of migrant workers from its application.

Article 89

1. Any State Party may denounce the present Convention, not earlier than five years after the Convention has entered into force for the State concerned, by means of a notification writing addressed to the Secretary-General of the United Nations.

2. Such denunciation shall become effective on the first day of the month following the expiration of a period of twelve months after the date of the receipt of the notification by the Secretary-General of the United Nations.

3. Such a denunciation shall not have the effect of releasing the State Party from its obligations under the present Convention in regard to any act or omission whi ch occurs prior to the date at which the denunciation becomes effective, nor shall denunciation prejudice in any way the continued consideration of any matter which is already under consideration by the Committee prior to the date at which the denunciation becomes effective.

4. Following the date at which the denunciation of a State Party becomes effective, the Committee shall not commence consideration of any new matter regarding that State.

Article 90

1. After five years from the entry into force of the Convention a request for the revision of the Convention may be made at any time by any State Party by means of a notification in writing addressed to the Secretary-General of the United Nations. The Secretary-General shall thereupon communicate any proposed amendments to the States Parties with a request that they notify him whether the favour a conference of States Parties for the purpose of considering and voting upon the proposals. In the event that within four months from the date of such communication at least one third of the States Parties favours such a conference, the Secretary-General shall convene the conference under the auspices of the United Nations. Any amendment adopted by a majority of the States Parties present and voting shall be submitted to the General Assembly for approval.

2. Amendments shall come into force when they have been approved by the General Assembly of the United Nations and accepted by a two-thirds majority of the States Parties in accordance with their respective constitutional processes.

3. When amendments come into force, they shall be binding on those States Parties that have accepted them, other States Parties still being bound by the provisions of the present Convention and any earlier amendment that they have accepted.

Article 91

1. The Secretary-General of the United Nations shall receive and circulate to all States the text of reservations made by States at the time of signature, ratification or accession.

2. A reservation incompatible with the object and purpose of the present Convention shall not be permitted.

3. Reservations may be withdrawn at any time by notification to this effect addressed to the Secretary-General of the United Nations, who shall then inform all States thereof. Such notification shall take effect on the date on which it is received.

Article 92

1. Any dispute between two or more States Parties concerning the interpretation or application of the present Convention that is not settled by negotiation shall, at the request of one of them, be submitted to arbitration. If within six months from the date of the request for arbitration the Parties are unable to agree on the organization of the arbitration, any one of those Parties may refer the dispute to the International Court of Justice by request in conformity with the Statute of the Court.

2. Each State Party may at the time of signature or ratification of the present Convention or accession thereto declare that it does not consider itself bound by paragraph 1 of the present article. The other States Parties shall not be bound by that paragraph with respect to any State Party that has made such a declaration.

3. Any State Party that has made a declaration in accordance with paragraph 2 of the present article may at any time withdraw that declaration by notification to the Secretary-General of the United Nations.

Article 93

1. The present Convention, of which the Arabic, Chinese, English, French, Russian and Spanish texts are equally authentic, shall be deposited with the Secretary-General of the United Nations.

2. The Secretary-General of the United Nations shall transmit certified copies of the present Convention to all States.

IN WITNESS WHEREOF the undersigned plenipotentiaries, being duly authorized thereto by their respective Governments, have signed the present Convention.

Status of ratification of the International Convention on the Protection of the Rights of All Migrant Workers and Members of their Families Number of States parties as of 24 November 2004: 27

References

Acuña, Rodolfo. 2000. *Occupied America: A history of Chicanos.* 4th ed. New York: Addison Wesley Longman.

Audre Lorde Project. 2000. *Silent screams: Police brutality against lesbian, gay, bisexual, two spirit, and transgender communities of color in New York City.* New York: Audre Lorde Project.

Albonetti, Celesta A. 1997. "Sentencing under the Federal Sentencing Guidelines: Effects of defendant characteristics, guilty pleas, and departures on sentence outcomes for drug offenses, 1991–92." *Law and Society Review* 31: 789–822.

Amnesty International. 1998. *United States of America: Rights for all.* New York: Amnesty International Publications.

_____. 2003. *United States of America: Death by discrimination—the continuing role of race in capital cases.* New York: Amnesty International Publications. http://www.amnestyusa.org/abolish/reports/dp_discrimination.html.

Audley, John J., Demetrios G. Papademetriou, Sandra Polaski, and Scott Vaughan. 2003. *NAFTA's promise and reality: Lessons from Mexico for the hemisphere.* Washington, D.C.: Carnegie Endowment for International Peace.

Báez, Iris. 2002. Interview by author. Bronx, New York, 13 August.

Baker, Al. 2002. Fire Department looks to diversify the ranks. *New York Times,* 3 April.

Barrios, Luis. 1998. "'Santa Maria' as a liberating zone: A community church in search of restorative justice." *Humanity and Society* 22, 1 (February): 55–78.

Bayley, David H., and Harold Mendelsohn. 1969. *Minorities and the police: Confrontation in America.* New York: Free Press.

Bender, Steven W. 2003. *Greasers and gringos: Latinos, law, and the American imagination.* New York: New York University Press.

Berg, Charles Ramírez. 2002. *Latino images in film: Stereotypes, subversion, resistance.* Austin, Texas: University of Texas Press.

Bernstein, Ilene Nagel, Edward Kick, Jan T. Leung, and Barbara Schultz. 1977. "Charge reduction: An intermediary state in the process of labeling criminal defendants." *Social Forces* 56: 362–84.

Black, Donald. 1980. *The manners and customs of the police.* New York: Academic Press.

Blauner, Robert. 1972. *Racial oppression in America.* New York: Harper & Row.

Blumstein, Alfred, and Joel Wallman, eds. 2000. *The crime drop in America.* New York: Cambridge University Press.

Bourgois, Philippe. 1995. *In search of respect: Selling crack in El Barrio.* Cambridge, United Kingdom: Cambridge University Press.

Broyles-González, Yolanda. 1994. *El Teatro Campesino: Theater in the Chicano movement*. Austin, Texas: University of Texas Press.

Buergenthal, Thomas, Dinah Shelton, and David Stewart. 2002. *International human rights in a nutshell*. 3d ed. St. Paul, Minnesota: West Group.

Butler, Smedley D. [1935] 2003. *War is a racket*. Los Angeles: Feral House.

Bureau of Justice Statistics. 1999. *Truth in sentencing in state prisons: Bureau of Justice Statistics special report (January 1999)*, NCJ 170032, by Paula M. Ditton, and Doris James Wilson. Washington, D.C.: U.S. Department of Justice.

_____. 2000. *Criminal victimization in the United States, 1995 (May 2000)*, NCJ 171129. Washington, D.C.: U.S. Department of Justice.

_____. 2002. *Hispanic victims of violent crime, 1993–2000: Bureau of Justice Statistics special report (April 2002)*, NCJ 191208, by Callie Marie Rennison. Washington, D.C.: U.S. Department of Justice.

_____. 2003a. *Criminal victimization in the United States, 2002, Statistical Tables (December 2003)*, NCJ 200561. Washington, D.C.: U.S. Department of Justice.

_____. 2003b. *Criminal Victimization, 2002: Bureau of Justice Statistics National Crime Victimization Survey (August 2003)*, NCJ 199994, by Callie Marie Rennison, and Michael R. Rand. Washington, D.C.: U.S. Department of Justice.

_____. 2003c. *Local police departments: Bureau of Justice Statistics law enforcement management and administrative statistics (January 2003)*, NCJ 196002, by Matthew J. Hickman, and Brian A. Reaves. Washington, D.C.: U.S. Department of Justice.

_____. 2003d. *Prisoners in 2002: Bureau of Justice Statistics bulletin (July 2003)*, NCJ 200248, by Paige M. Harrison, and Allen J. Beck. Washington, D.C.: U.S. Department of Justice.

Cabán, Pedro A. 1999. *Construction a colonial people: Puerto Rico and the United States, 1898–1932*. Boulder, Colorado: Westview Press.

Canedy, Dana. 2001. Troubling label for Hispanics: 'Girls most likely to drop out.' *New York Times*, 25 March.

Cannon, Lou. 2000. One bad cop. *New York Times Magazine*, 1 October.

Carrasco, Gilbert Paul. 1997. Latinos in the United States: Invitation and exile. In *Immigrants out! The new nativism and the anti-immigrant impulse in the United States*, ed. J. F. Perea, 190–204. New York: New York University Press.

Cassese, Antonio. 1996. *Self-determination of peoples: A legal reappraisal*. Cambridge, Great Britain: Cambridge University Press.

Césaire, Aimé. 2000. *Discourse on colonialism*. New York: Monthly Review Press.

Chambliss, Elizabeth. 2000. *Miles to go 2000: Progress of minorities in the legal profession*. Chicago: American Bar Association Commission on Racial and Ethnic Diversity in the Profession, American Bar Association.

Chang, Nancy. 2002. *Silencing political dissent: How post-September 11 anti-terrorist measures threaten our civil liberties*. New York: Seven Stories Press.

Chapman, Francisco. 2002. *Race, identity and myth in the Spanish-speaking Caribbean: Essays on biculturalism as a contested terrain of difference*. New York: Diaspora Publishing.

Chemerinsky, Erwin. 2001. "Symposium: The Rampart scandal: Policing the criminal justice system: An independent analysis of the Los Angeles Police Department's Board of Inquiry Report on the Rampart scandal." *Loyola of Los Angeles Law Review* 34: 545–655.

Chemerinsky, Erwin, with Paul Hoffman, Laurie Levenson, R. Samuel Paz, Connie Rice, and Carol Sobel. 2000. *An independent analysis of the Los Angeles Police Department's Board of Inquiry Report on the Rampart scandal, Los Angeles, California.* Los Angeles, California.

Chevingny, Paul. 1995. *Edge of the knife: Police violence in the Americas.* New York: New Press.

Citizens' Committee for Children of New York. 2000. *Keeping track of New York City's children: A Citizens' Committee for Children status report.* New York: Citizens Committee for Children of New York, Inc.

_____. 2002. *Keeping track of New York City's children: A Citizens' Committee for Children status report.* New York: Citizens Committee for Children of New York, Inc.

Clark, Ramsey. 1991. We never heard the truth, In *The U.S. invasion of Panama: The truth behind Operation "Just Cause,"* ed. The Independent Commission of Inquiry on the U.S. Invasion of Panama, 9–14. Boston: South End Press.

Cohn, D'Vera. 2003. Hispanics declared largest minority; Blacks overtaken in census update. *Washington Post,* 19 June.

Cole, David. 1999. *No equal justice: Race and class in the American criminal justice system.* New York: New Press.

_____. 2001. Formalism, realism, and the war on drugs. *Suffolk University Law Review* 35:241–55.

Cole, David, and James X. Dempsey. 2002. *Terror and the constitution: Sacrificing civil liberties in the name of national security.* New York: New Press.

Commission for Historical Clarification. 1999. *Guatemala, Memory of silence: Report of the Commission for Historical Clarification (Conclusions and recommendations).* Guatemala: Commission for Historical Clarification.

Convention on the Rights and Duties of States. 1933. Done at Montevideo, Dec. 26, 1933. Entered into force, Dec. 26, 1934; for the United States, Dec. 26, 1934. 49 Stat. 3097, T.S. No. 881, Bevans 145, 165 L.N.T.S. 19.

Crawford, James, ed. 1992. *Language loyalties: A source book on the official English controversy.* Chicago: University of Chicago Press.

_____. 2000. *At war with diversity: U.S. language policy in an age of anxiety.* Clevedon, England: Multilingual Matters, Ltd.

Crutchfield, Robert, Joseph G. Weis, Rodney L. Engen, and Randy R. Gainey. 1995. *Racial and ethnic disparities in the prosecution of felony cases in King County.* Olympia Washington State Minority and Justice Commission.

Cummins, Jim. 1993. Empowering minority students: A framework for intervention. In *Beyond silenced voices: Class, race, and gender in United States schools,* ed. L. W. and M. Fine, 101–17. Albany, New York: State University of New York Press.

_____. 2000. *Language, power and pedagogy: Bilingual children in the crossfire.* Clevedon, England: Multilingual Matters.

Danner, Mark. 1993. *The massacre at el Mozote.* New York: Vintage Books.

Dávila, Arlene. 2001. *Latinos, Inc.: The marketing and making of a people.* Berkeley: University of California Press.

Davis, Robert C., and Pedro Mateu-Gelabert. 1999. *Respectful and effective policing: Two examples in the South Bronx.* New York: Vera Institute of Justice.

DeCesare, Donna. 2003. From civil war to gang war: The tragedy of Edgar Bolanos. In *Gangs and society: Alternative perspectives,* ed. L. Kontos, D. Brotherton, and L. Barrios, 283–313. New York: Columbia University Press.

Delgado, Richard, and Jean Stefancic. 1992. "Images of the outsider in American law and culture: Can free expression remedy systemic social ills?" *Cornell Law Review* 77: 1258–97.

_____, eds. 1998. *The Latino/a condition: A critical reader.* New York: New York University Press.

Delpit, Lisa. 1995. *Other people's children: Cultural conflict in the classroom.* New York: The New Press.

DeNavas-Walt, Carmen, Robert W. Cleveland, and Marc I. Roemer. 2001. *Money Income in the United States: 2000.* Current Population Reports, Consumer Income, P60–213, U.S. Census Bureau, Washington, D.C.

Del Valle, Sandra. 2003. Langu*age rights and the law in the United States: Finding our voices.* Clevedon, England: Multilingual Matters.

Díaz-Stevens, Ana María. 1996. Aspects of Puerto Rican religious experience: A sociohistorical overview. In *Latinos in New York: Communities in transition,* ed. G. Haslip-Viera and S. L. Baver, 147–86. Notre Dame, Indiana: University of Notre Dame Press.

Donziger, Steven R., ed. 1996. *The real war on crime: The report of the National Criminal Justice Commission.* New York: HarperPerrenial.

Dorfman, Ariel, and Armand Mattelart. 1984. *How to read Donald Duck: Imperialist ideology in the Disney comic.* Trans. David Kunzle. New York: International General.

Dorfman, Lori, and Vincent Schiraldi. 2001. *Off balance: Youth, race and crime in the news.* Washington, D.C.: Building Blocks for Youth.

Ebright, Malcolm. 1994. *Land grants and law suits in Northern New Mexico.* Albuquerque, New Mexico: University of New Mexico Press.

Ehlers, Scott, Vincent Schiraldi, and Jason Ziedenberg. 2004. *Still striking out: Ten years of California's three strikes.* Washington, D.C.: Justice Policy Institute.

Engle, Charles Donald. 1971. Criminal justice in the city: A study of sentence severity and variation in the Philadelphia court system. Ph.D. diss., Temple University.

Eron, Leonard D., and L. Rowell Huesmann. 1990. The stability of aggressive behavior—even unto the third generation. In *Handbook of developmental psychopathology,* ed. M. Lewis and S. M. Miller, 147–56. New York: Plenum.

Escobar, Edward J. 1999. *Race, police, and the making of a political identity: Mexican Americans and the Los Angeles Police Department 1900–1945.* Berkeley: University of California Press.

Falcón, Angelo. 2002. *Opening up the courthouse doors: The need for more Hispanic judges.* New York: Puerto Rican Legal Defense and Education Fund.

Fanon, Frantz. [1963] 1986. *The wretched of the earth.* New York: Grove Press.

Fernandez, Ronald. 1994. *Prisoners of colonialism: The struggle for justice in Puerto Rico.* Monroe, Maine: Common Courage Press.

Ferrante, Joan, and Prince Browne, Jr., eds. 2001. *The social construction of race and ethnicity in the United States.* 2d ed. Upper Saddle River, New Jersey: Prentice Hall.

Feuer, Alan. 2003. Little but language in common; Mexicans and Puerto Ricans quarrel in East Harlem. *New York Times,* 6 September.

Flores, Glenn et al. 2002. "The health of Latino children: Urgent priorities, unanswered questions, and research agenda." *Journal of the American Medical Association* 288, 1 (July): 82–90.

Flores, Juan. 2000. *From bomba to hip hop: Puerto Rican culture and Latino identity.* New York: Columbia University Press.

Flynn, Kevin. 1999. Record payout in settlements against police. *New York Times,* 1 October.

Franklin, Benjamin. 1959. *The papers of Benjamin Franklin,* ed. L. W. Labarre. New Haven: Yale University Press.

Freidman, Warren, and Martha Hott. 1995. *Young people and the police: Respect, fear and the future of community policing in Chicago.* Chicago: Chicago Alliance for Neighborhood Safety.

Freire, Paulo. 1994. *Pedagogy of the oppressed.* New York: Continuum.

Fyfe, James J. 1981. "Who shoots? A look at officer race and police shooting." *Journal of Police Science and Administration* 9: 367–82.

Galeano, Eduardo. [1973] 1997. *Open veins of Latin America: Five centuries of the pillage of a continent.* New York: Monthly Review.

García, Mario T. 1994. *Memories of Chicano history: The life and narrative of Bert Corona.* Berkeley: University of California Press.

García Martínez, Alfonso. 1989. *Puerto Rico: Leyes fundamentales.* Río Piedras, Puerto Rico: Editorial Edil.

Gautier Mayoral, Carmen, and Maria Del Pilar Arguelles. 1978. *Puerto Rico y la ONU.* Río Piedras, Puerto Rico: Editorial Edil.

General Accounting Office. 1991. *The war on drugs: Narcotics control efforts in Panama.* GAO/NSIAD-91-233. Washington, D.C.

_____. 2004. *Tax administration: Comparison of the tax liabilities of foreign- and U.S.-controlled corporations, 1996–2000.* GAO-04-358. Washington, D.C.

Gereffi, Gary, David Spener, and Jennifer Bair, eds. 2002. *Free trade and uneven development: The North American apparel industry after NAFTA.* Philadelphia: Temple University Press.

Gleach, Frederic W. 2002. "Images of empire: Representations of the 1898 war." *Latino(a) Research Review* 5, 1 (Spring): 51–79.

Goldberg, Jeffrey. 1999. What cops talk about when they talk about race: The color of suspicion. *New York Times Magazine,* 20 June.

Goldewijk, Berma Klein. 2002. From Seattle to Porto Alegre: Emergence of a new focus on dignity and the implementation of economic, social and cultural rights. In *Dignity and human rights: The implementation of economic, social and cultural rights,* ed. B. K. Goldewijk, A. C. Baspineiro, and P. C. Carbonari, 3–16. Antwerp, Belgium: Intersentia/Transnational Publishers.

Goldewijk, Berma Klein, Adalid Contreras Baspineiro, and Paolo César Carbonari, eds. 2002. *Dignity and human rights: The implementation of economic, social and cultural rights.* Antwerp, Belgium: Intersentia/Transnational Publishers.

Gómez Quiñones, Juan. 1990. *Chicano politics: Reality and promise, 1940–1990.* Albuquerque, New Mexico: University of New Mexico.

Gonzalez, Juan. 1996. Her bravery shatters blue wall. *New York Daily News,* 27 September, 21.

_____. 2000. *Harvest of Empire: A history of Latinos in America.* New York: Viking.

Goodstein, Laurie, and Gustav Niebuhr. 2001. Attacks and harassment of Middle Eastern Americans rising. *New York Times,* 14 September.

Gootman, Elissa. 2003. Old tensions over immigrants surface after firebombing. *New York Times,* 14 July.

Grasmuck, Sherri, and Patricia R. Pessar. 1991. *Between two islands: Dominican international migration.* Berkeley: University of California Press.

_____. 1996. Dominicans in the United States: First- and second generation settlement, 1960–1990. In *Origins and destinies: Immigration, race, and ethnicity in America,* ed. S. Pedraza and R. G. Rumbaut, 280–301. Belmont, California: Wadsworth Publishing Company.

Green, Mark. 1999. *Investigation of the New York City Police Department's response to civilian complains of police misconduct: Interim report.* New York: Office of the Public Advocate.

Greenhouse, Steven. 2003a. Immigrants rally in city, seeking rights. *New York Times,* 5 October.

_____. 2003b. Wal-Mart raids by U.S. aimed at illegal aliens. *New York Times,* 24 October.

Hadden, Bob. 2003a. Government leaders crack down on gangs in Central America. *National Public Radio, Morning Edition,* 9 September.

_____. 2003b. Latino migration to the United States. *National Public Radio, Morning Edition,* 29 September.

Hagan, John, and Alberto Palloni. 1999. "Sociological Criminology and the mythology of Hispanic immigration and crime." *Social Problems* 46 (4): 617–32.

Haney López, Ian F. 2003. *Racism on trial: The Chicano fight for justice.* Cambridge, Massachusetts: Belknap/Harvard University Press.

Hannum, Hurst. 1990. *Autonomy, sovereignty and self-determination: The accommodation of conflicting rights.* Philadelphia, Pennsylvania: University of Pennsylvania Press.

Harris, David A. 2002. *Profiles in injustice: Why racial profiling cannot work.* New York: the New Press.

Harris, Fred R., and Roger W. Wilkins. 1988. *Quiet riots: Race and poverty in the United States—The Kerner Report twenty years later.* New York: Pantheon Books.

Hayden, Tom. 2000. We need peacemakers like Alex Sanchez. *Los Angeles Times,* 26 January.

Hayes-Bautista, David E., and Chapa, Jorge. 1987. "Latino terminology: Conceptual basis for standardized terminology." *American Journal of Public Health* 77: 61–68.

Healey, Joseph F. 2003. *Race, ethnicity, gender, and class in the United States: Inequality, group conflict, and power.* 3rd ed. Thousand Oaks, CA: Pine Forge Press.

Henkin, Louis. 1990. *The age of rights.* New York: Columbia University Press.

Hernández, Ramona. 2002. *The mobility of workers under advanced capitalism: Dominican migration to the United States.* New York: Columbia University Press.

Hernández, Ramona, and Silvio Torres-Saillant. 1996. Dominicans in New York: Men, women, and prospects. In *Latinos in New York: Communities in transition*, ed. G. Haslip-Viera, and S. L. Baver, 30–56. Notre Dame, Indiana: Notre Dame University Press.

Hernandez-Chávez, Eduardo. 1995. Language policy in the United States: A history of cultural genocide. In *Linguistic human rights: Overcoming linguistic discrimination*, ed. T. Skutnabb-Kangas, and R. Phillipson, 141–77. Berlin: Mouton de Gruyter.

Hernández-Truyol, Berta Esperanza. 1997. Reconciling rights in collision: An international human rights strategy. In *Immigrants out! The new nativism and the anti-immigrant impulse in the United States*, ed. J. F. Perea, 254–76. New York: New York University Press.

———. 1998. Bringing international human rights home. In *The Latino/a condition: A critical reader*, ed. R. Delgado, and J. Stefancic, 381–86. New York: New York University Press.

Herszenhorn, David M. 2003. City English scores show marked gain. *New York Times*, 21 May.

Hirschi, Travis, and Michael J. Hindelang. 1977. "Intelligence and delinquency: a revisionist review." *American Sociological Review*, 42: 571–87.

Hitchens, Christopher. 2001. *The trial of Henry Kissinger.* London: Verso.

Hoffman, Alison. 2003. *Looking for Latino regulars on prime-time television: The fall 2002 season.* Los Angeles, California: Chicano Research Report/UCLA Chicano Studies Research Center. Also available online at http//www.sscnet.ucla.edu/csrc/.

Holden, Robert H., and Eric Zolov, eds. 2000. *Latin America and the United States: A documentary history.* New York: Oxford University Press.

Holmes, Malcolm D., Harmon M. Hosch, Howard C. Daudistel, Dolores A. Perez, and Joseph B. Graves. 1993. "Judges' ethnicity and minority sentencing: Evidence concerning Hispanics." *Social Science Quarterly* 74: 496–506.

Hood, Roger. 1992. *Race and sentencing.* Oxford, England: Clarendon.

Hostos, Eugenio María de. 1999. *Estímulos de vida para cada día.* 2d ed., ed. V. Quiles-Calderín. San Juan, Puerto Rico: Instituto de Cultura Puertorriqueña.

Hsiao, Andrew. 2001. Mothers of invention: The families of police-brutality victims and the movement they've built. In *Zero tolerance: Quality of life and the new police brutality in New York City*, ed. A. McArdle and T. Erzen, 179–95. New York: New York University Press.

Human Rights Watch. 1998. *Shielded from justice: Police brutality and accountability in the United States.* New York: Human Rights Watch.

———. 2002. *Race and incarceration in the United States: Human Rights Watch briefing.* New York: Human Rights Watch. Also available online at http://hrw.org/backgrounder/usa/race/ pdf/race-bck.pdf.

_____. 2003. *Incarcerated America: Human Rights Watch backgrounder.* New York: Human Rights Watch. Also available online at http://hrw.org/backgrounder/usa/incarceration/us042903.pdf.

Independent Commission on the Los Angeles Police Department. 1991. *Report of Independent Commission on the Los Angeles Police Department.* Los Angeles: California, 9 July.

Institute of Medicine of the National Academy of Sciences. 2004a. *Insuring America's health: Principles and recommendations.* Washington, D.C.: The National Academies Press. Also available online at http://www.nap.edu.

_____. 2004b. *IOM report calls for universal health coverage by 2010; Offers principles to judge, compare proposed solutions* (Press Release). Washington, D.C.: The National Academies. Also available online at http://www4.nationalacademies.org/news.nsf.

Jay, John. [1788] 2003. Federalist No. 2. In *The Federalist Papers,* ed. C. Rossiter, 31–35. New York: Signet Classic.

Johnson, Marilynn S. 2003. *Street justice: A history of police violence in New York City.* Boston: Beacon Press.

Jordan, Mary, and Kevin Sullivan. 2003. Trade brings riches, but not to Mexico's poor. *Washington Post,* 22 March.

Journal of el Centro de Estudios Puertorriqueño. 1998. "Focus/en foco: 1898–1998, Part I." *CENTRO Journal of the Center for Puerto Rican Studies* 10, 1–2 (Fall): 5–223.

Karman, Andrew. 2000. *New York murder mystery: The true story behind the crime crash of the 1990s.* New York: New York University Press.

Kennedy, Randall. 1997. *Race, crime, and the law.* New York: Vintage Books.

Kessler, Judi. 2002. The impact of North American economic integration on the Los Angeles apparel industry. In *Free trade and uneven development: The North American apparel industry after NAFTA,* ed. G. Gereffi, D. Spener, and J. Bair, 74–99. Philadelphia: Temple University Press.

Kocieniewski, David and Robert Hanley. 2000. Racial profiling was routine. *New York Times,* 28 November.

Kontos, Louis, David Brotherton, and Luis Barrios, eds. 2003. *Gangs and society: Alternative perspectives.* New York: Colombia University Press.

Kontra, Miklós, Robert Phillipson, Tove Skutnabb-Kangas and Tibor Várady, eds. 1999. *Language: A right and a resource: Approaching linguistic human rights.* Budapest, Hungary: Central European University Press.

Kornbluh, Peter. 2003a. "Opening up the files Chile declassified." *NACLA Report on the Americas* 37, 1 (July/August): 25–31.

_____. 2003b. *The Pinochet file: A declassified dossier on atrocity and accountability.* New York: New Press.

Koss-Chioino, Joan D., and Luis A. Vargas. 1999. *Working with Latino youth: Culture, development, and context.* San Francisco, California: Jossey-Bass Publishers.

Krashen, Stephen D. 1996. *Under attack: The case against bilingual education.* Culver City, California: Language Education Associates.

_____. 1999. *Condemned without a trial: Bogus arguments against bilingual education.* Portsmouth, New Hampshire: Heinemann.

LaFeber, Walter. [1963] 1998. *The new empire: An interpretation of American expansionism, 1860–1898*, Reprint, with a new preface by W. LaFeber, Ithaca, New York: Cornell University Press.

_____. 1993. *Inevitable revolutions: The United States in Central America*. 2d ed. New York: W. W. Norton.

Lauren, Paul Gordon. 1998. *The evolution of international human rights: Visions seen*. Philadelphia, Pennsylvania: University of Pennsylvania Press.

LeoGrande, William, M. 1998. *Our own backyard: The United States in Central America, 1977–1992*. Chapel Hill, North Carolina: University of North Carolina Press.

Leone, Richard C., and Greg Anrig, Jr., eds. 2003. *The war on our freedoms: Civil liberties in an age of terrorism*. New York: Century Foundation.

Levy, Clifford J., and William K. Rashbaum. 2001. After the attacks: The airports. *New York Times*, 14 September.

Lewis, Gordon K. 1963. *Puerto Rico: Freedom and power in the Caribbean*. New York: Monthly Review.

Louima, Gariot. 2002. Bracero protest 'caravan" comes to L.A. *The Los Angeles Times*, 11 April.

Lyall, Sarah. 1988. 'Blunt force' is cited in a death in police custody. *New York Times*, 21 February.

Maldonado-Denis, Manuel. 1972. *Puerto Rico: A socio-historic interpretation*. New York: Vintage.

Martin, Elizabeth A., ed. 2002. *A Dictionary of Law: Oxford Reference Online*. Oxford University Press. http://www.oxfordreference.com/views/ENTRY.html?subview=Main&entry=t49.001994 (accessed July 2, 2003).

Martínez, Elizabeth. 1993. "Beyond black/white: The racisms of our time." *Social Justice* 20 (1–2): 22–34.

Martinez, Jr., Ramiro. 2002. *Latino homicide: Immigration, violence and community*. New York: Routledge.

Maxfield, Linda Drazga, and John H. Kramer. 1998. *Substancial assistance: An empirical yardstick gauging equity in current federal policy and practice*. Washington, D.C.: U.S. Sentencing Commission.

McArdle, Andrea. 2001. Introduction. In *Zero tolerance: Quality of life and the new police brutality in New York City*, ed. A. McArdle and T. Erzen, 1–16. New York: New York University Press.

McArdle, Andrea, and Tanya Erzen, eds. 2001. *Zero tolerance: Quality of life and the new police brutality in New York City*. New York: New York University Press.

McKinley, Jr., James C. 2004. Killings deepen the family's drama. *New York Times*, 10 December.

McWilliams, Carey. 1990. *North from Mexico: The Spanish-speaking people of the United States*. New York: Peaeger.

Meek, James. 2003. Inside Guantanamo: People the law forgot. *The Guardian*, 12 March.

Meeks, Kenneth. 2000. *Driving while Black*. New York: Broadway Books.

Meléndez, Miguel. 2003. *We took the streets: Fighting for Latino rights with the Young Lords*. New York: St. Martin's Press.

Memmi, Albert. [1965] 1991. *The colonizer and the colonized*. Boston: Beacon Press.

Menchaca, Martha. 1993. Chicano Indianism: A historical account of racial repression in the United States. *American Ethnologist* 20:583–603.

Méndez, Miguel A. 1993. "Hernandez: The wrong message at the wrong time." *Stanford Law and Policy Review* 4: 193–202.

_____. 1997. "Lawyers, linguists, story-tellers, and limited English-speaking witnesses." *New Mexico Law Review* 27: 77–99.

Méndez-Méndez, Serafín, and Diana Alverio. 2003. *Network brownout 2003: The portrayal of Latinos in network television news, 2002.* Washington, D.C.: National Association of Hispanic Journalists.

Miranda, Anthony. 2002. Interview by author. New York, 30 September.

Mirandé, Alfredo. 1987. *Gringo justice.* Notre Dame, Indiana: University of Notre Dame Press.

Moore, Joan and Harry Pachon. 1985. *Hispanics in the United States.* Englewood Cliffs, New Jersey: Prentice-Hall.

Morales, Iris. 1998. ¡PALANTE SIEMPRE PALANTE! The Young Lords. In *The Puerto Rican movement: Voices from the diaspora,* ed. A. Torres and J. E. Velásquez, 210–27. Philadephia: Temple University Press.

Morín, José Luis. 2000. "Indigenous Hawaiians under statehood: Lessons for Puerto Rico." *CENTRO Journal of the Center for Puerto Rican Studies* 11 (Spring): 4–25.

Morín, José Luis, and Manuel del Valle. 1990. Racially motivated violence: International remedies for human rights violations in the United States, *International Review of Contemporary Law,* 1: 61–68.

Mosisa, Abraham. 2002. "The role of foreign-born workers in the U.S. economy." *Monthly Labor Review* (May): 3–14.

Moya Pons, Frank. 1995. *The Dominican Republic: A national history.* New Rochelle, New York: Hispaniola Books.

Moynihan, Colin. 2004. Latino police officers and city settle suit. *New York Times,* 1 February, late edition.

Mumford Center. 2001. *Ethnic diversity grows, neighborhood integration lags behind.* Albany, New York: University at Albany. Also available online at www.albany.edu/mumford/census.

_____. 2002. *Hispanic populations and their residential patterns in the metropolis.* Albany, New York: University at Albany. Also available online at www.albany.edu/mumford/census.

National Advisory Commission on Civil Disorder. [1968] 1988. *The Kerner Report: The 1968 report of the National Advisory Commission on Civil Disorders.* Reprint, with new introductions by Fred R. Harris and Tom Wicker, New York: Pantheon Books.

Navarro, Mireya, and Marjorie Connelly. 2003. Hispanics in New York hold bleaker views. *New York Times,* 8 August.

New Jersey Black and Latino Caucus. 2002. "Report on discriminatory practices within the New Jersey State Police." *Seton Hall Legislative Journal* 26: 273–313.

New York City Civilian Complaint Review Board. 2003. *Status report: January–June 2003.* New York: New York City Civilian Complaint Review Board.

New York Times. 1997. 2 police officer groups file U.S. bias complaint, 18 April.

_____. 1999. Former police officer sues over dismissal, 7 April.

_____. 2003a. Harvesting poverty: The great catfish war. Editorial, 22 July.

_____. 2003b. Harvesting poverty: The long reach of king cotton. Editorial, 5 August.

_____. 2003c. Harvesting poverty: The rigged trade game. Editorial, 20 July.

_____. 2003d. Harvesting poverty: The unkept promise. Editorial, 30 December.

Ngũgĩ, Wa Thiong'o. 1986. *Decolonising the mind: The politics of language in African literature.* Portsmouth, New Hampshire: Heinemann.

Noel, Donald. 1968. "A theory of the origin of ethnic stratification." *Social Problems* 16: 157–72.

Noguera, Pedro A. 2001. Youth perspectives on violence and the implications for public policy. *In Motion Magazine*, 30 September. Also available online at http://inmotionmagazine.com/er/pnypref.html.

Oboler, Suzanne. 1995. *Ethnic labels, Latino lives: Identity and the politics of re-presentation in the United States.* Minneapolis, Minnesota: University of Minnesota Press.

Office of National Drug Control Policy. 2003. *Minorities and drugs.* Also available online at http://www.whitehousedrugpolicy.gov/drugfact/minorities/index.html.

Omi, Michael, and Howard Winant. 1994. *Racial formations in the United States: From the 1960s to the 1990s.* 2d ed. New York: Routledge.

Oquendo, Angel R. 1995. "Re-imagining the Latino/a race." *Harvard Blackletter Law Journal* 12: 93–129.

Palpacuer, Florence. 2002. Subcontracting networks in the New York City garment industry: Changing characteristics in a global era. In *Free trade and uneven development: The North American apparel industry after NAFTA,* ed. G. Gereffi, D. Spener, and J. Bair 53–73. Philadelphia: Temple University Press.

Pantoja, Antonia. 2002. *Memoir of a visionary: Antonia Pantoja.* Houston, Texas: Arte Público Press.

Passel, Jeffrey S., and Rebecca Clark. 1998. *Immigrants in New York: Their legal status, incomes, and taxes.* Washington, D.C.: Urban Institute. Also available online at http:// www.urban.org.

Pastor, Manuel, Jr. 1993. *Latinos and the L.A. Uprising.* Tomás Rivera Center Study, Occidental College, California.

Patterson, Gerald, John B. Reid, and Thomas J. Dishion. 1997. *Antisocial boys.* Eugene, Oregon: Castalia.

Pedraza, Sylvia. 1996. Cuba's refugees: Manifold migrations. In *Origins and destinies: Immigration, race, and ethnicity in America,* ed. S. Pedraza and R. G. Rumbaut, 263–79. Belmont, California: Wadsworth Publishing Company.

Perea, Juan F. 1995. "Los Olvidados: On the making of invisible people." *New York University Law Review* 70: 965–91.

_____. 1997a. *Immigrants out! The new nativism and the anti-immigrant impulse in the United States.* New York: New York University Press.

_____. 1997b. "The Black/White binary paradigm of race: The 'normal science' of American racial thought." *California Law Review* 85: 1213–58.

Perea, Juan F., Richard Delgado, Angela P. Harris, and Stephanie M. Wildman. 2000. *Race and races: Cases and resources for a diverse America.* St. Paul, Minnesota: West Group.

Pérez, Luis. 2004. Cops' work bias suit settled. *New York Newsday*, 31 January, Queens edition.

Pérez, Jr., Louis A. 1995. *Cuba: Between reform and revolution.* 2d ed. New York: Oxford University Press.

Petersilia, Joan, and Susan Turner. 1986. *Prison versus probation in California.* Santa Monica, California: Rand.

Pew Hispanic Center/Kaiser Family Foundation. 2002. *2002 National Survey of Latinos.* Washington, D.C.: Pew Hispanic Center/Kaiser Family Foundation.

Piatt, Bill. 1990. "Attorney as interpreter: A return to babble." *New Mexico Law Review* 20: 1–16.

Police Officer David. 2002. Interview by author. New York, 24 September.

Pollan, Michael. 2003. The (agri)cultural contradictions of obesity: A generation of U.S. farm policy promoting overproduction of corn has made us fat—and made Big Food happy. *New York Times Magazine,* 12 October.

Portes, Alejandro, and Richard Schauffler. 1996. Language acquisition and loss among children of immigrants. In *Origins and Destinies: Immigration, race, and ethnicity in America,* ed. S. Pedraza and R. G. Rumbaut, 432–43. Belmont, California: Wadsworth Publishing Company.

Rainwater, Lee, and Timothy M. Smeeding. 2003. *Poor kids in a rich country: America's children in comparative perspective.* New York: Russell Sage Foundation.

Rappleye, Charles. 2000. Harrassing homies: LAPD campaigns against a church-based gang-peace project. *LA Weekly,* 11–17 February.

Reiman, Jeffrey. 2001. *The rich get richer and the poor get prison: Ideology, class, and criminal justice.* Boston: Allyn and Bacon.

Reynoso, Cruz. 2000. Hispanics and the criminal justice system. In *Hispanics in the United States: An agenda for the twenty-first century,* ed. P. San Juan Cafferty and D. W. Engstrom, 277–315. New Brunswick, New Jersey: Transaction Publishers.

Riley, K. Jack. 1997. *Crack, powder cocaine, and heroin: Drug purchase and use patterns in six U.S. cities.* Washington D.C.: U.S. Department of Justice, National Institute of Justice.

Rivera Ramos, Efrén. 2001. *The legal construction of identity: The judicial and social legacy of American colonialism in Puerto Rico.* Washington, D.C.: American Psychological Association.

Rivera, Raquel Z. 2003. *New York Ricans from the hip hop zone.* New York: Palgrave.

Rodriguez, Orlando. 1996. *The new immigrant Hispanic population: An integrated approach to preventing delinquency and crime.* National Institute of Justice, Research Review: U.S. Department of Justice.

Romaine, Suzanne. [1989] 1992. *Bilingualism.* Oxford, United Kingdom: Blackwell Publishers.

Roorda, Eric Paul. 1998. *The dictator next door: The Good Neighbor Policy and the Trujillo regime in the Dominican Republic, 1930–1945.* Durham, North Carolina: Duke University Press.

Rosen, Fred, and Diedre McFadyen, eds. 1995. *Free trade and economic restructuring in Latin America.* New York: Monthly Review.

Rosenbaum, Robert J. 1998. *Mexicano resistance in the Southwest.* Dallas, Texas: Southern Methodist University Press.

Rosenberg, Tina. 2003. The Taint of the Greased Palm. *New York Times Magazine,* 10 August.

Said, Edward. 1993. *Culture and imperialism*. New York: Vintage Books.

Sánchez, Alex. 2001. Interview by author. Los Angeles, California, 18 July.

Sánchez, Marcela. 2003. Immigration reform growing at the grassroots. *Washington Post*, 2 October.

Sassen, Saskia. 1998. *Globalization and its discontents: Essays on the new mobility of people and money*. New York: The New Press.

Schaefer, Richard T. 2001. *Race and ethnicity in the United States*. 2d ed. Upper Saddle River, New Jersey: Prentice Hall.

_____. 2004. *Racial and ethnic groups*. 9th ed. Upper Saddle River, New Jersey: Pearson/Prentice Hall.

Schmidt, Hans. 1995. *The United States occupation of Haiti, 1915–1934*. New Brunswick, New Jersey: Rutgers University Press.

Schmitz, David F. 1999. *Thank God they're on our side: The United States and right-wing dictatorships, 1921–1965*. Chapel Hill, North Carolina: University of North Carolina Press.

Schoultz, Lars. 1998. *Beneath the United States: A history of U.S. policy toward Latin America*. Cambridge, Massachusetts: Harvard University Press.

Schulhofer, Stephen J. 2002. *The enemy within: Intelligence gathering, law enforcement, and civil liberties in the wake of September 11*. New York: Century Foundation.

Scott, Janny. 2001. Races still tend to live apart in New York, census shows. *New York Times*, 23 March.

Scott, Dale Peter, and Jonathan Marshall. 1991. *Cocaine politics: Drugs, armies, and the CIA in Central America*. Berkeley: University of California Press.

Sentencing Project. 2003. *Hispanic prisoners in the United States*. Washington, D.C.: Sentencing Project. Also available online at http://www.sentencingproject.org/pdfs/1051.pdf.

Silverman, Eli B. 1999. *NYPD battles crime: Innovative strategies in policing*. Boston: Northeastern University Press.

Sklar, Holly. 1995. *Chaos or community: Seeking solutions, not scapegoats for bad economics*. Boston: South End Press.

Skutnabb-Kangas, Tove. 2000. *Linguistic Genocide in education—or worldwide diversity and human rights?* Mahwah, New Jersey: Lawrence Erlbaum Associate, Publishers.

Skutnabb-Kangas, Tove, and Robert Phillipson, eds. 1995. *Linguistic human rights: Overcoming linguistic discrimination*. Berlin: Mouton de Gruyter.

Smith, Robert C. 1996. Mexicans in New York: Membership and incorporation in a new immigrant community. In *Latinos in New York: Communities in transition*, ed. G. Haslip-Viera, and S. L. Baver, 57–103. Notre Dame, Indiana: Notre Dame University Press.

Smith, Peter H. 2000. *Talons of the eagle: Dynamics of U.S.-Latin American relations*. 2d ed. New York: Oxford University Press.

Sohn, Louis B., and Thomas Buergernthal. 1974. *International Protection of Human Rights*. New York: Bobbs-Merrill Company.

Sotomayor, Sonia. 2002. "Raising the bar: Latino and Latina presence in the judiciary and the struggle for representation: Judge Mario G. Olmos memorial lecture: Latina judge's voice." *La Raza Law Journal* 13 (Spring): 87–93.

Spears, Jeffrey W. 1999. Diversity in the courtroom: A comparison of the sentencing decisions of black and white judges and male and female judges in Cook County Circuit Court. Ph.D. diss., University of Nebraska at Omaha.

Spitzer, Elliot. 1999. *The New York City Police Department's "Stop and Frisk" Practices: a Report to the People of the State of New York from the Attorney General.* New York: Civil Rights Bureau.

Spohn, Cassia. 1990. "The sentencing decisions of black and white judges: Expected and unexpected similarities." *Law & Society Review* 24: 1197–1216.

Spohn, Cassia, John Gruhl, and Susan Welch. 1987. The impact of the ethnicity and gender of defendants on the decision to reject or dismiss felony charges. *Criminology* 25: 175–91.

Stephanson, Anders. 1995. *Manifest destiny: American expansion and the empire of right.* New York: Hill and Wang.

Stiglitz, Joseph E. 2002. *Globalization and its discontents.* New York: W.W. Norton & Company.

Substance Abuse and Mental Health Services Administration. 2002. *Results from the 2001 National Household Survey on Drug Abuse: Volume 1. Summary of national findings.* Rockville, Maryland: Office of Applied Studies, NHSDA Series H-17, DHHS Publication No. SMA 02-3758.

_____. 2003. *The NHSDA report,* 15 August.

Tomlinson, John. 1991. *Cultural imperialism: A critical introduction.* Baltimore: Maryland: Johns Hoppkins University Press.

Torres, Andrés, and José E. Velázaquez. 1998. *The Puerto Rican movement: Voices from the diaspora.* Philadelphia: Temple University Press.

Torruella, Juan R. 1988. *The Supreme Court and Puerto Rico: The doctrine of separate and unequal.* Río Piedras, Puerto Rico: Universidad de Puerto Rico.

Treaty of Guadalupe Hidalgo. 1848. *Treaty of peace, friendship, limits, and settlement.* Done at Guadalupe Hidalgo, February 2, 1848. Entered into force May 30, 1848. 9 Stat. 922; T.S. No. 207; 9 Bevans 791.

Trías Monge, José 1997. *Puerto Rico: The trials of the oldest colony in the world.* New Haven: Yale University Press.

Trubeck, David M. 1984. Economic, social and cultural rights in the Third World: Human rights and human needs. In *Human rights in international law,* ed. T. Meron, 205–71. New York: Oxford University Press.

Uhlman, Thomas M. 1978. "Black elite decision Making: The case of trial judges." *American Journal of Political Science* 22: 884–95.

United Nations. 1945. Charter of the United Nations. Adopted 26 June 1945, entered into force 24 Oct. 1945, as amended by G.A. Res. 1991 (XVIII) 17 Dec. 1963, entered into force 31 Aug. 1965 (557 UNTS 143); 2101 of 20 Dec. 1965, entered into force 12 June 1968 (638 UNTS 308); 2847 (XXVI) of 20 Dec. 1971, entered into force 24 Sept. 1973 (892 UNTS 119).

_____. 1948. Universal Declaration of Human Rights. Adopted by the U.N. General Assembly, Dec. 10, 1948. U.N.G.A. Res. 217 A (III), U.N. A/810, at 71 (1948).

_____. 1951. Convention Relating to the Status of Refugees. Done at Geneva, July 28, 1951. Entered into force, Apr. 22, 1954. 189 U.N.T.S. 137.

_____. 1960. Declaration on the Granting of Independence to Colonial Countries and Peoples, G.A. Res. 1514, U.N. GAOR, 15th Sess., Supp. No.16, at 66, U.N. Doc. A /4684 (1960).

_____. 1966a. International Covenant on Civil and Political Rights. Done at New York, Dec. 16, 1966. Entered into force, Mar. 23, 1976. U.N.G.A. Res. 2200 (XXI), 21 U.N. GAOR, Supp. (No. 16) 52, U.N. Doc. A/RES/6316 (1967), *reprinted in* 6 I.L.M. 368 (1967).

_____. 1966b. International Covenant on Economic, Social and Cultural Rights. Done at New York, Dec. 16, 1966. Entered into force, Jan. 3, 1976. U.N.G.A. Res. 2200 (XXI), 21 U.N. GAOR, Supp. (No. 16) 49, U.N. Doc. A/RES/6316 (1967), *reprinted in* 6 I.L.M. 360 (1967).

_____. 1966c. International Convention on the Elimination of All Forms of Racial Discrimination. Done at New York, Mar. 7, 1966. Entered into force, Jan. 4, 1969. 660 U.N.T.S. 195, *reprinted in* 5 I.L.M. 352 (1966).

_____. 1977. United Nations General Assembly resolution 32/130. Adopted 16 December 1977, G.A. Res. 32/130 (1977).

_____. 1979a. Code of Conduct for Law Enforcement Officials. Adopted 7 December 1979, G.A. Res. 34/169 (1979).

_____. 1979b. Convention on the Elimination of all Forms of Discrimination against Women. Done at New York, Dec. 18, 1979. Entered into force, Sept. 3, 1981. U.N.G.A. Res. 34/180 (XXXIV), 34 U.N. GAOR. Supp. (No. 46) 194, U.N. Doc. A/34/830 (1979), reprinted in 19 I.L.M. 33 (1980).

_____. 1984. Convention against Torture and Other Cruel, Inhuman or Degrading Treatment or Punishment. Done at New York, Dec. 10, 1984. Entered into force, June 26, 1987. U.N.G.A. Res. 39/46 Annex, 39 U.N. GAOR, Supp. (No. 51) 197, U.N. Doc. E/CN.4/1884/72, Annex (1984), *reprinted in* 23 I.L.M. 1027 (1984).

_____. 1989. Convention on the Rights of the Child. Done at New York, Nov. 20, 1989. A/Res/44/25 (1989) *reprinted in* 28 I.L.M. 1457 (1989).

_____. 1990. International Convention on the Protection of the Rights of All Migrant Workers and Members of Their Families. Adopted 18 December 1990, G.A. Res. 45/158, (1990).

_____. 1991. *Fact Sheet No. 16 (Rev.1), The Committee on Economic, Social and Cultural Rights.* Geneva, Switzerland: United Nations. Also available online at http://www.unhchr.ch/html/menu6/2/fs16.htm.

_____. 1992. Declaration on the Rights of Persons Belonging to National or Ethnic, Religious and Linguistic Minorities. Adopted 18 Dec. 1992, G.A. Res. 47/135, reprinted in 32 ILM 911 (1993), 14 HRLJ 54 (1993).

_____. 1994a. Agreement on the establishment of the commission to clarify past human rights violations and acts of violence that have caused the Guatemalan population to suffer, U.N. Doc. A/48/954/S/1994/751, Annex II, Done at Oslo, June 23, 1994.

_____. 1994b. *Human rights: A compilation of international instruments, volume 1 (part 1), Universal instruments.* New York: United Nations.

_____. 2003a. *Report of the Special Committee on the Situation with regard to the Implementation of the Declaration of the Granting of Independence to Countries and Peoples for 2003,* U.N. Doc. A/58/23 (Part I), 3 July 2003.

_____. 2003b. *Special Committee decision of 10 June 2003 concerning Puerto Rico. Special Committee on the Situation with regard to the Implementation of the Declaration of the Granting of Independence to Countries and Peoples for 2003*, U.N. Doc. A/AC.109/2003/22, 10 June 2003.

United Nations Development Programme. 2003. *Human development report 2003*. New York: Oxford University Press.

United Nations Human Rights Committee. 1994. *General comment no. 24 (52) on issues relating to reservations*, U.N. Doc. CCPR/C/21/Rev.1/Add. 6 (1994).

Urban Institute. 2002. *Immigrants in nation's two largest cities report extensive unmet food needs: Greatest hardship among those who speak limited English*. Washington, D.C.: Urban Institute. Also available online at http://www.urban.org/url.cfm?ID= 900483.

U.S. Bureau of the Census. 2001a. *Money Income in the United States: 2000*. Current Population Reports, Consumer Income, P60–213. Prepared by Carmen DeNavas-Walt, Robert W. Cleveland, and Marc I. Roemer, Bureau of the Census. Washington, D.C.

_____. 2001b. *The Hispanic population: Census 2000 Brief*. Publication No. C2KBR/01-3. Prepared by Betsy Guzmán, Bureau of the Census. Washington, D.C.

_____. 2002a. *Poverty in the United States: 2001*. Current Population Reports, Consumer Income, P60–219. Prepared by Bernadette D. Procter, and Joseph Dalaker, Bureau of the Census. Washington, D.C.

_____. 2002b. *The Hispanic population in the United Status: March 2002*. Current Population Reports, P20–545. Prepared by Roberto R. Ramirez and G. Patricia de la Cruz, Bureau of the Census. Washington, D.C.

_____. 2003a. *Health insurance coverage in the United States: 2002*. Current Population Reports, Consumer Income, P60–223. Prepared by Mills, Robert J., and Shailesh Bhandari, Bureau of the Census. Washington, D.C.

_____. 2003b. *Hispanic population reaches all-time high of 38.8 million, new census estimates show*. United States Commerce News, Economics and Statistics Administration, Bureau of the Census. Washington, D.C. Also available online at www.census.gov/Press-Release/www/2003/cb03-1000.html.

_____. 2003c. *Net worth and asset ownership of households: 1998–2000*. Household Economic Studies, P70–88. Prepared by Shawna Orzechowski, and Peter Sepielli, Bureau of the Census. Washington, D.C.

_____. 2003d. *Poverty in the United States: 2002*. Current Population Reports, Consumer Income, P60–222. Prepared by Bernadette D. Procter, and Joseph Dalaker, Bureau of the Census. Washington, D.C.

_____. 2003e. *Young, diverse, urban: Hispanic population reaches all-time high of 38.8 million, new Census Bureau estimates show* (Press Release No. CB03-100). Washington, D.C.: Public Information Office, B. Bernstein and M. Bergman.

U.S. Commission on Civil Rights. 2000. *Police practices and civil rights in New York City: A report of the United States Commission on Civil Rights*, Washington, D.C.

U.S. Department of Health and Human Services. 2003. *Monitoring the Future National Survey Results on Drug Use, 1975–2002, Volume II: College Students & Adults Ages 19–40*, by Lloyd D. Johnston, Patrick M. O'Malley, and Jerald G. Bachman, National Institute on Drug Abuse and University of Michigan. Bethesda, Maryland.

U.S. Department of Justice. 2001. *Crime in the United States, 2000, Uniform Crime Reports*. Washington, D.C.: U.S. Department of Justice.

_____. 2002. *Crime in the United States, 2001, Uniform Crime Reports*. Washington, D.C.: U.S. Department of Justice.

U.S. Department of State. 1898. *Treaties and other international agreements of the United States of America, 1776–1949*, Treaty of Peace (Treaty of Paris), 30 Stat. 1754; T.S. 343.

_____. 1905. *Papers relating to the foreign policy of the United States, with the annual message of the President transmitted to Congress, 6 December 1904*. Washington, D.C.: GPO.

U.S. House. 2002. *Homeland Security Act of 2002*. 107th Cong., 2nd sess., H.R. 5005.

U.S. News and World Report. 2003. Did you know? http://www.usnews.com/usnews/edu/grad/rankings/law/lawindex_brief.php (accessed December 18, 2003).

U.S. Public Law 107-56. 170th Cong., 1st sess., 3 January 2001. *Uniting and Strengthening America by Providing Appropriate Tools Required to Intercept and Obstruct Terrorism (USA PATRIOT) Act of 2001*.

U.S. Senate. 1900. *Congressional Record*, 56th Cong., 1st sess., 30 April. Washington, D.C.

_____.1975a. Select Committee to Study Governmental Operations with Respect to Intelligence Activities. *Alleged assassination plots involving foreign leaders: An interim report, November 20, 1975*. Washington, D.C.: GPO.

_____.1975b. Select Committee to Study Governmental Operations with Respect to Intelligence Activities. *Covert action in Chile, 1963–1973: Staff report*. Washington, D.C.: GPO.

U.S. Sentencing Commission. 2001. *2001 Sourcebook of Federal Sentencing Statistics*. Washington, D.C.: U.S. Sentencing Commission.

Villarruel, Francisco A., and Nancy E. Walker, with Pamela Minifree, Omara Rivera-Vázquez, Susan Peterson, and Kristen Perry. 2002. *Dónde está la justicia? A call to action on behalf of Latino and Latina youth in the U.S. justice system*. Washington, D.C.: Michigan State University/Building Blocks for Youth.

Walker, Samuel, Miriam Delone, and Cassia Spohn. 2004. *The color of justice: Race, ethnicity, and crime in America*. 3d ed. Belmont, California: Thomson/Wadsworth.

Wallach, Lori, and Michelle Sforza. 1999. *The WTO: Five years of reasons to resist corporate globalization*. New York: Seven Stories Press. Quoting United Nations Development Program (UNDP), Human Development Report 1999, Geneva: UNDP (1999): 3.

Weiser Benjamin. 1999a. 14 minority officers sue police force, alleging bias in disciplinary practices. *New York Times*, 10 September.

_____. 1999b. City violated officers' right to free speech, judges rule. *New York Times*, 19 November.

_____. 1998. U.S. asserts police officer planned to lie. *New York Times*, 25 June.

Welch, Susan, Michael Combs, and John Gruhl.1988. "Do black judges make a difference?" *American Journal of Political Science* 32: 126–36.

Wilbanks, William. 1987. *The myth of a racist criminal justice system*. Belmont California: Wadsworth.

Wright, Bruce.1987. *Black robes, white justice*. Secaucus, New Jersey: Lyle Stewart Inc.

Zea, María, Virginia A. Diehl, and Katherine S. Porterfield. 1997. Central American youth exposed to war violence. In *Psychological interventions and research with Latino populations*, ed. J. G. García and M. C. Zea, 39–55. Boston: Allyn and Bacon.

Zentella, Ana Celia. 1999. Language policy/planning and U.S. colonialism: The Puerto Rican thorn in the English-only's side. In *Sociopolitical perspectives on language policy and planning in the USA*, ed. T. Huebner and K. D. Davis, 155–71. Amsterdam: John Benjamins.

Zernike, Kate. 2003. Woman accused of leading smuggling in which 19 died. *New York Times*, 17 June.

Zinn, Howard. 2003. *People's history of the United States: 1492–present*. New York: Perennial Classics.

INDEX

About the Author

José Luis Morín is an Associate Professor and Chairperson of the Puerto Rican/Latin American Studies Department at John Jay College of Criminal Justice, City University of New York. He teaches in the areas of criminal justice, civil rights, international human rights, international criminal justice, U.S. foreign policy in Latin America, and Latino/a and ethnic studies. Prior to joining the faculty at John Jay College, he was a Visiting Professor at the University of Hawai'i at Mānoa, where he taught courses on international law and Indigenous Peoples' rights. He has also worked for many years as a civil rights and international human rights attorney.